Dyer Daniel Lum

A Concise History
OF THE
GREAT TRIAL
OF THE
Chicago Anarchists
IN 1886

Elibron Classics
www.elibron.com

Elibron Classics series.

© 2005 Adamant Media Corporation.

ISBN 1-4021-6287-1 (paperback)
ISBN 1-4021-2176-8 (hardcover)

This Elibron Classics Replica Edition is an unabridged facsimile of the edition published in 1887 by Socialistic Publishing Society, Chicago.

Elibron and Elibron Classics are trademarks of Adamant Media Corporation. All rights reserved.

This book is an accurate reproduction of the original. Any marks, names, colophons, imprints, logos or other symbols or identifiers that appear on or in this book, except for those of Adamant Media Corporation and BookSurge, LLC, are used only for historical reference and accuracy and are not meant to designate origin or imply any sponsorship by or license from any third party.

A Concise History

— OF THE —

GREAT TRIAL

— OF THE —

Chicago Anarchists

IN 1886.

CONDENSED FROM THE OFFICIAL RECORD.

By DYER D. LUM.

PUBLISHED BY THE
SOCIALISTIC PUBLISHING SOCIETY.
271 WEST 12TH STREET, CHICAGO, ILL.

A Concise History

— OF THE —

GREAT TRIAL

— OF THE —

Chicago Anarchists

IN 1886.

CONDENSED FROM THE OFFICIAL RECORD.

By DYER D. LUM.

CHICAGO, ILL.
Socialistic Publishing Company,
274 WEST TWELFTH STREET.

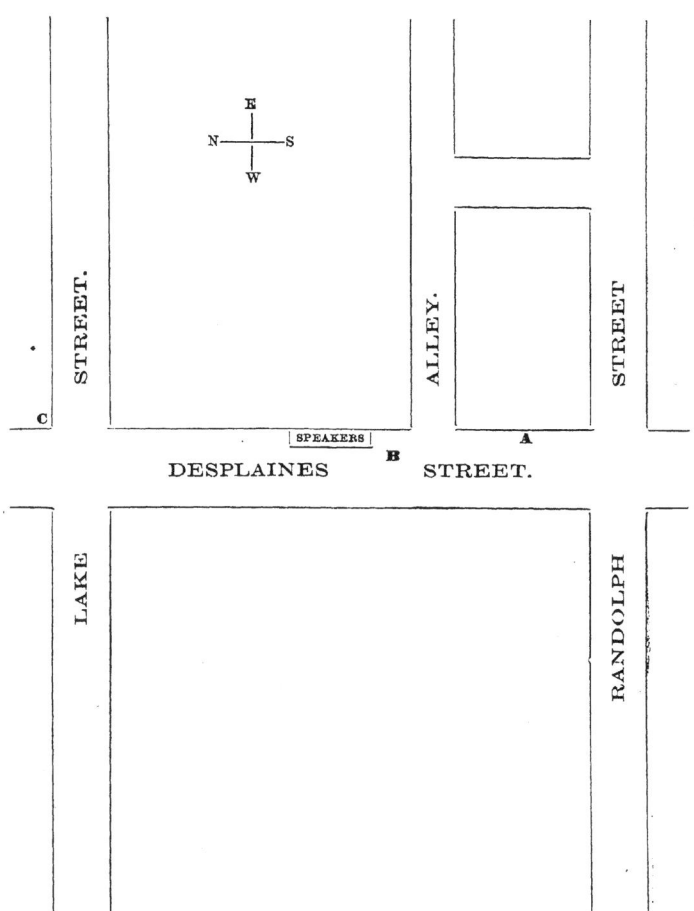

A. Where the bomb was thrown.
B. Where the bomb exploded.
C. Zepf's Hall.

PREFACE.

A bomb! A dynamite bomb! Such was the startling intelligence which went over the wires from the city of Chicago on the night of May 4th, 1886. Who threw it? After a long and protracted trial the question remains unanswered. Whether thrown by some one indignant at the raid by the police upon a peaceable meeting, an individualistic attempt to resist invasion, or thrown by some hireling to break the great eight-hour movement which, at the time, seemed likely to compel the acquiesence of manufacturers in the growing demand for shorter hours of toil, the trial did not reveal.

Yet, eight men were placed on trial for their lives, their houses searched without process of law; they were subjected to personal abuse by city officials, denounced and virtually tried and condemned by a press whose existence, as caterers to capitalists, laid in creating a scarecrow and imparting to it some semblance of reality.

Property alone found voice; Labor, aghast, awaited developments. Some regarded it as the opening of a new struggle between these two classes, which were now clearly seen to have a defined and divergent existence. Capital and Labor were asserted to be pitted against each other in a new "irrepressible conflict." Others, alarmed at the danger to vested rights and existing social conditions, with equal impetuosity and want of logic, fell back on the law and demanded extreme measures of repression; a reign of terror set in. Property trembled for its existence before a phantom; every way-side bush seemed a secret danger; fear paralyzed reason, and force—arbitrary and illegal—held full sway.

Anarchy, that dread spectre that Siberian snows had not frozen; to which under the synonym of Nihilism our dilettanti had given a quasi interest, struck the same alarm in Chicago as it brought to the palace of the Czars. Nor was a reign of terror lacking to the great body of wage workers. Labor Unions found their doors closed by the police. "Suspects" were arrested, imprisoned, and their homes searched by detectives without warrants.

Now that the sentence of death has been passed upon the men accused of "murder," law "vindicated" and order restored; when society has resumed the even tenor of its way and respectable and legal jobbery can again be safely carried on, it were well to ask: Upon what evidence were they convicted?

In the following pages an attempt is made to condense the testimony, omitting nothing essential to the case. The testimony is taken from the official record prepared by counsel for the Supreme Court, not from the newspaper reports. After carefully reading hundreds of pages of testimony, scrupulously scanning the addresses of counsel for the State and carefully weighing all the facts in the case, the writer is still at a loss to account for the verdict upon other grounds than that of class prejudice. Prejudice as strong and envenomed as moved the narrow minds of loyal Frenchmen in their persecution of the Huguenots, or which inspired the breasts of loyal Englishmen in hounding Roundheads to death. True, religion did not enter into the controversy as in France and England. The nineteenth century has passed beyond that stage of controversy. Having passed through and won freedom in disputes regarding religious and political faiths, the great controversies of this age are necessarily economic, questions of a social nature. The Holy Inquisition no longer exists to compel acceptance of a religious creed, but the State remains to crush out social heretics who will not accept its doctrine that wrong is right and glaring injustice to be Christian civilization. The popular god has but changed his vestments. The dark-robed priests no longer gather around the stake to gloat over the dying agony of the daring unbeliever in their rightuousness and authority; the cross no longer cramps intellect and fosters injustice by the strong hand of power. But the same dominating genius prevails and finds expression in other directions. Heresy in social beliefs is still as vigorously denounced as ever in former times under other dominating beliefs. Society to-day, as in the past centuries, can rely on a horde of hirelings to relentlessly pursue, villify and punish the heretic who dares to question and resist the existing order of things. The old question, the only fundamental question of modern civilization, Authority versus Liberty, is still with us. Again, as of old, the cry has gone forth from pulpit, press and tribune—That which is must remain, while at the same time the evil genius of authority, enforcing control over others, from its very nature is constantly usurping new privileges and establishing more restrictions.

The eight social heretics of Chicago who dared to defend their beliefs when tried for an act, of which it was openly admitted they were not personally guilty, have challenged the attention of the world and the admiration of the oppressed of all lands. Though John Brown's body has long been at rest—still, more than ever can it be said, his soul is marching on!

A CONCISE HISTORY
— OF THE —
Great Trial of the Chicago Anarchists in 1886.

CHAPTER I.
THE EIGHT-HOUR MOVEMENT.

The Haymarket tragedy and the trial of the Anarchists are indissolubly connected with the great eight-hour strike of May 1, 1886. To understand the trial and the position of the prisoners on trial we must obtain a view of that movement and of the prisoners' relation thereto. Many and diverse have been the reports circulated in this regard, some claiming that the prisoners were opposed to the eight-hour struggle; others, that they were its champions; while others again — and this has been the theory of the press — that they but seized upon this occasion to bring about a conflict with the constituted authorities and thereby precipitate a revolution. Happily, their own expressions are a matter of record, and they can, as they should, be placed before the public.

The one great characteristic of all public questions which have engaged the attention of statesmen in the nineteenth century is that they have been essentially of an economic nature. Forms of religion and of government are questions of the past; they no longer distract the discussions of cabinets nor excite the popular heart. The huge black-lettered folios of polemic lore which constituted the "living issues" of the seventeenth century gave place in the next to disquisitions on the political rights of man. Parliaments ceased to worry over theology and devoted their energies to combat and suppress the writings of Junius, Rousseau and Paine.

With the triumph of the American and French revolutions, new issues began slowly to force themselves upon public attention. It is self-evident that they have not been religious in their nature. Have they been political? Such we have thought them to be, but each year proves that they are more and far broader. All the great questions of the day, since England began factory legislation in 1802, have been Economic! Freedom of commerce! Corn laws! Tariffs! Strikes!

All have the same inspiration in various degrees of intelligible articulation. It stirred the heart of the English chartist; it moved the pulses of the European workmen in 1848; it found audible voice in the Commune of Paris in 1871; to-day the red flag of labor groups the sons of all nationalities into one common brotherhood.

State patriotism is as obsolete as church creed. Nations still go to war, but it is now for a *market*. England and Russia contend for midland Asia. France, Italy, Spain and Germany seek new colonial dependencies for purely commercial reasons. It has become a question of exports and imports. The productions of labor must find an outlet to new markets to sustain commercial supremacy. Home producers cannot buy that into which they have too often hammered and woven their lives. A foreign market must be sought and won by other lives. The 110,585 boys and girls under thirteen years of age employed in English textile factories may be ragged, but English fabrics must be exported to find them in bread.

As early as September, 1832, a convention of farmers and mechanics of New England was convened at Boston. In January, 1834, a meeting to form a general trades' union was called in the same city. On the Fourth of July following a grand banquet was held at Faneuil Hall; and it is a noteworthy fact that so indifferent were all not immediately interested, that the committee of arrangements apologized for the absence of a clergyman, and stated that application was made to twenty-two religious associations for the use of a church in which to deliver the oration, but their request was in every case refused. Consequently they sat down to their banquet without a clerical blessing.

At that day, and for long since, the tariff was a vital question to America. To-day the desperate struggle of all European powers for a foreign market has overshadowed it with a far deeper one. True, so-called statesmen still harp in the old strain, but workmen are annually growing indifferent to their statistics and eloquence. At that period, so far as there was a labor movement, it was almost entirely confined to Massachusetts. In fact, in 1833, '34 and '35 a labor party presented to the voters of that state a gubernatorial ticket, but few, however, felt an interest in the matter. It was not till 1850 that Massachusetts adopted, in most of the trades, the ten-hour plan. In the large mills a longer working day, however, still prevailed, being twelve hours, or fourteen hours more per week, than in English mills. In other states but little attention, if any, was bestowed upon legislation on hours of labor.

Immediately upon the close of the civil war an agitation for the lessening of the hours of labor began in earnest. The great changes made in our system of production during the interval, the colossal fortunes made by men in army contracts, with the rapid progress towards centralization of capital under the American system of protective tariff, gave the movement a more wide-spread character. The New England Eight-Hour League, endorsed with the eloquent support of Wendell Phillips, aroused more attention one year than had been evoked in the preceding thirty. Growing out of this was the Labor Congress, which was held in the city of Baltimore in 1866.

On June 24, 1878, the national eight-hour law passed and in the same year a National Labor Union was formed at a convention held at Cincinnati with Richard F. Trevellick as president and an executive for each of the several states of the Union. The Eight-Hour law of 1868, applying to government employes, was never rigidly enforced. Government set the example of ignoring it and petitions to Congress were treated with disdain.

The remarkable increase in the production of wealth by the rapid development of " labor-saving " machinery gave stability to the movement. Muscles of steel were taking the place of those of flesh, and strong stalwart men, anxious and eager to toil for others, found themselves " superfluous." Without entering further into the history of the movement, I quote here a letter submitted to the Committee on Depression in Labor and Business of the XLVI Congress. It will be interesting as showing in brief the argument for the shortening of the hours of labor, and instructive in considering the paucity of results which have followed such appeals. It is as follows:

Hon. Hendrick B. Wright, *Chairman Congressional Committee on the Depression of Labor:*

Sir:— At your request, I gladly avail myself of the opportunity so kindly presented to lay before your honorable committee a few thoughts which I think have a practical bearing on the subject-matter of your investigation. As the general question as to the causes of the recent depression of labor opens up a broad and almost endless discussion, I shall beg leave to confine myself strictly to what I consider one of the causes, and wherein remedial legislation will prove beneficial.

I allude to the necessity for a reduction of the hours of labor. The subject came before Congress in 1868, in which year what is known as the national eight-hour law went into effect. Though still on the statute book, its observance is not generally nor uniformly enforced. As a recommendation from your committee could not but have weight in the struggle being waged by workingmen to secure its enforcement, I shall briefly sketch some of the arguments with which we press the matter upon our legislators. Dismissing the question at once whether a law remaining unrepealed should not be enforced, let us see if good reasons do not exist why it should be enforced upon its own merits.

First, we ask it in the name of political economy. All political economists are agreed that the standard of wages is determined by the cost of subsistence, rather than by the number of hours employed. Wages are recognized as resulting from the necessary cost of living in any given community. "The natural and necessary rate of wages," of which we sometimes hear, is such a rate as will supply, to use the words of Adam Smith, " not only the commodities that are indispensably necessary for the support of life, but whatever the custom of the country renders it indecent for creditable people even of the lowest order to be without."

The cost of subsistence for an average family determines the rate, and it is for this reason that single men can save more if they will. They reap the advantage from being exceptions to the general custom. Women's wages are always lower because custom has not made others dependent upon them. Wages have been and will be regulated by existing conditions of living. In 1444 the rate of wages in England, for agricultural labor, averaged about four pence a day, but the price of board was only two pence.

In Rome under Diocletian and Constantine Chlorus, an agricultural laborer received, on an average, equal to twelve and a half cents a day but the cost of subsistence was in proportion.

Second, we ask it in the interest of civilization. The battle for the reduction of the hours of labor is a struggle for a wider civilization. Civilization demands a prosperous and contented people, with increased wants and means to supply them. To refuse aid to willing hands to cultivate our idle lands, to import a servile race, that thereby the cost of subsistence may be reduced to a far lower standard and a lower level for all be reached, and to insist on long hours of toil when thousands are standing idle, all are heavy blows aimed at the very foundation of our modern civilization.

A decrease in the hours of labor means rest, and rest, is invariably accompanied by increased wants. Release the poor drudge in the mine or the factory from his long hours of toil, and give him daily hours of recreation and leisure and you at once raise him in the social scale. Rest cultivates.

We insist that every reduction in the hours of labor heretofore made has elevated the working people; that increased leisure has invariably produced new wants, has added to the necessaries of life, and consequently has raised the social condition of the people. The setting apart of one day in seven for rest wherein no man shall labor, is a prime factor in the growth of civilization. We never hear the charge that wage workers receive seven days' pay for six days' work, simply because conscientious conviction has become hardened into national custom. The cost of subsistence—what will support a family, not what equity requires—is the test by which the standard of wages is determined. For once the reformer and the political economist agree, and the question arises, shall eight hours a day, like six days a week, become firmly fixed as a national custom, so far as the government can establish it?

The whole history of the short-hour movement in England proves conclusively that every reduction of time in the United Kingdom has invariably been followed by an increase of wages. When the agricultural laborers in certain counties of England secured additional rest, but a short period was needed to see a marked difference in their social condition. Flowers began to blossom around their cottage walls, the broken gate was mended and the garden more carefully cultivated. Inside of these humble dwellings where the laborer had formerly entered at the conclusion of a long days' labor only to throw his wearied body down to rest, articles of comfort began to come in, and a general feeling of manliness and pride was awakened. With increased comfort came increased wants; increased wants brought a higher standard of wages than in those counties where the hours had not been reduced.

Third, the changed relations between production and consumption demand it. Should the changed condition of our industrial system, arising from the rapid development of mechanical appliances, whereby hand labor has been so largely superceded, call for remedial legislation? Political economists recognize the evil and propose to meet it by such measures as will preserve to the people what custom has heretofore rendered it indecent to be without. To do this less hours of daily toil are essential. A reduction of hours means less idle hands, more persons profitably employed. By increasing the number of employed, consumption will be stimulated, over-production checked, and a more balanced relationship between the two established.

In the manufacture of cotton fabrics one girl today can do what two generations ago would have required the united labor of 100 women, and in woolens the use of machinery has laid aside 70 per cent of the laborers. In cutting and harvesting grain one man now does the work that formerly would have required 384 men to perform. In Massachusetts the effect of machinery is strikingly shown in the boot and shoe trade. In 1845 the number of hands employed, 45,877, produced 20,896,312 pairs of boots and shoes; in 1875 the number of hands employed, 48,090, produced 59,762,866 pairs. In thirty years the total production has nearly trebled, while the number of persons employed is but slightly in excess of what it was in 1845, and far below the number employed in 1855, when the census showed 77,827.

From 1865 to 1875 the number of establishments in this trade in Massachusetts increased from 206 to 1,461. The examination of the tables given in the state census shows that in the ten years cited, establishments have increased sevenfold; capital invested has nearly doubled; the value of stock used has increased nearly three-fifths; the number of pairs made has increased nine-tenths. Yet in the same period the number of persons employed in this one industry has fallen off from 52,821 to 48,090!

If we look at the other industries, wherever we find an increased number of persons employed we will notice that the increase in production is far greater in proportion. The conquest of man over nature is rapidly augmenting in results, but the question whether the people are in like manner benefitted has but to be asked to be answered. Are peace and contentment more promptly realized? Are the pangs of hunger more readily alleviated? Are the necessities of life more easily attained? or, do privation and poverty remain as marked as in the preceding century? Has not what improvement exists in the material condition of the workingman directly followed from the additional leisure acquired through reduction in the hours of labor, rather than from any other source whatever?

Machinery in the boot and shoe trade in Massachusetts has increased production, swelled the capital invested and augmented profits, but has it lessened the toil of the poor drudge employed, brought increased comfort to his hearth, or placed him in any higher social condition? Labor has been *saved* to the employer only; the tireless muscles of the inanimate machine have not only displaced the living muscles in many cases, but in others have increased the strain upon them by requiring an increased speed to keep up with the machine.

Professor Huxley says that the seven and a half millions of workers in England can produce as much in six months as would have required one hundred years ago the entire working force of the whole world to equal.

Mr Gladstone, in a careful estimate of the production of wealth in Great Britian during the present century and up to the year 1870, finds that the aggregate that has been acquired in this period is equal to that of the whole previous period from the landing of Julius Cæsar, 55 years before the birth of Christ, and that the wealth produced between 1850 and 1870 was fully equal to that of the first half of the present century.

Shall not labor enter into the benefits arising from this increased wealth more directly?

John Stuart Mill says:

"It is questionable if all the mechanical inventions yet made have lightened the day's toil of any human being. They have enabled a greater population to live the same life of drudgery and imprisonment, and an increased number of manufacturers and others to make fortunes; they have increased the comforts of the middle class, but they have not begun to effect those great changes in human destiny which it is their nature to accomplish."

Sir, your committee, I trust, will recognize the importance of this question of the reduction of the hours of labor. The great industrial revolution which we are undergoing, the change of human activity from warlike to industrial pursuits, which constitutes the essential characteristics of modern civilization, and the happiness of the producing classes, which forms the foundation of a republican form of government, alike demand your consideration. The enforcement of the national eight-hour law would be accepted by workingmen everywhere as a signal proof that their prayer has been heard and the first step taken toward the universal acceptance of eight hours as a normal day's work.

It was to the government that the credit is due for the reduction from eleven and twelve hours to ten, in the order issued by President Van Buren. May we not hope that the government may also follow in his footsteps, and further modern civilization and human happiness by establishing eight hours as a day's work in all national workshops, thereby preparing for its adoption as a national custom?

I remain, sir, very respectfully,   SAMUEL C. HUNT.
Boston, Mass., November 10, 1879.

Such was the logic and polity of eight-hour advocates in 1879. Their sole hope at that time lay in legislation. In the following year a National Eight-Hour Committee was organized, of which Albert R. Parsons was a member, to further this end. But Congress did nothing, and slowly hope withered and faith in legislation died out.

In October, 1884, the Federation of Trade and Labor Unions of the United States and Canada, then in session in Chicago, resolved on a different line of action. They resolved that on and after the first day of May, 1886, eight hours should constitute a day's work, and determined to use every endeavor to make the movement a success. In November, 1885, a few individuals in Chicago, prominent among whom were George A. Schilling, William Gleeson and Joseph Gruenhut, met and organized the "Eight-Hour Association of Chicago." They issued a manifesto embodying the following planks:

1. The reduction of the hours of labor will require a proportionate increase in the number of men employed, and will thus lessen, if it does not remove, the competition among workmen, which competition is now admitted by all to be the sole cause of low wages.
2. The reduction of the hours of daily labor will proportionately decrease production, and the employment of a greater number of men will relatively increase consumption, thus destroying the bugaboo of overproduction which now afflicts the dabblers in political economy, and frightens so many well-meaning but unthinking people.
3. The reduction of the hours of daily labor, without a decrease of pay, is a necessary consequence of invention and improved methods of production.
4. The reduction of the hours of labor does not necessarily involve a diminution of the gross societary product.

The association concluded its manifesto by asking the following question, which has become significant in the light of subsequent events:

Do you think that capitalists are justified in using all the powers of the government and society to reduce the working people into wage slavery, and to accumulate all the results of societary work into the hands of a small number of millionaires and soulless corporations, and in case of a general movement for eight hours' daily work among the people of the United States would you demand the interference of the army, the militia, police and sheriff's posse, and employ Pinkerton's hirelings and other mercenaries to coerce the people into submission, and would not such course, if adopted, inevitably lead to bloodshed, anarchy, destruction and social death?

Owing to the activity of this association the movement in Chicago became general, and other cities aimed to emulate it by their co-operation. The Trade and Labor Assembly, believing eight hours the Mecca of the labor movement, swung into line and issued the following circular letter:

To all Trade and Labor Associations of Chicago and Vicinity:

FELLOW-WORKERS—The first of May has been set apart for the general inauguration, as far as possible, of the eight-hour system. That time is near at hand, and as the Trades Assembly of Chicago is the most influential representative body of organized labor west of New York city, it is, therefore, quite natural that the working people and the public generally will hold it responsible to a very great extent for the success or failure of this movement. There never was a time in the history of this country when there was such an activity among the workers for the betterment of their condition. Chicago, true to her pluck and energy in all things, stands first and foremost in this grand and beneficent movement, and as we look over the field to-day there seems to be but one thing which threatens to defeat the successful inauguration of the eight-hour day—the exorbitant demands our fellow-workers are likely to make on the question of wages. In this connection we wish to call your attention to a circular issued by this body on January 14, 1886, to manufacturers and employers of labor generally in Chicago and vicinity:

"The workingmen of Chicago are ready to make sacrifices in wages in order that more people may find employment, and for the general good of the whole community. Surely such a self-sacrificing spirit should meet with a cordial response from the employing class."

The above was given out in good faith by our eight-hour committee at the time, and we see no good reason why it should not be adhered to now. The Bricklayers and Stonemasons' Union and the Cigarmakers' International Union—two of the most perfect organizations in this city—have agreed to accept a corresponding reduction in wages, and we hope that their example will be followed generally, unless there is an absolute certainty that the old standard of wages can be retained without any trouble.

When the eight-hour day has become an actuality, the idle workers re-employed, the boss looking for more hands, the question of better pay will be easily solved, but we implore you not to lumber the cart down with issues that are likely to lead to strikes, lockouts, etc., and possibly to the defeat of the eight-hour movement.

We further advise all trades that have not yet completed their arrangements to immediately select suitable committees, with instructions to confer with the employers in their respective trades, so that this question may be solved as near as possible by mutual consent. Fellow-workers, the victory is assured if you will act determinedly and judiciously. THE EIGHT-HOUR COMMITTEE.

CHARLES W. ROWAN, *President,*
WM. HOLLISTER, *Secretary, Trade and Labor Assembly.*

These extracts are given for the purpose of recalling the fact that the issue had become clearly defined and that the representatives of labor and capital were distinctly arrayed against each other. All unions were pledged to the effort, and there was every reason to believe that it would be crowned with success. The industrial barons of the day were powerless against such general combination on the part of workmen, and could only trust to time or craft to resume the old order of affairs.

Having thus briefly outlined the causes which led up to the eventful week in May, we must pause to consider the relation of the prisoners to that movement and their connection therewith. In October, 1883, a group of men—grown weary of the hope-deferred that all attempts at remedial legislation had brought—met at Pittsburgh, Pa., and revived the International Working-People's Association. To this convention August Spies and Albert R. Parsons were delegates, and took a prominent part in its proceedings. Departing from the methods of the old Socialistic Labor Party, they abjured political action as a method of the present order and powerless as an instrument against it. In an address to the workingmen of America, presenting in vivid colors the inequalities of the present social system, the necessity for revolutionary action was distinctly advocated. The following extract will more clearly define their position:

" As in former times a privileged class never surrendered its tyranny, neither can it be expected that the capitalists of this age will give up their rulership without being forced to do it. If there ever could have been any question on this point, it should long ago have been dispelled by the brutalities which the bourgeois of all countries—in America as well as in Europe—constantly commits as often as the proletariat anywhere energetically move to better their condition. It becomes, therefore, self-evident that the struggle of the proletariat with the bourgeois will be of a violent revolutionary character.

"We could show by scores of illustrations that all attempts in the past to reform this monstrous system by peaceful means, such as the ballot, have been futile, and all such efforts in the future must necessarily be so, for the following reasons:

"The political institutions of our time are the agencies of the propertied class; their mission is the upholding of the privileges of their masters; any reform in your own behalf would curtail these privileges. To this they will not and can not consent, for it would be suicidal to themselves."

The International, as an avowed revolutionary organization, soon numbered several groups in Chicago. In the *Arbeiter-Zeitung*, the *Vorbote* and the *Fackel* they had earnest advocates among the German-speaking people. In October, 1884, an American organ of the International, the *Alarm*, was founded, and secured quite an extensive circulation among the trade unions of Chicago. Public meetings were called in public squares and on the lake front and a thorough system of popular agitation inaugurated. At these meetings probably the most untiring and indefatigable speakers were August Spies, Samuel Fielden and Albert R. Parsons. In summer in the open air, and in winter in halls, the Chicago "groups" kept up an incessant agitation.

Although pursuing a different line of action from that adopted by the Eight-Hour Association, it was impossible that so formidable an economic movement as had been organized to take place on May 1, should not engage their attention. At first the leading spirits in the International held themselves aloof. In their warfare upon the existing social organization ameliorative measures could hardly command their active support. Not that they were opposed to a reduction of the hours of labor, but because the movement did not strike at the root of the evil.

As all of the prisoners were connected with the International Working People's Association their position becomes a question of importance. In the editorial columns of the *Alarm*, for December 12, 1885, appears an article headed "No Compromise."

The following is an extract:

We of the International are frequently asked why we do not give our active support to the proposed eight-hour movement. Let us take what we can get, say our eight-hour friends, else by asking too much we may get nothing.

We answer: Because we will not compromise. Either our position that capitalists have no right to the exclusive ownership of the means of life is a true one, or it is not. If we are correct, then to accede the point that capitalists have the right to eight hours of our labor, is more than a compromise, it is a virtual concession that the wage system is right. If capitalists have the right to own labor or to control the results of labor, then clearly we have no business dictating the terms upon which we may be employed. We cannot say to our employers: Yes, we acknowledge your right to employ us, we are satisfied that the wages system is all right, but we, your slaves, propose to dictate the terms upon which we will work. How inconsistent; and yet that is exactly the position of our eight-hour friends. They presume to dictate to capital, while they maintain the justness of the capitalistic system, they would regulate wages while defending the claims of the capitalists to the absolute control of industry.

A. R. Parsons, the editor of the *Alarm*, who had been formerly prominently identified with eight-hour organizations, was equally explicit. In his paper for October 31, 1885 he said:

"The private possession or ownership of the means of production and exchange places the propertyless class in the power and control of the propertied class, since they can refuse bread or the chance to earn it to all the wage-classes who refuse to obey their dictation. Eight hours, or less hours, is, therefore, under existing conditions a lost battle. The private property system employs labor only to exploit (rob) it, and while that system is in vogue the victims—those whom it disinherits—have only the choice of submission or—starvation!"

Mr. Spies was equally emphatic, and as the statement of his views is essential to the understanding of his position in the course of events which preceeded the Haymarket meeting, it is herewith cited from the *Alarm* of September 5, 1885:

"A man whose name is Edmonston, and whom the irony of fate has awarded the office of secretary in a national labor organization, has written a reply to some remarks which appeared in the *Alarm* in connection with the eight-hour proclamation. He is evidently one of those fellows who think because 'God gave them an office he also furnished them with sense.' Instead of showing our position in regard to the eight-hour question to be unattainable he throws a lot of vile epithets at the Anarchists whom he looks upon in his stupidity as men with 'disordered brains.' The simpleton knows about as much on the subject of economics as the average ass knows about Homerian poetry.

"We do not antagonize the eight-hour movement, — viewing it from the standpoint that it is a social struggle we simply predict that it is a lost battle, and we prove that though even the eight-hour system should be established at this late day, the wage-workers would gain nothing. They would still remain the slaves of their masters.

"Suppose the hours of labor should be shortened to eight, our productive capacity would thereby not be diminished. The shortening of the hours of labor in England was immediately followed by a general increase of labor-saving machines, with a subsequent discharge of a proportionable number of employees. The reverse of what had been sought took place. The exploitation of those at work was intensified. They now performed more labor, produced more than before.

"Now, for a man who desires to remain a wage slave, the introduction of every new improvement and machine is a threatening competitor. The *anorganic* machine works cheaper than the *organic* being! Mr. Edmonston views wage slavery as the very corner-stone of civilization. Hence to be consistent, he ought to be opposed to the reduction of the hours of labor. His position is, it seems, that eight hours would give work to the unemployed and save us from over-production. This, however, will not be the case. If the strike should turn out successful, the eight-hour system would result in the extermination of every small manufacturer and small shopman. They and those whom they now employ would be thrown in the labor market. Production would increase through larger establishments, greater subdivision of labor, etc., while the consuming power of the working class would, if not decrease, remain as it is.

"What E. calls 'over-production' would still remain. For this anomaly will remain just so long as the propertied class have the privilege to distribute the world's goods as they choose.

" 'But,' interjects Mr. E., 'Capital was, and rightfully is, but the servant of labor, and when it assumes to be more, it oversteps its bounds, and becomes a trespasser, liable to correction.'

"How naive! We should think that capital was 'overstepping its bounds' when it refuses to be the servant of more than 2,000,000 men and probably as many women in this country. These people are starving, many have starved—why, Mr. E., don't you correct the trespasser? We should like to see you do it!

"If you say 'capital is the servant of labor,' you lie! it is the servant of its possessor. Does labor possess capital? No. The fellows with the 'disordered brain' would make labor the possessor of capital. But this you don't want, yet you say 'capital ought rightfully be the servant of labor.'

"Now in regard to the eight-hour strike next spring, a few practical words to our friends. The number of organized wage-workers in the country may be about 800,000, the number of unemployed about 2,000,000. Will the manufacturing kings grant your modest request under such circumstances? No sir! the small ones cannot, and the big one will not. They will fill your place by drawing from the army of the unemployed.... You will interfere.... Then comes the police and militia!"

Whatever their individual views and expectations were regarding the "eight-hour reform,"—the Internationalists are not narrow-minded theorists, and hence, instead of opposing the movement, they gave it their full support. And possessing the confidence of the great body of wage-workers, whose cause they had for years espoused, they naturally became the champions of the movement, owing to their recognized ability, intelligence and sincerity.

CHAPTER II.
THE GREAT STRIKE.

While both sides were preparing themselves for the great conflict on the coming first of May, trouble had arisen in the McCormick Harvester factory, which still further intensified public feeling. On the 16th of February, 1886, at 9.30 A. M. the works were closed down and 1,200 men were "locked out." The employes of that establishment had been for some time perfecting their organization and at last had presented a petition for the redress of certain grievances and a general advance of wages. The dispute arose over an additional demand that a guarantee should be given that no man in the factory, or any one serving on a committee, should be discharged for having acted as a representative of his comrades. This was absolutely refused. A strike in the factory in the preceeding April had been adjusted on the basis that none of the men who served on committees, etc., and made themselves conspicuous in behalf of their fellow workmen, would be discharged for so doing. This agreement has been wantonly violated, and every man who had incurred the displeasure of Mr. McCormick was not only discharged, but black listed, in many cases being unable to obtain employment in other shops. On the 2d of March the locked-out men assembled in mass meeting and were addressed at length by A. R. Parsons and Michel Schwab. The meeting had been called not only for the purpose of stating their grievances, but to protest against the armed force which had been enlisted against them—four hundred uniformed police and three hundred Pinkerton detectives, all armed to the teeth. To beseech an employee not to take the place of another became an attack on the State, and these armed men employed by the State came forth at the behest of capital, struck down the peaceable citizens, clubbed and searched them, and cast them into the patrol wagons and hustled them off to prison. The banditti of "law and order" maintained the legal right of capital to do what it pleased with labor, and the authorized "pickpockets" searched every workman for weapons of defense!

These stormy scenes but intensified the general feeling of resistence and determination to unite in making the strike of May 1 all embracive. Meetings were held nightly in various portions of the city and the prisoners became prominent as orators or organizers. Their frequent speeches at meetings held on the lake front had made the names and faces of most of them familiar to workmen. The *Arbeiter-Zeitung*, on which Spies and Schwab were editors, entered ardently on the work and was instrumental in bringing about a reduction in hours from fourteen and sixteen to ten for the bakers, brewers and other unions. The speakers of the International were engaged nearly every evening, either in addressing or organizing unions. On the Sunday preceding the first of May the Central Labor Union held an immense eight-hour demonstration, at which there were estimated present 25,000 persons and who were addressed by Spies, Parsons, Fielden and Schwab.

The eventful day at last arrived. Fully 25,000 men laid down their tools and by the fourth of May this number was doubled. On the first of May the *Arbeiter-Zeitung* contained the following article from the pen of Mr. Spies:

"The dies are cast! The first of May, whose historical significance will be understood and appreciated only in later years, is here. For twenty years the working people of the United States have whined and have begged their extortionists and legislators to introduce an eight-hour system. The latter knew how to put the modest beggar off and thus year after year has passed by. At last, two years ago, a number of trades organizations took the matter up and resolved that the eight-hour work day should be established on May 1, 1886.

"That is a sensible demand, said the press, howled the professional imposters, yelled the extortionists. The impudent Socialists, who wanted everything and would not content themselves with rational demands of this kind, were treated to the customary shower of epithets.

"Thus things went on. The agitation progressed and everybody was in favor of the shortening of the work day. With the approach of the day, however, on which the plan was at last to be realized, a suspicious change in the tone of the extortionists and their priestcraft on the press became more and more noticeable.... What had formerly in theory been modest and rational, was now impudent and senseless. What had formerly been lauded as a praiseworthy demand, when compared with Socialism and Anarchism, changed now suddenly into 'criminal Anarchism' itself. The cloven feet of the hellish crew, panting for spoils, became visible. They had intonated the eight hour hymn simply to lull their dupes, workingmen, to sleep, and thus keep them away from Socialism.

"That the workingmen would proceed in all earnestness to introduce the eight-hour system was never anticipated by these confidence men; that the workingmen would develop such stupendous power, this, they never dreamed of. In short, today, when an attempt is made to realize a reform so long striven for; when the extortionists are reminded of their promises and pledges of the past, one has this and the other has that to give as an excuse. The workers should only be contented and confide in their well-meaning exploiters and some time between now and doomsday everything would be satisfactorily arranged.

"Workingmen, we caution you. You have been deluded time and time again. You must not be led astray this time.

"Judging from present appearances, events may not take a very smooth course. Many of the extortionists, aye, most of them, are resolved to starve those to 'reason' who refuse to submit to their arbitrary dictates, i. e., to force them back into their yoke by hunger. The question now arises—will the workmen allow themselves to be slowly starved into submission, or will they inoculate some modern ideas into their would-be murderers' heads?"

As illustrative of the hatred earned by thus championing the cause of their fellow-workers, attention is called to the following leader in the editorial columns of the Daily *Mail* of the same day, May 1.

"BRAND THE CURS.

"There are two dangerous ruffians at large in this city; two sneaking cowards who are trying to create trouble. One of them is named Parsons. The other is named Spies. Should trouble come they would be the first to skulk away from the scene of danger, the first to attempt to shield their worthless carcasses from harm, the first to shirk responsibility.

"These two fellows have been at work fomenting disorder for the last ten years. They should have been driven out of the city long ago. They would not be tolerated in any other community on earth.

"Parsons and Spies have been engaged for the past six months in perfecting arrangements for precipitating a riot today. They have taken advantage of the excitement attending the eight-hour move-

ment to bring about a series of strikes and to work injury to capital
and honest labor in every possible way. They have no love for the
eight-hour movement, and are doing all they can to hamper it and
to prevent its success. These fellows do not want any reasonable
concessions. They are looking for riot and plunder. They haven't
got one honest aim nor one honorable end in view.

"Mark them today. Keep them in view. Hold them personally
responsible for any trouble that occurs. *Make an example of them if
trouble does occur!*"

Certainly a more personally vindictive article than any that the
prosecution have been able to produce from the pen of either Spies or
Parsons. How these gentlemen have borne themselves when "trouble"
came is a matter upon which no question can be raised; how far the
implied threat has influenced their conviction is not, however, beyond
question.

On the third of May the strike had become general. On that day
a riot occurred near the McCormick works, arising out of an attack
by the strikers on the "scabs" who had taken their places. Police
were quickly hurried to the spot and opening a murderous fire soon
cleared the field. It was to protest against the growing tendency to
shoot workmen on slight provocation that the now famous meeting at
the Haymarket was called. Mr. Spies, in his autobiography, has
given a succinct account of those two important meetings which preceded the throwing of the bomb, and as he was one of the principal
actors on both occasions his own account of the affair is here quoted:

"On Monday, May 3, the strike became general. The *Arbeiter-
Zeitung* of that day gives a complete review of the local movement,
which is most interesting; it also bears evidence of the intense excitement that existed. Several large processions were held, among which
that of about 500 brave tailor girls who marched through the principal
part of the city was the most noteworthy. This novel procession was
perfectly orderly; nevertheless, several assaults were made upon it by
the police. A general strike of the freight handlers on the Northwestern Road broke out, which thickened the cloud that hung ominously over the city.

"I was invited by the Central Labor Union to address a mass
meeting of striking lumber-shovers in the afternoon on Twenty-second
street and Blue Island avenue. I did not intend to go to the meeting.
I was completely exhausted from the exertions of the last few days;
but a committee called on me and insisted that I must come along.
It was an immense gathering, fully 10,000 persons must have been

present. Several short speeches had already been made when I arrived. When the chairman introduced me, some men in the audience cried out: 'He is a Socialist, we don't want any Socialistic speeches!' But as soon as I began to speak all became quiet and silent. I spoke with unusual calmness and moderation. The essence of my remarks was that they, the strikers, should stand firmly together and they then would carry the day. The effect of my speech may best be judged by the fact that at its conclusion the audience elected me unanimously as spokesman of a committee, which had been appointed to confer with the lumber-yard owners with regard to bringing the strike to a close.

" During my speech I heard some voices in the rear, which I did not understand, and saw about 150 men leave the prairie, running up the Black Road towards McCormick's Reaper works (one-quarter mile south of where the meeting was). Five minutes later I heard pistol-shooting in this direction, and upon inquiry was informed that the striking molders of McCormick's works were trying to make the 'scabs' who had taken their places stop work.

" About this time — I was just closing my speech — a patrol-wagon rattled up the street, filled with policemen; a few minutes later about seventy-five policemen followed the patrol-wagon on foot, who were again followed by three or four more patrol-wagons. The shooting continued, only, that instead of the single shots regular volleys were now fired. I left the meeting and hastened up to McCormick's. A long line of freight cars were standing on the railroad track in front of the high board inclosure of the factory building. Between these cars and the fence was the battle-field, or better the target range of the police. All I could see was that about 150 men, women and small boys were chased by as many or more policemen who emptied their revolvers in rapid succession upon the fleeing and screaming 'mob.'

" To say that I was horrified at the sight of this is only expressing vaguely what I felt. I saw several persons carried and led away by their friends — they had been shot. A young Irishman, who seemed to know me, came running up to me, and said: " What kind of a h— of union is that down there! (pointing to the lumber-shovers' meeting.) They must be nice fellows to stand by and have their brothers shot down like dogs by these —— !"

" 'Have many been hurt?' I inquired.

" 'Many? I should think so! I helped carrying two away, who seemed to be killed. Nobody knows how many have been shot and killed!' was his reply, adding, 'Have you no influence with those men down there? If you have, for God's sake, bring them up here!'

" I have seen this identical man a few weeks ago in the jail, and upon inquiry learned that he was a *detective!*

" I ran back to the meeting, which in the meantime had been adjourned. The people were leaving it in small knots, going home, some of them indifferent and unconcerned at the news from McCormick's, others shaking their heads in indignation. I was frantic, but my senses returned as I glanced over the stolid faces of these people; there was no response there! And, seeing that I could be of no possible assistance here, I took a car, without uttering another word, and rode down town to my office. Just in what frame of mind I was, I cannot describe. I sat down to address a circular to the workingmen — a short account of what had transpired and a word of advice: that they should not be so foolish as to try to resist an armed organized 'mob,' in the employ of the capitalists, with empty hands,— but I was so excited that I could not write. I dictated a short address, but tore it up again, after I had read it, and then sat down — the compositors were waiting for the copy, it being after the regular hours — and wrote the now famous so called '*Revenge Circular*' in English and German.* The word 'Revenge' was put on as a headline by one of the compositors (without my knowledge) who 'thought it made a good heading.' I ordered the circular printed and told the office assistant to have them taken to the different meetings that were held in the evening. There were only a few hundred of them circulated. After I had given this order I went home."

We interrupt this sketch by Mr. Spies at this point to call attention to the fact that on the trial Ludwig Zeller, of the Central Labor

---

* The circular read as follows:

Revenge! Workingmen, to arms. Your masters sent out their bloodhounds, the police. They killed six of your brothers at McCormick's this afternoon; they killed the poor wretches because they had the courage to disobey the supreme will of your bosses; they killed them because they dared to ask for the shortening of the hours of toil; they killed them to show you, free American citizens, that you must be satisfied and contented with whatever your bosses condescend to allow you or you will get killed. You have for years suffered unmeasurable iniquities; you have worked yourselves to death; you have endured the pangs of want and hunger; your children you have sacrificed to the factory lords,— in short, you have been miserable and obedient slaves all these years. Why? To satisfy the insatiable greed, to fill the coffers of your lazy thieving masters. When you ask them now to lessen the burden they send their bloodhounds out to shoot you — kill you. If you are men, if you are the sons of your grandsires who have shed their blood to free you, then you will rise in your might, Hercules, and destroy the hideous monster that seeks to destroy you! To arms! We call you to arms! YOUR BROTHERS.

Union, swore that Spies was selected to address the Lumber-Shovers' Union meeting in response to an invitation for some one who would keep it "quiet and orderly." In this connection also, as preliminary to the narration of the Haymarket meeting of May 4, the editorial of the *Arbeiter-Zeitung* (by Schwab) of the above date, a translation of which was read during the trial by the prosecution, is here given:

"Blood has flowed. It had to be, and it was not in vain, that Order drilled and trained its bloodhounds. It was not for fun that the militia was practiced in street fighting. The robbers who know best of all what wretches they are; who pile up their money through the miseries of the masses; who make a trade of the slow murder of the families of workingmen, are the last ones to stop short at the direct shooting down of the workingmen. 'Down with the Canaille,' is their motto. Is it not historically proven that private property grows out of all sorts of violence. Are these capitalistic robbers to be allowed by the canaille, by the working classes, to continue their bloody orgies with horrid murders? Never! The war of classes is at hand. Yesterday workingmen were shot down in front of McCormick's factory, whose blood cries out for revenge! Who will deny that the tigers who rule us are greedy for the blood of the workingman? Many sacrifices have been offered upon the altars of the golden calf amid the applauding cries of the capitalistic band of robbers. One need only think of Cleveland, New York, Brooklyn, East St. Louis, Fort Worth, Chicago, and many other places, to realize the tactics of these despoilers. It means, 'Terrorize our working cattle.' But the workingmen are not sheep, and will reply to the white terror with the red terror. Do you know what that means? You soon will know. Modesty is a crime on the part of workingmen, and can anything be more modest than this eight-hour demand? It was asked for peacefully a year ago, so as to give the spoilsmen a chance to reply to it. The answer is, drilling of the police and militia regulations of the workingmen seeking to introduce the eight-hour system, and, yesterday, blood flowed. This is the way in which these devils answer the modest prayer of their slaves.

"Sooner death than life in misery, if workingmen are to be shot at. Let us answer in such a way that the robbers will not soon forget it.

"The murderous capitalistic beasts have been made drunk by the smoking blood of workingmen; the tiger is crouching for a spring; its eyes glare murderously; it moves its tail impatiently, and all its muscles are tense. Absolute necessity forces the cry, 'To Arms! To Arms!' If you do not defend yourselves you will be torn and mutilated by the fangs of the beast. The new yoke which awaits you in case of a cowardly retreat is harder and heavier than the bitter yoke of your present slavery. All the powers opposed to labor have united; they see their common interest in such days as these; all else must be subordinate to the one thought — How can the wealthy robbers and the hired bands of murderers be made harmless?

"The papers lie when they say that the workingmen who were near McCormick's yesterday shot first. It is a bold and shameless lie of the newspaper gang. The police shot among the workingmen without a word of warning, and, of course, the latter replied to the fire. Why be so ceremonious with the 'canaille?' Had they been not men, but sheep or cattle, they must have reflected before shooting. But a workingman is quickly replaced. Yet these well-fed fellows boast at their costly meals, in the company of their mistresses, of the splendid working of Law and Order.

"Shabbily-dressed women and children in miserable huts weep for husbands and fathers. In palaces they still fill goblets with costly wine, and pledge the health of the bloody banditti of Order. Dry your tears, ye poor and suffering! Take heart, ye slaves! Rise in your might and level the existing robber rule with the dust."

In the same issue appeared also the following:

"The heroes of the club yesterday pounded brutally with their cudgels a number of girls, many of whom were mere children. Whose blood does not course more swiftly through his veins when he hears of this outrage? Whoever is a man must show it to-day. Men to the front!"

It was followed in the afternoon by the following dodger, which was scattered broadcast through the streets of the city:

"ATTENTION, WORKINGMEN! Great mass-meeting to-night, at 7:30 o'clock, at the Haymarket, Randolph street, between Desplaines and Halsted. Good speakers will be present to denounce the latest atrocious acts of the police — the shooting of our fellow-workmen yesterday afternoon.   "THE EXECUTIVE COMMITTEE."

We will now resume Mr. Spies' narrative of the events of May 4th:

"On the following morning about 9 or 10 o'clock, A. Fischer, one of our compositors, asked me if I would not come to a general mass-meeting which would take place at the Haymarket in the evening and 'make a speech' on the brutality of the police and the situation of the eight-hour strike. I replied that I was hardly able to speak, but if there was no one to take my place I should come. Delegates of a number of unions had called the meeting, he said. I made no further inquiries. About 11 o'clock a member of the Carpenters' Union called on me and asked that the hand-bill he showed me be printed in the *Arbeiter-Zeitung* as an announcement. It was the circular calling the Haymarket meeting, and at the bottom it contained the words — 'Workingmen, bring your arms along!'

"'This is ridiculous!' said I to the man, and had Fischer called. I told him that I would not speak at the meeting if this was the circular by which it had been called.

"'None of the circulars are as yet distributed; we can have these words taken out,' the man said. Fischer assented, and I told them that if they did that it would be all right.

"I never for a moment anticipated that the police would wantonly attack an orderly meeting of citizens. And I never saw a disorderly meeting of workingmen. The only disorderly meetings I have ever witnessed were the republican and democratic pow-wows. I went home about four o'clock P. M. to take a little rest before going to the meeting. The reaction following the excitement of the previous day had set in. I was very tired and ill-humored. After supper my brother Henry called at our house. I asked him to come along to the meeting, which he did. We walked slowly down Milwaukee avenue. It was warm; I had changed my clothes; the revolver I was in the habit of carrying was too large for the pocket, and inconvenienced me. Passing Frank Stauber's hardware store, I left it with him. It was about 8:15 o'clock when we arrived at Desplaines and Lake streets. I was under the impression that I was to speak in German, which generally follows the English. That is the reason why I was late. Small and large groups of men were standing around, but there was no meeting. Not seeing anyone who might be supposed to be entrusted with the management of the meeting, I jumped upon a wagon, inquired for Mr. Parsons (who I thought had been invited), and called the meeting to order. Parsons was not there. 'I saw Parsons at the corner of Halsted and Randolph streets; I think he is speaking there,' said a reporter to me. I told the crowd to wait a few minutes while I went out in search of Parsons. Not finding him I returned to the wagon, where somebody told me Parsons, Fielden and others were holding a meeting in the office of the *Arbeiter-Zeitung*. I sent one of our employes over to the office to call Parsons and Fielden, and began to address the meeting. I spoke about twenty minutes.

"Then Parsons spoke. The audience was very quiet and attentive. Parsons confined himself to the eight-hour question, but spoke at great length. While he was speaking I asked Mr. Fielden if he would not make a few remarks. He didn't care to speak, but would say a few words and then adjourn the meeting. I said, 'All right, do so.' It was about ten o'clock when Fielden began to speak. A few minutes later a dark and threatening cloud moved up from the north. The people—or, at least, two-thirds of them—fearing it would rain, left the meeting. 'Stay,' said Fielden, 'just a minute longer; I will conclude presently.' There were now not more than two hundred persons remaining. One minute later two hundred policemen formed into line at the intersection of Randolph street and marched upon the little crowd in double quick step.

" Raising his cane in an authoritative way, Captain Ward—directing his words to Fielden (I was standing just behind Fielden in the wagon)—said: 'In the name of the people of the State of Illinois I command this meeting to disperse!'

" 'Captain, this is a peaceable meeting,' retorted Mr. Fielden, while the captain turned around to his men and gave a command which I understood to be, 'Charge upon them!' At this juncture I was drawn from the wagon by my brother and several others, and I had just reached the ground when a terrible detonation occurred. 'What is that?' asked my brother. 'A cannon, I believe,' was my reply. In an instant the fusilade of the police began. Everybody was running. All this was as unexpected as if suddenly a cloud had burst. I lost my brother in the throng and was carried away toward the north. People fell, struck by the bullets, right and left. As I crossed the alley north of Crane's factory, a lot of officers ran into the alley, some of them exclaiming that they were hurt. They had evidently been shot by their own comrades, and sought protection in the alley. I was in a parallel line with them, and the bullets whistled around my head like a swarm of bees. I fell once or twice over others who had 'dropped,' but otherwise escaped unhurt into Zepf's saloon, at the corner of Lake street. Here I heard for the first time that the loud report had been caused by an explosion, which was thought to have been the explosion of a bomb. I could learn no particulars, and about a half hour afterward took a car and rode home to see if my brother had been hurt. He had received a dangerous wound. Turning aside when I had answered, 'It's a cannon, I believe,' he beheld the muzzle of a revolver deliberately aimed at my back. Grasping the weapon, the bullet struck him in a vital part.* (He recovered.)

---

*NOTE.—There is no question at all but that detectives had been stationed in the crowd to kill the obnoxious speakers at the instant the police would charge upon the crowd.

"The next morning the papers reported that the police had been searching for me all night and that they had orders to arrest me. Nobody had been at my house during the night; the report was a lie. I went to the office at my regular hour and began to work. About nine o'clock Detective Jim Bonfield made his appearance and told me the chief of police wanted to have a talk with me. I went along with him to the central station. Two other detectives arrested Schwab and my brother Christ, who had come to the office to learn what had occurred on the previous night. The fact that his name was Spies sufficed to arrest him and charge him with having committed murder."

The reign of terror which prevailed during the month of May would form the subject of a lengthy and interesting chapter, but space forbids entering into details. A brief reference to a few leading points must suffice:

On the night of the Haymarket meeting, Mr. Parsons, one of the alleged "conspirators to destroy the city," took with him his wife and his two young children and a lady friend, who occupied seats in an adjoining wagon until the appearance of rain drove them away. At the time of the explosion of the bomb the only ones of the eight prisoners present were Spies and Fielden. And in this connection it will be well to recall out of the regular order some of the testimony which remained unimpeached, bearing directly on the attack by the police.

On the 2d of August Hon. Carter H. Harrison, the mayor of Chicago, was placed on the witness stand as the first witness for the defense. His testimony as to the character of the meeting was clear and decisive. Following are extracts:

Q. Did you attend the Haymarket meeting on Desplaines street on the 4th of May last?

A. A part of it, not the whole. During May 4th, probably about noon, information came to me of the issuance of a circular of a very peculiar character, and a call for a meeting at the Haymarket that night. I called the chief of police and directed him that if anything should be said at that meeting as was likely to call out a recurrence of such proceedings as at McCormick's factory the meeting should be immediately dispersed. I believed that it was better for myself to be there and to disperse it myself instead of leaving it to any policemen. I thought my order would be better obeyed. I went there then for the purpose, if I felt it necessary for the best interests of the city, to disperse that meeting.

Q. How long did you remain at the meeting?

A. It was about five minutes before eight o'clock when I arrived. I should judge from the time when the bomb sounded and the time it took me to walk home, that I left the meeting between 10 and 10:05 o'clock. I heard all except probably a minute or a minute and a half of Mr. Spies' speech, and all of Mr. Parsons' up to the time I left, with the exception of a break when I left him talking and went over to the station. I was absent five or ten minutes. It was near the close of Parsons' speech. *I should judge he was looking toward a close.* I went to the station to speak to Captain Bonfield, and had determined to go home, but instead of going home I went back to hear a little more, *and then left.*

Q. Up to the time that you went to the station and had this interview with Mr. Bonfield, what was the tenor of the speeches?

A. With the exception of a portion in the earlier part of Mr. Spies' address, which, for probably a minute, was such that I feared it was leading up to a point where I should disperse the meeting, it was such that I remarked to Captain Bonfield *that it was tame.* The portion of Mr. Parsons' speech attracting most attention was the statistics as to the amount of returns given to labor from capital, and showing, if I remember rightly now, that capital got eighty-five per cent and labor fifteen per cent. It was what I should call a violent political harangue against capital.

Q. Was any action taken by you while you were at the meeting looking to the dispersal of the meeting?

A. *No!*

Q. Do you recollect any suggestion made by either of the speakers looking toward the immediate use of force or violence toward any person?

A. *There was none.* If there had been I should have dispersed them at once.

Q. How long was the interview that you had with Inspector Bonfield?

A. Probably five minutes.

Q. Will you please state what it was?

A. I went back to the station and said to Bonfield that I thought that the speeches were about over; *that nothing had occurred yet or was likely to occur to require interference, and I thought he had better issue orders to his reserves at the other stations to go home.* He replied that he thought about the same way, as he had men in the crowd who were reporting to him.

Q. Did you see any weapons in the hands of the audience?

A. No, sir; none at all.

Upon cross-examination by the State the specific reasons for the mayor's attendance at the meeting, and their utterly groundless nature, were clearly brought out. The entire cross-examination is here given:

MR. GRINNELL.—Had you heard rumors of an attempt to burn the Milwaukee and St. Paul freight house that evening which led you to go to the meeting?

A. The rumor that I adverted to was this. Shortly after my reaching the station Capt. Bonfield told me that he had just received information that this meeting, or part of it, would go to the St. Paul freight house, then filled with what they called scabs, and blow it up. There was also an intimation that this meeting might be merely a ruse to attract the attention of the police to the Haymarket, while the real attack, if any should be made that night, should be at McCormick's. It was with reference to these rumors that I listened to the speeches.

Q. And listening in that way to the speeches you ascertained that there was no invitation to go to the St. Paul depot?

A. None.

Q. And therefore you concluded that there was no organization to destroy property that night?

A. That is the fact.

Q. Now, what was the order you gave to Bonfield?

A. That the reserves held at the other stations might be sent home, because I had learned that all was quiet in the Second District —the southwest. Bonfield said he had already given such an order.

Q. Did you hear Parsons' call to arms?

A. I don't remember it. *I think I should have noticed such language.*

CAPTAIN BLACK.—Where did you hear that rumor about the McCormick affair?

A. *That was something that I apprehended myself.*"

It is thus clearly established that the meeting at the Haymarket was perfectly peaceable. Nothing is shown to have occurred in the short time which elapsed between the departure of the mayor for home and the order given by Inspector Bonfield to six companies of police, numbering 174 men, to march to and disperse the meeting. Why, then, was the order given?

The Chicago *Times* of the next morning, in its narration of the affair, said:

"It was about ten minutes after ten and just at that moment a large squad of police moved up from the Desplaines street station *for the purpose of arresting Spies, Schwab, Parsons and Fielden.*"

Barton Simonson, a traveling salesman of irreproachable character, and known to the officers of police stations by his prominence in efforts made by Christian organizations to establish soup-houses for the destitute, followed Mayor Harrison on the stand. The following extract is pertinent in this connection:

"I spoke to Capt. Bonfield about the trouble at McCormick's and he said that the greatest trouble the police had in dealing with the Socialists was that they had their women and children with them at the meetings so that the police could not get at them. *He said he wished he could get a crowd of about three thousand of them together without their women and children* AND HE WOULD MAKE SHORT WORK OF THEM."

The witness said that he was not a Socialist nor an Anarchist, and had never affiliated with either. He had merely attended the meeting from curiosity and had, though not intentionally, preserved in his pocket the hand-bill or dodger calling the meeting, which he offered in evidence. It did *not* contain the words "Workingmen, arm yourselves and appear in full force."

He said he heard Spies say on opening, "This meeting was not called to incite to riot." He gave a synopsis of Spies' speech which agreed in the main with accounts already given. The witness said that he had never before attended a Socialistic meeting, and he thought "all the remarks were a little wild." When the clouds came up some suggested an adjournment, but Fielden said he was nearly through and twice said "in conclusion." When the witness heard the police order to the meeting to disperse he heard distinctly above the commotion the two words "peaceable meeting." These words came from the direction of the wagon [where Fielden was speaking.] He heard nothing from the wagon or from Fielden about "Here comes the bloodhounds." After the explosion the witness saw the flashing of many pistol shots from the police, *but none from the surrounding crowd*. Other witnesses corroborated him not only on these points, but also that among the fleeing fugitives were a large number of the police who sought shelter or safety in flight; and thus confirming what the writer has been repeatedly assured of by eye witnesses—that the large number of policemen wounded by balls were shot by their own frightened comrades. The number of citizens shot will probably never be known. One was found dead, and twelve wounded were reported as removed to the county hospital. Of the police, one, Officer Degan, was killed, while sixty-six others were wounded by pieces of the bomb and pistol shots, six of them fatally.

The Chicago *Tribune* of May 5 said:

"There was no warning given. The crowd was rapidly dispersing. The police, marching slowly, were in a line with the east and west alley when something like a miniature rocket suddenly rose out of the crowd on the east sidewalk, in a line with the police. It rose about twenty feet in the air, describing a curve, and fell right in the middle of the street and among the marching police. It gave a red glare while in the air. The bomb lay on the ground for a few seconds, then a loud explosion occurred, and the crowd took to their heels, scattering in all directions. Immediately after the explosion the police pulled their revolvers and fired on the crowd. An incessant fire was kept up for nearly two minutes, and at least 250 shots were fired. The air was filled with bullets. The crowd ran up the streets and alleys and were fired on by the now thoroughly enraged police. Then a lull followed. Many of the crowd had taken refuge in the halls or entrances of halls and saloons. As the firing ceased they ventured forth, *and a few officers opened fire on them.*"

At half-past eleven, curiosity and a desire to find friends drew a large number to the spot and another charge was made and two volleys fired, which dispersed the crowd, though there was no indication that they were Socialists.

The *Tribune* gives the following list of wounded citizens carried off by the police:

"ROBERT SCHULTZ, No. 88 Harrison street, waiter at No. 165 Ashland avenue, just coming from the Lyceum. Shot in the leg.

"JOHN SACHMAN, No. 103 South Desplaines street; was lounging along Randolph street when he was shot in the leg.

"FRANK WROSCH, residence in the cheap lodging houses. 'I just stopped and listened,' he groaned, 'and then the fire came to my shoulders and sides.' He will probably die. Not a Socialist.

"CHARLES SCHUMAKER, No. 19 Fry street, was with two friends. They ran away and he was shot in the back. It is doubtful if he will recover.

"EMIL LOTZ, keeper of a small shoe shop at No. 25 North Halsted street; when he got through work he went out to hear the speeches and was shot in the shoulder.

"JOHN EDBUND, a carriagemaker at 1138 Milwaukee avenue; clubbed in the head.

"PETER LEY, 536 West Huron street, shot in the back.

"JOE KUCKER, a hanger-on around West Side 'barrel houses,' and boarding at No. 116 Randolph street; shot in the side.

"B. LePlant, Earl Park, Ind.; 'I bought some peanuts and was eating them when the bomb went off,' he said, 'then a shot broke my leg and I fell. In a second a shot went through my shoulder *and a policeman kicked me.*'

"Frank Kadereit, a member of the Central Labor Union and residing at the corner of Mohawk street and North avenue, wounded on the head and right shoulder by a policeman's club.

"Thomas Haha, of 157 Eagle street, was shot in the back and leg. He was carried into a hallway at 182 West Madison street, where he lay groaning. He was able to walk to the patrol wagon, in which he was carried to the county hospital. He was *probably* a rioter, but he claimed to be an unoffending citizen.

"Fritz Kaderit, a German workingman; scalp wound from some blunt instrument. *He was locked up.*

"In a search of the dead Bohemian only twelve cents was found upon him. Not a trace of a name could be found. He was apparently about 35 years of age.

"Every drug store in the vicinage was crowded with wounded getting their injuries dressed and then carried home by their friends.

"It was a common spectacle to see men having their wounds dressed on the sidewalk. The street cars going in every direction contained men who had been wounded but were still strong enough to help themselves away."

It was the old, old story; merciless brutality and inoffensive victims. The capitalistic *Tribune* confesses this in plain words. It says on May 5:

"Goaded to madness the police were in that state of mind which permitted of no resistance, and in a measure *they were as dangerous as any mob of Communists*, for they were blinded by passion and unable to distinguish between the peaceable citizen and the Nihilist assassin. For squares from the Desplaines street station companies and squads of officers cleared the streets and mercilessly clubbed all who demurred at the order to go."

"Who threw the bomb? is a query the police have still to solve," said the Chicago *Herald* of the 6th; and the query has not yet been solved.

Hundreds were arrested and locked up as "suspects." The entire force of the *Arbeiter-Zeitung* were taken in charge and orders given to have the paper suppressed.

A. R. Parsons was not to be found; but the police arrested his wife and some other ladies known to be their friends. The papers report Mrs. Parsons as wearing a "flaming red handkerchief" about her throat and the following colloquy ensued:

"You still wear the red ribbon," remarked Detective Palmer to her, alluding to the handkerchief.

"Yes," she defiantly answered, "and I'll die under it, too."

Nearly everyone known to be in sympathy with the International Working People's Association were "run down" and submitted to the "pumping process" by detectives, sworn at and even threatened with revolvers and ropes. The whole force of the city was employed to secure evidence to convict by any and every means. The character of some of the "evidence" thus obtained will be apparent in a review of the testimony. But before entering upon the history of the trial we desire to give the speeches made at the Haymarket meeting by Spies and Parsons.

CHAPTER III.
THE HAYMARKET SPEECHES.

At the request of his attorney, Mr. Spies wrote out the substance of his remarks on the evening of May 4th, which agrees in tenor with the memories of those who heard it. Mr. Parsons also made notes of his address at the meeting, and repeated it under oath before the jury*

The Speech Delivered by August Spies at the Haymarket, May 4, on the Occasion of the Bomb-Throwing.

FRIENDS:—The speakers of the evening not having arrived I shall entertain you a few minutes. I am told that a number of patrol wagons, carrying policemen, were sent to Desplaines street station, and I understand that the militia have been called under arms. There seems to prevail the opinion in certain quarters that this meeting has been called for the purpose of inaugurating a riot, hence these warlike preparations on the part of so-called "law and order." However, let me tell you at the beginning that this meeting has not been called for

---

*The Chicago *Times* of August 10 contained the following statement in regard to this speech:

"The climax in the Anarchist trial was reached yesterday. Schwab, Spies and Parsons told their respective stories to the jury from the witness-chair, to a spell-bound audience of spectators, an amazed jury, and a surprised judge. * * Parsons was composed and eloquent. * * * His brother, General W. H. Parsons, sat with eyes fixed upon him during the time he was upon the stand. As soon as Mr. August Spies retired Mr. Parsons took the stand, and in a quiet, deferential tone answered the questions put to him in a firm voice, not appearing to

any such purpose. The object of this meeting is to explain the general situation of the eight-hour movement, and to throw light upon various incidents in connection with it.

For more than twenty years have the wage workers of this country begged and prayed their masters, the factory lords, to reduce their burdens. It has been in vain. They have pointed out the fact that over a million of willing and strong hands were in a state of enforced idleness and starvation, that to help them to obtain employment it would not only be advisable, nay, it was necessary to reduce the hours of daily toil of those who were fortunate enough in having found a buyer for their muscles, their bones and their brain. The masters of this earth have treated them with contempt, have condemned them to vagabondage whenever they insisted. The legislatures have been called upon, one petition has succeeded the other, but with no avail.

At last the condition of the disinherited producers has become unbearable. Seeing that neither " boss" nor law would concede anything to them, they have organized for the purpose of helping themselves—a wise and prudent resolution.

All over the land we behold vast armies of producers, no longer begging, but demanding that eight hours shall henceforth constitute a normal working day. And what say the extortionists to this? They demand their pound of flesh, like Shylock. They will not yield one iota. They have grown rich and powerful on your labor. They amass stupendous fortunes, while you, who bring them into existence, are suffering from want. In answer to your pleadings they ask for the bodies of your little children, to utilize them in their gold mints, to make dollars out of them. Look at the slaves of McCormick! When they tried to remonstrate with their master he simply called upon the " protectors of these free and glorious institutions"—the police—to silence them. And they did silence them.

You have no doubt heard of the killing and wounding of a number of your brothers at McCormick's, yesterday. Mr. McCormick told a

---

be in the least unnerved by his peculiar position. At length he was asked to give the substance of his Haymarket speech, and he did so, and if the jury, the court, and the audience have been entertained since the trial began, they were entertained by the chief agitator of the Chicago Anarchists. He pulled out of his pocket a bundle of notes, and began at the jury in tones which betokened that the speaker was primed for the finest speech of his life. Luckily for him the witness-chair was a swinging one. He held his notes in his left hand, and, together with the swaying of his body, gesticulated with his right arm. From low, measured tones he went on from eloquence to oratory, and from oratory to logic, and from logic to argument."

SPEECH OF AUGUST SPIES. 37

Times reporter that Spies was responsible for that massacre committed by the most noble Chicago police. I reply to this that McCormick is an infamous liar. (Cries of "Hang him.") No, make no idle threats. There will be a time, and we are rapidly approaching it, when such men as McCormick will be hanged; there will be a time when monsters who destroy the lives and happiness of the citizens (for their own aggrandizement) will be dealt with like wild beasts. But that time has not yet come. When it has come you will no longer make threats, but you will go and "do it."

The capitalistic press, like the "respectable gentleman" McCormick, howls that the Anarchists are responsible for the deeds of violence now committed all over this country. If that were true one would have to conclude that the country was full of Anarchists, yet the same press informs us that the Anarchists are very few in number. Were the "unlawful" acts in the Southwestern strike committed by Anarchists? No, they were committed by Knights of Labor—men who never fail to declare, whenever there is an opportunity, that they are law-and-order-abiding citizens. The attack upon McCormick's yesterday—was it made by Anarchists? Let us see. I had been invited by the Central Labor Union to address a meeting of lumber-yard laborers on the Black road. I went out there at the appointed time, about three o'clock in the afternoon. There were at least ten thousand persons assembled. When I was introduced to address them a few Poles or Bohemians in the crowd cried out: "He's a Socialist." These cries were followed by a general commotion and derision. "We want no Socialist; down with him." These and other exclamations I was treated to. Of course, I spoke anyway. The crowd became quiet and calm, and fifteen minutes later elected me unanimously a delegate to see their bosses. Nevertheless, you can see that these people are not Socialists or Anarchists, but "good, honest, law-abiding, church-going Christians and citizens." Such were the persons who left the meeting, as I afterward learned, "to make the scabs at McCormick's quit work." In my speech I never mentioned McCormick. Now you may judge for yourselves whether the Anarchists were responsible for the bloodshed yesterday or not.

Who is responsible for these many "lawless" acts, you ask me? 1 have told you that they are generally committed by the most lawful and Christian citizens. In other words, the people are by necessity driven to violence; they can't carry the burden heaped upon them any longer. They try to cast it off, and in so doing break the laws. The law says they must not cast it off, for such an act would alter, yea, revolutionize the existing order of society. These acts of violence are the natural outgrowth of the present industrial system, and every one is responsible for them who supports and upholds that system.

What does it mean when the police of this city, on this evening, rattle along in their patrol wagons?

What does it mean when the militia stands warlike and ready for bloody work at our armories?

What are the gatling guns and cannon for?

Is this military display of barbarism arranged for your entertainment?

All these preparations, my friends, are *made in your behalf.*

Your masters have perceived your discontent.

They do not like discontented slaves.

They want to make you contented at all hazards, and if you are stubborn they will force or kill you.

Look at the killing of your brothers at McCormick's yesterday. What did they do? The police tell you they were a most dangerous crowd, armed to their teeth. The fact is, they, like ignorant children, indulged in the harmless sport of bombarding McCormick's slaughter house with stones. They paid the penalty of this folly with their blood.

The lesson I draw from this occurrence is that workingmen must arm themselves for defense, so that they may be able to cope with the government hirelings of their masters.

I see Mr. Parsons has arrived. He is a much abler speaker in your tongue than I am, therefore I will conclude by introducing him.

A. R. Parsons on the Rights and Wrongs of Labor.

Captain Black.—"Now, Mr. Parsons, going back to the meeting, retracing our steps for a moment—will you tell us, please, what was the substance of your speech that night, as fully as you can remember?"

THE SPEECH.

"I have taken some notes of reference since then to refresh my memory. I recollect distinctly of mentioning all of these points, but I could not recall them seriatim unless I put them on paper, and that is the reason I have done so.

"When I was introduced I looked at the crowd and observed that it was quite a large crowd. I am familiar with public speaking and with crowds, and I should estimate there were three thousand men present, and I consider myself a judge in such matters. The street was packed from sidewalk to sidewalk, north and south of the wagon, but especially south of the wagon, for a considerable distance. I faced the south.

I first called the attention of those present to the evidence of discontent among the working classes, not alone of Chicago, not alone of the United States, but of the civilized world, and I asked the question, if these evidences of discontent, as could be seen in strikes and lockouts and boycotts, were not indications that there was something radically wrong in the existing order of things in our social affairs. I then alluded to the eight-hour movement, and spoke of it as a movement designed to give steady employment to the employed, work to the idle, and thereby bring comfort and cheer to the homes of the destitute and relieving the unrelieved and wearisome toil of those who worked not alone ten hours, but twelve, fourteen and sixteen hours a day. I said that the eight-hour movement was in the interests of civilization, of prosperity, of the public welfare, and that it was demanded by every interest in the community, and that I was glad to see them assembled on that occasion to give their voice in favor of the adoption of the eight-hour workday.

I then referred again to the general condition of labor throughout the country. I spoke of my recent travels through the States of Pennsylvania and Ohio, where I had met and addressed thousands and thousands of workingmen. I told of the Tuscarora Valley and of the Hocking Valley and of the Monongahela Valley—among the miners of this country, where their wages averaged 24½ cents a day. I showed, of course, these were not wages they received while at work, but that the difficulty was they did not get the day's work, and consequently they had to sum up the totals and divide it. Throughout the year it amounted to 24½ cents a day. I asked if this was not a condition of affairs calculated to arouse the discontent of the people, and to make them clamor for redress and relief. I pointed to the fact that in the city of Pittsburgh a report was made by, I think, the Superintendent of Police of that city, stating that at the Bethel Home, a charitable institution in that city, from January 1, 1884, to January 1, 1885, there were 26,374 destitute men—tramps—American sovereigns—who had applied for a night's lodging and a morsel of food at one establishment alone in the city of Pittsburgh. I referred, of course, to many other places and similiar things, showing the general condition of labor in the country.

I then spoke of the eight-hour movement—that it was designed to bring relief to these men and to the country. I thought surely that there was nothing in it to excite such hostility on the part of employers and on the part of monopoly and corporations against it, as was witnessed in different parts of the country. I referred to the refusal of the corporations and monopolists to grant and concede this modest request of the working class, and their attempts to defeat it. I then referred to the fact that in the face of all these causes producing these effects, the monopolistic newspapers, in the interests of corporations, blamed such men as I—blamed the so-called agitators, blamed the workingmen—for these evidences of discontent, this turmoil and confusion, and so-called disorder. I called the attention of the crowd specifically to that fact—that we were being blamed for this thing, when, on the contrary, it was evident to any fair-minded man that we were simply calling the attention of the people to this condition of things and seeking a redress for it. I impressed that upon the crowd specifically, and I remember that in response to that several gentlemen spoke up loudly and said: 'Well, we need a good many just such men as you to right these wrongs and to arouse the people.'

I spoke of the compulsory idleness and starvation wages, and how these things drove the workingmen to desperation—drove them to commit acts for which they ought not to be held responsible; that they were the creatures of circumstances, and that this condition of things was the fault, not of the workingmen, but of those who claimed the right to control and regulate the rights of the workingmen. I pointed out the fact that monopoly, in its course in grinding down labor in this country and in refusing to concede anything to it—refusing to make any concessions whatever—that in persisting in such course it was creating revolutionists, and if there was a single revolutionist in America, monopoly and corporations were directly responsible for his existence. I specifically called attention to this fact, in order to defend myself from the charges constantly being made through the mouthpiece of monopoly—the capitalistic press.

I called attention to the Chicago *Times* and other newspapers. I called the attention of the working-people that night to the strike of 1877, when the Chicago *Times* declared that hand-grenades ought to be thrown among the striking sailors who were then upon a strike on the river wharves in this city, in order to teach them a lesson, and that other strikers might be warned by their fate. I said that the Chicago *Times* was the first dynamiter in America, and as the mouthpiece of monopoly and corporations it was the first to advocate the killing of people when they protested against wrong and oppression. I spoke of the Chicago *Tribune*, which at that day advocated that when bread was given to the poor strychnine should be placed on it. I also called attention to *Frank Leslie's Illustrated Paper*, which declared in an editorial that the American toiler must be driven to his task either by the slave-driver's lash or the immediate prospect of want. I spoke of the New York *Herald*, and its saying that lead should be given to any tramp who should come around. Whenever a workingman, thrown out of employment and forced to wander from place to place in search of work, away from family and home, asked for a crust of bread, the New York *Herald* advised those to whom he applied to fill him with lead instead of bread.

I called attention to what Tom Scott, the railway monopolist, said during the strike of 1877, "Give them the rifle diet and see how they like that kind of bread." I referred to Jay Gould when he said we would shortly have a monarchy in this country, and to a similar statement in the Indianapolis *Journal*.

Then I referred to how monopoly was putting these threats into practice. They not only used these threats but they put them into practice, and I cited East St. Louis, where Jay Gould called for men and paid them $5 a day for firing on harmless, innocent, unarmed workingmen, killing nine of them and one woman in cold-blooded murder. I referred to the Saginaw valley, where the militia were used to put down strikes. I referred to Lemont, Ill., where defenseless and innocent citizens and their town were invaded by militia of the State of Illinois, and without any pretext men, women and children were fired upon and slaughtered in cold blood. I referred to the McCormick strike on the previous day, and denounced the action of the police on that day as an outrage.

I asked the workingmen if these were not facts, and if monopolies and corporations were not responsible for them, and were they not driving the people into this condition of things. And then I used some words of some phrase in connection with the use of the military and the police and the Pinkerton thugs to shoot down workingmen, to drive them back into submission and starvation wages.

I then referred to the *Chicago Mail* of Monday, to which my attention had been called on Tuesday afternoon. In an editorial it asserted that Parsons and Spies incited the trouble at McCormick's factory the day before and ought to be lynched or driven out of the city. Now the truth is, I was at Cincinnati at that time. I called attention to the fact that the newspapers were wickedly exciting the people against the workingmen. I denied the newspaper charge that we were sneaks and cowards, and defied them to run us out of the city.

I pointed to the fact that the capitalistic press were the subsidized agents and organs of monopoly, and that they held stocks and bonds in corporations and railroads, and that no man could be elected an alderman in this city unless he had the sanction of some one of the corporations and monopolies of this city. Then I said, I am not here, fellow workingmen, for the purpose of inciting anybody, but to tell the truth, and to state the facts as they actually exist, though it should cost me my life in doing so. I then referred to the Cincinnati demonstration, at which I was present the Sunday previous. I said that the organizations of workingmen in that city—trades unions and other organizations—had a grand street parade and picnic. They sent for me to go down there and address them. It was an eight-hour demonstration. I attended on that occasion and spoke to them. I referred to the fact that they turned out in thousands and that they marched with Winchester rifles, two or three companies of them. I suppose there were about two hundred men at the head of the column, the Cincinnati Rifle Union. I said that at the head of the procession they bore the red flag—the red flag of liberty, fraternity, equality of labor, all over the world—the red flag of emancipated labor. I pointed out that every other flag repudiated the workingman, outlawed the workingman, and that he had no shield and no flag but the red one.

I then referred to our country, and to men saying this was a movement of foreigners, and so on. I pointed out the fact that the desire for right and the thirst for liberty and for justice was not a foreign affair at all; it was one that concerned Americans as well as foreigners, and that patriotism was a humbug in this connection; that it was used to separate the people, to divide them, and to antagonize them against each other; that the Irish were separated and their national feeling was kept alive as against an Englishman in order that the exploiters and depredators among them might more easily make them victims and use them as their tools. I referred in that connection to land monopoly and showed how the farms of this country were being driven into land tenures like those of Europe. I called attention to an article which appeared in the North American *Review* last December, which I think was by an American statistician of this country, in which it was stated that over three hundred and fifty millions of dollars in mortgages were held on farms west of the Alleghanies by capitalists living in the little State of Connecticut, demonstrating that Americans need not go abroad to find the evils of land monopoly. I stated that over fifty per cent, perhaps two-thirds, of the farms in the states of Illinois, Wisconsin and Michigan were under mortgage, and that landlordism was making it impossible for the toilers to pay for these farms, and that they were breaking them up, forcing them to become tenants, and instituting the European system in this country. I said I did not regard that as a question of patriotism, nor a foreign question, but an American question concerning Americans.

I referred to the banking monopoly of the country, by which a few men are empowered to make money scarce in order that they may control markets, run corners on the different mediums of exchange, and produce a panic in the country by making money scarce. They made the price of articles dear, threw labor out of employment, and brought on bankruptcy. I said that monopoly owned labor and employed its armed hirelings to subjugate the people.

In the light of these facts and of your inalienable right to life, liberty and the pursuit of happiness, I said, it behooves you, as you love your wives and children, if you would not see them perish with want and hunger, yourselves killed or cut down like dogs in the streets —Americans, as you love liberty and independence, arm! arm yourselves! A voice then said to me, "we are ready now." I answered, "No, you are not." I did not understand exactly what the gentleman said, but I made that reply, as has been testified to by many here. I called attention to the fact that the Constitution of the United States gave the right to every man to keep and bear arms, but monopoly was seeking to deprive the citizen of that right. I called attention to the fact that the Constitution guaranteed us the right of free speech, of free press, and of unmolested assembly, but that corporations and monopoly, by paid-for decisions of courts, had trampled these rights under foot, or were attempting to do so.

I called attention to the fact that the Government of the United States was in the hands of the money power, and that from this fact —the sway of this money power—it was almost impossible for a poor man to get justice in a court of law; that law was for sale, just like bread; if you had no money you could get no bread, and without money you could get no justice; that justice was almost beyond the reach of the poor, and that the producers were made and kept poor by the grinding processes of the corporations and monopolies.

I then called attention to Socialism and explained what it was. I gave them Webster's definition of it—that it meant a more equitable arrangement of society, a more just and equitable arrangement of social affairs; that there was nothing in the word or in the purposes of Socialism for anybody to become alarmed at. On the contrary, it should be hailed with delight by all, as it was designed to make all happy and prosperous.

I then spoke in this connection of the wage system of industry, and showed that it was a despotism, inherently and necessarily so, because under it the wage-worker was forced and compelled, under penalty of hunger, to work on such conditions and at such terms as the employers of labor may see fit to dictate to him. This I defined to be slavery, hence I said they were wage-slaves, and that the wage system was what Socialism proposed to displace. I then showed the power that the wage system gave to the employing class by the lockout, the blacklist, and the discharge; that I myself had been blacklisted because I exercised my right of free speech as an American, because I saw fit to be a member of a labor organization; that I had been deprived repeatedly of my bread for that reason by my employer.

I then called attention to the United States census for the year 1880, and I showed that the returns made there—statistically gotten up by a republican administration—these returns showed that eighty-five cents from every dollar produced went to the profit-taking classes, and that fifteen cents was the average sum received by the producing class for having produced the whole dollar. This labor bureau showed that in manufactures the daily average product of the workers amounted to ten dollars per day, and their wages or share of the product averaged $1.15 per day. I said that this was wrong, and that in the face of such a condition of things we could expect nothing but poverty, destitution, want and misery. I showed how under this system the workingmen of the United States were really doing ten hours' work for two hours' pay; that the employers say to the men: "You want to work only eight hours. Do you mean to say that we must give you ten hours' pay for eight hours' work?" I said: Gentlemen, fellow workmen, let us answer these men and say and prove to them by the official statistics of the United States census that we are not receiving now but two hours' pay for ten hours' work; that that is what the wages of the country on the average represent. I spoke of corporations crowding the workingmen to the wall, and summed it up in some such words as these: Now, for years past the Associated Press, manipulated by Jay Gould and other traitors to the republic and their infamous minions, have been sowing the seeds of revolution. These seeds, I thought, could be summarized about as follows:

To deprive labor of the ballot.

To substitute a monarchy for the republic.

To rob labor and then make poverty a crime.

To deprive small farmers of their land, and then convert them into serfs to serve a huge landlordism.

To teach labor that bread and water are all that it needs.

To throw bombs into crowds of workingmen who were opposed to laboring for starvation wages.

To take the ballot by force of arms from the majority when it is used against the interests of corporations and capital.

To put strychnine upon the bread of the poor.

To hang workingmen to lamp-posts by mobs in the absence of testimony to legally convict them.

To drive the poor working classes into open mutiny against the laws, in order to secure their conviction and punishment afterward.

These threats and diabolical teachings, I said, had been openly and boldly uttered by the great conspiracy—the solid Associated Press and monopolies of this country—for years, against the liberties of the poor, and the workingman of America was as sensitive to the wrongs imposed upon him as would be the possessor of millions. I said that this was the seed from which had sprung the labor movement, and it was as natural as cause and effect.

[The workingmen present appeared to be very much interested. I never saw a more quiet, orderly, interested gathering of men—and I have spoken to a great many in my life—than was present on that occasion.]

I called their attention to the fact that labor paid for everything —paid all the expenses of the government, of the police, of the armies, of legislators, of congressmen, of judges—paid everything. Labor paid it all. That I, as a tenant—I used my own case as an illustration— paid all the taxes. Said I: Now, the landlord claims that he pays the taxes. What are the facts? When I pay him my rent, I in fact pay the taxes. He claims that he makes all the repairs on the house, and paints it up and does all such things. He does not do anything of the kind. He is simply my agent to look after these things, and I, as his tenant, pay for it all. So it is with all tenants.

I said that labor bears all the burdens but derives none of the benefits of our present civilization. I referred to the fact that it was through these methods that the working people, who produced all the wealth, were kept poor, and being poor they were ignorant. That our school teachers had yet to learn the fact that the great need of the people was more material comforts before it would be possible for them to become amenable to the influences of educational forces; that ignorance was the result of poverty; that intemperance was the result of poverty, and for every man who was poor because he drank I could show twenty men who drank because they were poor. I said that this poverty, this discord, this commotion in the civilized world was because of the social disease, the cramming of people into hovels and dens unfit for animals to live in; it was the cause of the death of the young, of old age coming upon middle age; that it was the cause of crime; that poverty was at the root and bottom of war, of discord and of strife, and that this poverty was an artificial, unnatural poverty which Socialism proposed to remedy.

I was at this time, as you understand, gentlemen, making a speech for Socialism. I had been talking especially for Socialism. I then spoke as a trades-unionist. I am a member of my union and of the Knights of Labor. I said that these organizations differed somewhat with Socialism in that they hoped to receive and obtain redress within the present system, but that was not possible, in my belief; that a study of social affairs and of historical development had taught me that the system itself was at fault, and that as long as the cause remained the effects would be felt; that every trades union, every assembly of the Knights of Labor, every organization of workingmen, had for its ultimate end—let its course be what it might—the emancipation of labor from economic dependence, and whether they sought it or not, events and the developments of this existing wage system would of necessity force or drive these men into Socialism as their only savior, and the only means by which they could live—that they could exist in the end in no other way. If I remember rightly I then said that strikes were attempts to right these wrongs on the part of the unions and the Knights of Labor; that I did not believe in strikes; I did not believe that redress could be had by that method; that the power was in the hands of the employer to refuse; that if the men went on a strike the employer could meet the strike with a lockout, and could keep them out until they were so hungry that they would through their destitution be compelled to return and accept the terms of the employer; therefore, strikes must of necessity fail—as a general thing.

I called attention to the scabs, and said that the unionist made war on the scabs. Now, said I, here is the distinction between a Socialist and a trades-unionist. The unionist fights the scab. What is a scab? As a general thing, a man who, being out of employment and destitute, is driven by necessity to go to work in some other man's place at less wages than has previously been paid. He is at once denounced as a scab by the unionists, and war is made upon him. Now, Socialists don't do this; they regard these men as the victims of a false system and to be pitied. The scabs might be compared to fleas on a dog. The unionists want to kill the fleas, but the Socialists would kill the dog; that dog is the wage system of slavery.

I then pointed to the ballot—how we were swindled at the ballot box and defrauded and cheated, how we were bulldozed and intimidated and bribed and corrupted—yes, corrupted by the very money that had been stolen from us. Men would come to us when we were poor and give us bread-money if we would vote their ticket, and we often did it through necessity, and for these and other reasons, through this intimidation, bribery and corruption, the workingmen had but little to expect from the ballot—that a man who could not control his bread stood a poor chance to control his ballot. I said we had petitioned and passed resolutions, and had done everything in our power for redress; in fact, there was a rebuff on every occasion.

I then said to them: Gentlemen, Socialism means the free association of the people for the purpose of production and consumption — in other words, universal co-operation. Socialism is the abolition of the private ownership or monopoly of the resources of life, the means of subsistence — capital; placing the means of life in the hands of the whole people for their joint use and equal benefit. This is the sum total of Socialism, and the only permanent solution of the difficulties between capital and labor. I said that monopoly and corporation had formed a gigantic conspiracy against the working classes. I then called upon them to unite, to organize, to make every endeavor to obtain eight hours; that the less-hours movement meant a peaceful solution of the labor trouble; that if the employers in this and all other countries would concede this demand it meant peace. If they refused — it meant war; not by the working classes, not by laborers, but by monopolists and corporations upon the lives, liberty, and happiness of the working classes.

I said that capital in the hands of corporations and monopoly deprived the laborers of their labor product, of their right to live, and was driving labor into open revolt and forcing people to defend themselves and to protect and maintain their right to self-preservation, and self-preservation would compel the workers to abolish the government which enslaves them. I said the monopoly conspiracy originated in the great railroad strike of 1877, that this conspiracy since that time had proposed to use force, and that they used force. Vanderbilt said 'the public be damned.' The New York *World* and other papers had said that the American laborer must be contented with the wages he received, and not expect any more wages than his European brother, and be contented with that station in life to which it had pleased God to call him. I then appealed to them to defend themselves, their rights and their liberties — to combine, to unite, for in union there was strength.

That, gentlemen, was the subject of my hour's speech at the Haymarket.

CAPTAIN BLACK — When you were referring in your speech to Jay Gould or to the Southwestern system, do you remember any interruption from the crowd, or any response connected with the name of Gould?

A. Yes. I omitted that. Some one said "Hang him." My response to that was. that this was not a conflict between individuals, but for a change of system, and that Socialism designed to remove the causes which produced the pauper and the millionaire, but did not aim at the life of individuals.

Mr. Fielden's speech was not reported. Some of the papers of the next day contained a condensed report, but as it was brought out on the evidence that the reporter had been charged only to report "incendiary passages," perfect reliance cannot be placed on the reports they submitted for acceptance. Mr. Fielden, in his speech before sentence was passed upon him went sufficiently into the details of his speech, to which the reader is referred.

CHAPTER IV.

THE EMPANELING OF THE JURY.

On May 18th the Grand Jury began the examination of witnesses, Judge Rogers having charged them "that Anarchism should be suppressed." On the 25th they indicted August Spies, Michel Schwab, Albert R. Parsons, Adolph Fischer, Samuel Fielden, Louis Engel, Louis Lingg, Oscar Neebe, Rudolph Schnaubelt and Wilhelm Seliger, for the murder of Mathias J. Degan, and others for conspiracy, riot and unlawful assembly. Schnaubelt left the city and never returned. Neebe had not been arrested at first, but immediately on the suppression of the *Arbeiter-Zeitung* he had stirred himself so energetically in its behalf that it soon bid fair to stand on a firmer basis than ever. He was then arrested, but on June 14 he was admitted to bail in the sum of $17,000, his share in the "conspiracy" and its results not considered to be so well established as that of the other prisoners. Seliger turned informer and was not included with the others.

The trial was commenced before Judge Gary in the Criminal Court June 21, and the sensation of the day was the return and surrender of A. R. Parsons, who walked quietly into court with his counsel, Captain Black, and took his seat beside his indicted comrades. And in this connection the following story, related by a reporter in one of the city dailies, is too good to be lost:

THE EMPANELING OF THE JURY.

The question is often asked, "Do detectives detect?" It is fair to presume that in some cases they do not. Schnaubelt, whom it is now believed is the man who threw the Haymarket bomb, was firmly in the clutches of the detectives, but after being questioned by Lieutenant John Shea, was allowed to go on his way unmolested.

During the trial of the Anarchists a party of newspaper men and several Central Station detectives were standing one afternoon in front of the Criminal Court building. A little wiry fellow, with black hair and mustache and piercing black eyes, walked by briskly with Captain Black and entered the court house.

"I'll bet a dollar to a nickel," said a newspaper reporter, "that that little man is A. R. Parsons."

"Nonsense," said one of the detectives, "not in a thousand years. Why, man, don't you suppose I know Parsons when I see him? He isn't within five hundred miles of Chicago. Say, we detectives have been looking for him," and, as if this settled the matter, the detective entered the building. He had no sooner reached the stairway that leads to Judge Gary's court-room than an officer met him and exclaimed, "Parsons has just given himself up." The detective nearly fainted, and for several weeks he kept out of the way of the newspaper man.

Twenty-one days were consumed in the effort to secure twelve men who were esteemed competent to give the accused an unbiased trial on the evidence. But as the question of what was and what was not "bias" entered largely into the effort, and forms an important part of the history of the trial, let us examine the process of selecting "twelve men, good and true."

The right of trial by "an impartial jury" is a Constitutional provision, and it is a well-known principle that all statutes *must be construed* in conformity with the Constitution. The statute (March 12, 1874,) provides "that in the trial of any criminal cause, the fact that a person called as a juror has formed an opinion or an impression, based upon rumor or newspaper statements (about the truth of which he has expressed no opinion,) shall not disqualify him to serve as a juror in such case, if he shall, upon oath, state that he believes that he can fairly and impartially render a verdict therein, in accordance with the law and the evidence, and the court shall be satisfied of the truth of the statement."

In cases which have since arisen this statute has received a construction, and the essence of these cases is that this statute declares to be competent a juryman who has a *slight* opinion, or an opinion based upon rumor or newspaper statements, and where he will swear and the court is satisfied that such opinions will not affect him in the rendition of a fair and impartial verdict. This was always the construction of the law. In the first case in which this statute came under consideration, (September Term, 1874, 74 Ill., 361,) Mr. Justice Schofield, delivering the opinion of the court, says:

"The juror, Broubaker, we do not think was competent. He is unable to state that he could sit as an impartial juror in the case. He was, among others, asked this question: 'You think that you have heard reports which *you believe* to be true, in respect to the defendants, which would have a tendency, in some degree, to bias your mind in this respect?' and he answers: 'It may have.'

"When the juror has been exposed to influences, the probable effect of which is to create a prejudice in his mind against the defendant, which it would require evidence to overcome, to render him competent it should appear that he can, when in the jury box, *entirely* disregard those influences, and try the case without in any degree being affected by them." Judgment reversed.

Let us now proceed to the examination of jurors as illustrating Judge Gary's rulings, bearing in mind that the number of peremptory challenges permitted to each prisoner arraigned was twenty.

M. T. CAREY, on the first day, stated that he had read an account of the case, had talked of it, *believed what he had heard and read to be true*, and had formed *and expressed* an opinion as to the guilt or innocence of the defendants. He also expressed the belief that he could try the case fairly. He was asked the question whether that was *such an opinion as would require evidence to remove.* The court decided that this was an incompetent question, because it called for the opinion of the juror as to the future effect of evidence on his mind. This juror was subsequently challenged for cause, but upon another ground.

CLARENCE H. HILL stated that he had read accounts of the Haymarket meeting, had conversations in reference to it, and upon the information derived from all sources, had formed an opinion as to the guilt or innocence of the defendants, which he still entertained, and which was *based upon his belief in what he had read;* and that he was prejudiced against Socialists, Anarchists, etc. He was finally asked:

Q. You have no opinions, biases or prejudices, which *it would require evidence to overcome?*

A. Yes, sir; I have.

The juror was challenged for cause, the challenge was overruled, and he was thereupon challenged peremptorily by defendants.

W. N. UPHAM was another who was examined on the first day. He stated that he had read the newspaper accounts of the Haymarket affair, and had conversation with various persons upon the subject; that from all sources of information he had formed an opinion upon the guilt or innocence of some of the defendants, which he believed he *had expressed to others; that he believed to be true the statement which he had heard and read, and that he expressed a belief that what he had heard was true.* Subsequently, upon a direct question by the court, to-wit:

Q. The question is whether you have ever formed or expressed an opinion as to the guilt or innocence of any one of these eight men of the murder of Officer Degan?

A. I can't say what I have expressed in words, but *my opinion was that some of them are guilty.*

He also said he believed that he could render a fair verdict on the evidence.

THE COURT.— That is not any ground of challenge under the law!

He stated further that he had the same opinion as to the guilt of some of the defendants, and then the question was asked as to whether testimony would be required to remove that opinion before he would be unbiased and free to act upon the evidence. The question was objected to, quite freely argued, and the objection was then sustained by the court. The juror was then challenged for cause, the challenge was overruled, and then challenged peremptorily.

E. F. SHEDD, examined on June 23d, stated that he had read of the Haymarket affair in the papers, and at the time formed an opinion as to the guilt or innocence of the defendants, which opinion he still entertained, no circumstances having occurred to change it. That such opinion was formed from the belief by him of the truth of the statements which he had heard and read, and that he *had expressed* the opinion to others. He said also: " I would have my opinion, my own opinion, until it was set aside by the whole testimony," and that *it would require evidence to remove the opinion which he had.* He was thereupon challenged for cause and the court overruled the challenge.

The same person was thereupon interrogated, and stated that he *had a prejudice* against Communists, Anarchists and Socialists as a class, which was of such a character that it would *prevent his listening to the testimony and rendering an impartial verdict* if it were conceded or proved that the defendants belonged to such class. He stated further:

" I think the mere fact of their being Communists *would influence my opinion as a juror.*"

Q. And therefore you would not find the same verdict upon the same evidence as you would if they were not so — you would require additional evidence.

A. Yes, sir; and that he *would find the defendants guilty upon less evidence than if they were law-abiding citizens.*

But having stated that he thought he could try the cause fairly, the challenge for cause was overruled and another peremptory challenge used.

WILLIAM NEIL stated that he had heard and read about the Haymarket difficulty, and believed enough of what he had so heard *to form an opinion* as to the guilt or innocence of *some* of the defendants, but thought *strong evidence* to the contrary would change that opinion; that he *had expressed* said opinion and that "it would take pretty strong evidence to change my opinion." And again he said: "It would take pretty strong evidence to remove the impression that I now have." That he believed his opinion, based upon what he had heard and read, would accompany him through the trial, and *would influence* him in determining and getting at a result. But he also stated that he believed he could give a fair verdict on whatever evidence he should hear. Thereupon the juror was challenged for cause on all his answers, and particularly on the ground that he had expressed the opinion which he still entertained, which challenge was overruled, and thereupon was challenged peremptorily.

JAMES S. OAKLEY stated that he had heard and read of the Haymarket difficulty, and believed enough of what he had so read and heard *to form an opinion* as to the guilt or innocence of some of the defendants, which opinion he *had expressed* and still entertained. He was asked if that opinion was so strongly and firmly fixed that it would take strong evidence to the contrary to overrule it. This question was refused by the court. He also stated that he believed that he could determine the question of the guilt or innocence of the defendants on the evidence alone. He still further stated as follows:

Q. Still you think that the opinion you now have and what you have heard and read would influence you in arriving at a verdict?

A. I do.

Q. *You do think it would influence you?*

A. *I do.*

He was further asked as to his prejudice against Socialists, Anarchists, etc., and admitted that he had such a prejudice, and was then asked: "If it should be proven or conceded on the trial of this case that some of them are Anarchists or Communists, would this opinion of yours, in regard to these classes, influence you in arriving at a just and impartial verdict?" The question was refused by the court. Mr. Oakley again stating that he had expressed his opinion as to the guilt or innocence of the defendants, or some of them, was challenged for cause on all his answers, and particularly on the ground of the expression of his opinion. The challenge was overruled and another peremptory challenge rendered necessary.

Pages might be filled with similar evidence; but for the purpose of introducing some of the rulings of the court, and its peculiar method in "coaching" jurors, a few more should be cited.

H. F. CHANDLER stated that he had heard and read of the Haymarket affair, and from what he had so read and heard, had formed an opinion as to the guilt or innocence of one or more of the defendants, which he still entertained and which he *had expressed*. That he believed in the truth of the statements he had read and heard, and had never questioned it. The following questions and answers thereupon ensued:

Q. Is that a decided opinion as to the guilt or innocence?

A. *It is a decided opinion;* yes, sir.

Q. Your mind is pretty well made up now as to their guilt or innocence?

A. Yes, sir. Well, it will take evidence to satisfy me on that point. I don't know. I have simply heard one side of the case. I have just read the newspaper matter. I have formed an opinion as far as that goes.

Q. Would it be hard to change your opinion.

A. It might be hard; I can't say. I don't know whether it would be hard or not.

He also stated that he had a strong prejudice against Socialists, Anarchists and Communists, and was then asked if that prejudice would influence his verdict; which question was refused by the court. He further stated that he thought he had expressed his opinion as to the guilt or innocence of the defendants quite frequently; and was thereupon challenged for cause.

Certainly not a very marked case of *impartiality*, but the court thereupon took him in hand and he was led to state that he had an opinion as to whether the defendants did the act which caused the death of Degan, but that that opinion was based wholly upon what he had heard and read and not from conversation with any person who was present at the time of the transaction. While it may not be apparent that this in the least mitigates the fact that the juror was not competent to decide impartially, the court thought otherwise and laid down the following ruling: "It don't seem to me that it makes any difference in the competency of a juror whether he has simply *formed* an opinion, or *expressed* an opinion which he has formed. I don't see how it makes a particle of difference in his state of mind. *Every man is in favor of justice* and fair dealings as between other people where his *own interests* are not affected; and, as I have said before, I think it must be — I think it is the nature of any man to find out the truth of any transaction, that he will, when the original sources are presented to him, follow them, and not any hearsay that he has ever heard." The challenge for cause was thereupon overruled and resort rendered necessary to another peremptory challenge.

D. F. SWAN presents another typical instance. He had heard and read about the Haymarket trouble; had formed an opinion as to the guilt or innocence of the defendants, or some of them, which he still entertained, and had frequently expressed. The opinion was *firmly fixed in his mind* at the time of his examination. He stated, however, that he believed he could be governed by the evidence and the law; that he had discussed the case with his neighbors and friends, and was *prejudiced* in a general way against labor organizers. The court refused to allow him to be questioned as to whether his admitted prejudice against Socialists, Anarchists, etc., would influence his verdict. Being challenged for cause, the court interrogated him as follows:

Q. Have you any feeling against either of them, other than such as grows out of what you have heard about their connection with the Haymarket?

A. No, sir.

Q. That is the only feeling you have?

A. Yes, sir.

Q. And that feeling is based upon the assumption — you have taken it for granted that what you have read and heard about them was true, substantially?

A. Yes, sir.

Q. Now, do you believe that you can sit here as a juror and listen to the evidence on both sides that may be presented here on their trial, and from that evidence only make up your mind fairly and impartially as to what the real truth is about their connection with the matter?

A. I guess I could.

Q. Without any reference to what you have heard about it heretofore, or what you have read about it?

A. Yes, sir.

That was sufficient; his "firmly-fixed opinion," his prejudice "against labor organizers," counted for nought. However narrow his mind, his "guess" that he was broadminded enough to rise above his own narrowness, inherent in his nature from the very nature of the case, was enough for an American judge, between whom and Jeffries there had elapsed two centuries, to overrule the challenge for cause and compel resort to the rapidly diminishing number of peremptory challenges. An Orangeman trying a Roman Catholic for an alleged assault; a politician investigating a "bloody outrage" at the South; even a judge of the supreme court sitting on an electoral commission, might affirm ability to rise above prejudice and firmly-fixed opinions, but instances are rare.

GEORGE N. PORTER said that he had both formed and expressed an opinion as to the guilt or innocence of the defendants, which opinion he thought *would bias his judgment.* He would try to go by the evidence, but *what he had read would have a great deal to do with his verdict.* His mind was certainly biased now, and it would take a great deal of evidence to change it. Whereupon Mr. Porter was challenged for cause.

On examination by the State, in answer to the question whether he believed he could determine alone from the proof the guilt or innocence of the defendants, without consulting his opinion, or without being influenced by it, he said: " I hardly know how to answer that question, I should certainly try to." Being asked the same question over again he said: " Well, I rather think I could." In answer to the court, Mr. Porter said: " I think what I have read and heard before I came into court would have some influence with me." He was afraid that what he had read and heard before would have some effect upon the kind of verdict which he should render. He was finally led to say he believed he could fairly and impartially try the case and render a verdict according to the law and the evidence; at least, he would certainly try to. Whereupon challenge for cause was overruled.

The defendant's counsel pushed the inquiry still further and Mr. Porter admitted that he had a prejudice against Communists, Socialists and Anarchists, and said that he should certainly *try* to go by the evidence, but he thought in this case it would *be awful hard work for him to do it.* He should try very hard to do it, and he *believed* he could. He was asked whether he had ever expressed his opinion that he believed the narration. He said: " Well, I don't know that I ever said it in that many words, but I meant that, of course, certainly."

Q. You don't know, then, that you ever did say that you believed what you heard, or that you believed what you had read?

A. Why, we have talked about it there a great many times, and I have always expressed my opinion. I believe what I have read in the papers — *believe that the parties are guilty.*

Q. Now, then, you say that you did, in the discussion of it, in substance, say that you believed what you have read in the papers?

A. Yes, sir; I have.

Q. And it was from what you have read in the papers that you formed an opinion?

A. Yes, sir.

Challenge for cause was hereupon renewed. It would seem to be awful hard work to "coach" this juryman up to the proper point of impartiality to fairly try the case; the court, however, again took him in hand. Being asked whether he had expressed an opinion as to the truthfulness of the account itself which he had read or heard, he said:

"Well, that is a pretty hard question to answer; I don't know. I have expressed myself as believing it. I don't know."

Q. Well, believing—

A. Believing what I read in the papers.

Q. Believing the opinion that you had about the case and the defendant, *or* believing the story as it was printed?

A. Why, believing, of course, the opinion of the defendants, and the story, believing it all, believing it just as I read it in the newspapers. * * * *

Q. Did you ever express any opinion as to whether the newspapers had got bodily or the substance of the story right or not?

A. Oh, I don't know that I ever did that; no, sir.

This last was sufficient to overrule the challenge and to oblige the issuance of another peremptory challenge. In other words, he had never expressed an opinion on what he had never thought about; or, in view of his previous replies, he had never expressed an opinion against his own expressed opinion! and therefore was fully qualified to sit on the jury!

H. N. SMITH, in his examination, exhibits very clearly on his part, if not on that of the court, a decided bias. He said he had formed *quite a decided opinion* as to the guilt or innocence of the defendants; had read the newspapers at the time; had had frequent conversations in regard to the matter; had expressed his opinion and still entertained it. He said he was afraid he would listen a little *more intently* to testimony which concurred with his opinion than to testimony on the other side.

Q. That is, you would be willing to have your opinion strengthened and would hate very much to have it dissolved?

A. *I would.*

Q. Under these circumstances, do you think you could render a fair and impartial verdict?

A. I don't think I could.

Q. You think you would be prejudiced?

A. I think I would be prejudiced *because my feeling is very bitter.*   *   *   *   *

Q. The question is whether or not your prejudice would in any way influence you in coming to an opinion, arriving at a verdict?

A. I think it would.

Q. You think it would take less testimony as a juryman to come to a conclusion which you now have than to come to the opposite conclusion?

A. Yes, sir.

Q. That is your best judgment now?

A. Yes, sir.

Whereupon the state took him in hand as a promising juror and induced him to retract his statement that he thought his "decided opinion" and "bitter feeling" must influence his verdict, and led him to state that he thought he would nevertheless act fairly. The court then followed this up and the juror then stated that he didn't know any of the defendants; he had a personal feeling; some of the officers were personal friends of his, but he had no feeling toward any of the defendants upon any ground *other* than what he had heard or read. He had talked with persons who were at the Haymarket at the time of the excitement, but the name of no man was mentioned.

The challenge for cause was overruled and another peremptory challenge sacrificed. One more instance and we will pass on to the accepted jury.

JAMES H. WALKER said he had formed an opinion on the question of the guilt or innocence of the defendants of the murder of Mr. Degan, which opinion he still entertained and had expressed to others. Asked as to whether this opinion would influence his verdict, he replied:

"Well, I am willing to admit that my opinion would handicap my judgment, possibly. I feel that I could be governed by the testimony."

Further on he was asked:

"Then your belief is that you could listen to the testimony and other proof that might be introduced, and the charge of the court, and decide upon that alone, uninfluenced and unbiased by the opinion that you now have?

A. *No*, I don't say that.

Q. That is what I asked you.

A. I said *I would be handicapped.*"

He also stated that he was *prejudiced* against Socialists, Anarchists and Communists.

The following question was then asked him:

Q. Now, considering all prejudice, and all opinions that you now have, is there anything which, if the testimony was equally balanced, would require you to decide one way or the other in accordance with your opinion or your prejudice?

A. If the testimony was equally balanced I should hold my present opinion, sir.

Q. That is, you would throw your opinion upon the scale, which would give it greater weight, your present opinion would turn the balance of the scale in favor of your present opinion? That is, assuming that your present opinion is that you believe the defendants guilty—or some of them—now suppose, if the testimony were equally balanced, your present opinion would warrant you in convicting them, you believe, assuming that your present opinion is that they are guilty?

A. I presume it would.

Q. Well, you *believe* it would—that is your present belief, is it?

A. *Yes.*

Thereupon counsel for defense challenged Mr. Walker for cause.

Upon examination by the State's Attorney he, like the others, answered the usual questions satisfactorily, and thereupon was interrogated by the court, as follows:

THE COURT.—Mr. Walker, I suppose you know that the law is that no man is to be convicted of any crime unless the evidence upon his trial, unless that evidence proves that he is guilty beyond a reasonable doubt?

A. Yes, sir.

Q. Now, this *confusion* about opinions and verdicts I want to clear up if I can. I suppose you know that no man is to be tried upon prior impression or prior opinion of the jurors that are called into the case?

A. Yes, sir.

Q But only on the evidence. That you are familiar with, of course. Now, do you believe that you can fairly and impartially render a verdict without any regard to rumor and what you may have in your mind in the way of suspicion and impression, etc., but do you *believe* that you can fairly and impartially render a verdict in accordance with the law and evidence in the case?

A. I shall try to do it, sir.

Q. But do you *believe* that you can sit here and fairly and impartially make up you mind from the evidence, whether that evidence prove that they are guilty beyond a reasonable doubt or not?

A. I think I could, but I should feel that I was a little *handicapped in my judgment*, sir.

THE COURT.—*Well, that is a sufficient qualification for a juror in the case. Of course, the more a man feels that he is handicapped, the more he will be guarded against it.*

The counsel for the defense, in their brief before the Supreme Court, make the following remarks upon this ruling:

"We beg leave to state that not only is the remark given above contrary to experience, but to all the authorities. According to the remark of the court, the stronger the opinion of the juror against the defendant, and the more bias and prejudice he has, the better juryman he will make; because, having this hostile opinion and this bias and prejudice, he will be conscious of it, and will isolate it from himself, and that will leave his mind to act on the evidence alone. The common experience is that a previously-formed opinion or prejudice is like the sand-drift that permeates and mixes with everything, or like green spectacles that color everything within the vision. The authorities all agree that the defendants are not bound to take such a juryman, or, as the Chief Justice says in the Burr case, '*the law will not trust him.*' Judge Gary seems to think that the Constitution is all wrong. This provision should have been that a defendant should be entitled to a juryman '*handicapped*' by previous opinions and prejudices, and the more he is *handicapped* the better the juryman will be."

The attitude (for it would be improper to say bias) of the court may be illustrated by giving here a carefully formulated question which was propounded to a large number of the proposed jurors, but which in every instance was refused by Judge Gary, although Mr. Grinnell, the state's attorney, said: "I will not object to that question." It was as follows:

"Suppose it should appear that the meeting held at the Haymarket square was a meeting called by Socialists or Anarchists and was attended by them and others; suppose that it should further appear that the bomb which is alleged to have caused the death of Mr. Degan was thrown by some one in sympathy with the Anarchists or Socialists: Now, I will ask you, provided it was not established beyond all reasonable doubt that these defendants actually threw the bomb, or aided, participated in or advised the commission of that wrong, would the fact that they are Socialists or Communists have any influence upon your mind in determining their innocence?"

CHAPTER V.
THE JURY IN THE CASE.

Under such rulings as have been cited, the defendants being limited in their number of peremptory challenges by statutory regulation, it is evident that counsel for the defense were constrained to secure a jury as best they could, accepting only the least objectionable out of those presented for examination.

Taking now the jurors who were accepted, we find fully illustrated the great difficulties under which the defendants labored, and the, from the start, almost hopeless result of the trial, which led the defendants to anticipate the verdict which was attained.

I. MAJOR JAMES H. COLE, of Lawnsdale, was the first chosen. He was born in Utica, N. Y.; 53 years of age. Was a captain and major in the Forty-first Ohio Infantry, and during his life as a railroad constructor and contractor has been a citizen of Vermont, Ohio, Iowa, Tennessee and Illinois. He is an Episcopalian.

He was asked the same questions as quoted in the preceding chapter. The rulings of the court were the same, refusing to allow said questions to be answered, as in other instances. In answer to questions which were permitted, he stated that he was prejudiced against Socialists, Anarchists and Communists as a class. The rulings of the court, however, prevented inquiries as to whether that prejudice would influence his verdict, or the weight he would give to the testimony of the defendants, if they should be sworn, and to their witnesses, in his determination of the cause.

II. SCOTT G. RANDALL, born in Erie county, Pennsylvania; was 23 years of age and raised on a farm. Had lived in Chicago three years, and at the time was salesman for J. C. Vaughan & Co., seedsmen, 45 La Salle street. There was nothing marked in his examination.

III. THEODORE E. DENKER, Woodlawn; was born in Wisconsin; 27 years of age; shipping clerk for H. H. King & Co. He was examined on the fourth day of the trial. He admitted that he had heard of the Haymarket affair and that he had expressed an opinion as to the guilt or innocence of the defendants of the murder charged, which he still entertained; that he believed what he had read and heard upon the subject, and that he thought that the opinion was such as would prevent him from rendering an impartial verdict. He was therefore challenged for cause.

Mr. Grinnell, the state's attorney, then asked him if he believed he could determine the guilt or innocence of the defendants upon the proof presented in court, without reference to his prejudice or opinion and regardless of what he had heard, and he stated that he believed he could. Thereupon the court asked this question:

"Do you believe that you can fairly and impartially try the case and render an impartial verdict upon the evidence as it may be presented here and the instructions of the court?" To which he replied: "Yes, I think I could." The court then overruled the challenge for cause, and he was re-examined by defendants and again admitted that he had formed an opinion of the guilt or innocence of the defendants, which he had expressed freely and without hesitation. He persisted, however, in stating that he believed that he could lay aside his prejudice or opinion and try the case fairly, and was finally accepted.

After the trial, however, in support of the motion for a new trial, the defendants introduced the affidavits of Thomas J. Morgan,— well-known as an old-time antagonist to Anarchy and Anarchists,— and of Thomas S. Morgan, who both testified unequivocally that on the morning of the 6th of May Denker stated to them, and in their hearing, referring to Spies, Fielden, Schwab and Fischer particularly, who had been arrested on the 5th of May for alleged complicity with the Haymarket affair, and referring to Spies: "*He and the whole damned crowd ought to be hung.*" This remark, the affiants declared, was made with much feeling and emphasis.

Mr. Denker, in his affidavit in rebuttal, denied having made the remark sworn to by the Morgans, yet again admitted that he had an opinion which he had freely expressed. The two affidavits remain unimpeached, and the sole ground on which they were refused consideration was that the party accused *denied the charge!* Further, in Denker's affidavit he simply denies having made the quoted remark *to the Morgans*, but does not deny that it expressed his conviction, nor that he might or did not make the remark to others.

IV. CHARLES B. TODD, 1013 West Polk street; born in Elmira, N. Y.; 47 years of age; served in the Sixth New York Heavy Artillery; was a salesman in the Putnam clothing house; Baptist. He stated that from all sources of information, from what he had read and heard concerning the Haymarket affair, he had formed an opinion upon the guilt or innocence of the defendants of the crime of murder, which opinion he had freely expressed in conversation with others.

V. FRANK S. OSBORNE, 134 Dearborn avenue; born in Columbus, Ohio; 39 years of age; Episcopalian. He is head salesman in the retail carpet department of Marshall Field, the millionaire. He was the foreman of the jury.

VI. ANDREW HAMILTON, 1521 Forty-first street; hardware merchant at 3913 Cottage Grove Avenue. Belongs to no church, though his wife is a Baptist. Upon examination he stated, in substance, that he had said somebody ought to be made an example of in connection with the Haymarket affair, and that if it should be proved that the defendants were the men whose names he saw in the papers, connected with the affair, then he thought they should be made examples of. His other answers proving satisfactory, he was sworn.

VII. CHARLES A. LUDWIG, 4101 State street; 27 years of age; born in Milwaukee; book-keeper in the wood-mantel shop of C. L. Page & Co. Is an active member of the Immanuel Baptist Church. He admitted a prejudice against Socialists, Communists and Anarchists, but his other answers were comparatively unobjectionable.

VIII. JAMES H. BRAYTON, Englewood; born in Lyons, N. Y.; principal of the Webster school at Wentworth avenue; 40 years of age. By education a Methodist. His selection is said to have prevented a hunting and fishing excursion for the summer. He stated that he had taken some interest in Socialistic theories, and as a result of his investigations he had a prejudice against Anarchists, Socialists and Communists. He had formed an opinion of the nature and character of the crime perpetrated at the Haymarket, and, based upon his reading, as to the guilt or innocence of the defendants.

IX. ALANSON H. REED, 3442 Groveland Park; born in Boston; 49 years of age; of the firm of Reed & Sons, of Reed's Temple of Music, 136 State street. He is a Free-thinker, but alluded to by the Chicago *Daily News* at the time as "one of Chicago's best citizens." He also stated that he had formed an opinion concerning the commission of the offense at the Haymarket, and from newspaper reports had an opinion concerning the guilt or innocence of the defendants, or some of them, and that he had a prejudice derived from his reading against Socialists, Anarchists and Communists. He also stated that the opinion which he formed, touching the guilt or innocence of the defendants, was both from what he read in the papers and what he heard, but principally from the newspaper reports.

X. JOHN B. GREINER, No. 70 North California avenue; born in Columbus, Ohio; 25 years of age; stenographer in the freight department of the Chicago & Northwestern railway. He said that from his reading concerning the Haymarket affair he had formed an opinion as to the guilt of the defendants, or some of them. In the course of his examination the following colloquy ensued :

Q. The distinction is this, whether or not your opinion is that an offense was committed at the Haymarket merely, or whether it is that the defendants are connected with the offense that was so committed?

A. Well, it is evident that the defendants are connected with it from their being here, as far as that is concerned.

Q. You regard that as being evidence?

A. Well—well, I don't know exactly; I would expect, of course, that it connected them, or they would not be here.

Q. Well, that would infer that somebody thought so, anyhow, or else the whole thing would be a very foolish proceeding. So then the opinion you have has reference to the guilt or innocence of some of these men, or all of them? Now, is that opinion one, Mr. Greiner, which would influence your verdict if you should be selected as a juror to try the case, do you believe?

A. I certainly think it would affect it to some extent. I don't see how it could be otherwise.

Juror Greiner, in his youthful innocence, thus held that accusation was presumptive evidence of guilt!

XI. GEORGE W. ADAMS, Evanston; born in Indiana; 27 years of age; travels in the State of Michigan as commercial agent for Geo. W. Pitkin & Co., dealers in liquid paints, Clinton street. He admitted upon examination that he had formed an opinion that some of the defendants were guilty of the crime committed at the Haymarket, which opinion he still entertained. But upon his further statement that his opinion was not a strong one, he was sworn.

In the case of Mr. Adams, as in that of Mr. Denker, upon the motion for a new trial before Judge Gary, an affidavit was filed impeaching Mr. Adams' alleged impartiality. It was made by Michael Cull, who stated that shortly after the Haymarket affair he had a conversation with said Adams, at which a number of other persons were present, in which said Cull stated: "That the police had no right to interfere with the meeting; that if they, the police, had let the meeting alone they would have gone home in a short while;" to which said Adams replied that the police ought to have shot them all down; that they, the defendants, had no rights in this country, and that "if I was on the jury I would hang all the damned buggars." Further, that Adams evinced considerable bitter feeling against the defendants. It is true that an affidavit was filed in behalf of the State which denied the charge. But the fact stands with reference to Mr. Adams that after first stating that he had formed no opinion as to the guilt or innocence of the defendants as to the Haymarket affair, he subsequently, on cross-examination, admitted that he had formed such an opinion; while Cull's affidavit, if believed, shows the expression of a strong feeling adverse to the defendants.

XII. Howard T. Sanford, Oak Park; born in New York City and son of Lawyer Sanford, compiler of the Superior Court reports of New York; 24 years of age; formerly he was a petroleum broker in New York, but for a little over a year past had been voucher clerk in the auditor's office of the Chicago & Northwestern railway. He was the last juror examined, on the twenty-second day of the proceedings, July 25.

He stated that he had an opinion from what he had read and heard as to the guilt or innocence of the eight defendants of the throwing of the bomb. He also said that he had a decided prejudice against Socialists, Communists and Anarchists. He was thereupon challenged for cause by the defendants despite his statement that he believed he could fairly and impartially render a verdict in the case. He was then questioned by the State as follows:

Q. Have you ever said to any one whether or not you believed the statement of facts in the newspapers to be true?

A. I have never exactly expressed it in that way, but still I have no reason to think they were false.

Q. The question is not what your opinion of that was. The question simply is—it is a question made necessary by our statute, perhaps.

A. Well, I don't recall whether I have or not.

Consequently the challenge for cause was promptly overruled. Previous to the examination of this juror the defendants had exhausted all their peremptory challenges, and although they refused to accept Mr. Sanford as a competent juror, he was accepted by the State and sworn.

Another affidavit on the motion for a new trial merits attention in this connection, relative to the conduct of the special bailiff who had in charge the summoning of the jurors. Application was made for leave to examine in open court one Otis Favor. The reason therefor was given in an affidavit of E. A. Stevens, a well-known citizen of irreproachable character and president of the Secular Union, who stated that Favor was an intimate acquaintance of the special bailiff Ryce, and that affiant had learned from Favor that while said Ryce was serving the venires in the present case he stated to said Favor, and to others in Favor's presence, in substance, this:

"I am managing this case, and I know what I am about. Those fellows will hang as certain as death. I am summoning as jurors such men as they will be compelled to challenge peremptorily, and when they have exhausted their peremptory challenges they will have to take such jurors as are satisfactory to the State."

Judge Gary, however, refused to order the examination of Mr. Favor upon this application, although it appeared that while Mr. Favor refused to present himself or to make an affidavit in the matter, he would, however, if compelled, substantiate the charge as true. Here was a vital point, affecting the fate, if not the lives, of eight men; the case was still in court awaiting final disposition, and courts have always exercised plenary power to compel the appearance and testimony of witnesses; but on technical points all sense of justice was waived and, if not intentionally at least in effect, the special bailiff was screened from all investigation as to his alleged villainous action.

In conclusion we present the complaints made by the counsel for the defendants on Judge Gary's rulings on the qualification of jurors:

1. Judge Gary, in this trial, recognized the statute alone as the basis of the right of trial by jury. He absolutely ignored the constitutional right of trial by an *impartial jury*, and construed the statute broadly against the defendants in reference to its meaning, as though it were the only provision in existence in reference to the right named, and the only source of the right of trial by jury.

2. The court held that jurors were competent who had *formed and expressed* an opinion of the guilt or innocence of the accused, based on newspaper reports and rumors, and held such opinions at the time of their examination and which it would require evidence to remove, provided they could swear that they could " fairly and impartially render a verdict therein."

3. The court held that a juryman who had *formed and expressed* an opinion of the guilt or innocence of the accused, based upon rumors or newspaper articles, and had also, in the past, expressed an opinion of the truth or falsity of such rumors or articles, is thereby disqualified as a juror; but the present statement by the juror, at the time of his examination on his *voir dire*, that he believed then what he had heard and read to be true, and that he had *formed and expressed* an opinion of the guilt or innocence of the defendants, based on what he had so heard, read or believed, did not disqualify him.

In other words, Judge Gary held that, if a proposed juryman, who had formed and expressed an opinion as to the guilt or innocence of the accused, based upon newspaper accounts and rumors, had also expressed an opinion about the truth of such newspaper accounts and rumors, previous to his examination as a juror, that in itself disqualified him. But if he, for the first time during his examination, stated that he then believed such accounts and rumors to be true, and still had such an opinion of the guilt or innocence of the accused, that, in itself, did not disqualify him.

In his construction of the statute Judge Gary introduced the words " and expressed" after the word "formed," and makes it read, "formed and expressed;" and introduces after the words in parenthesis "about the truth of which he had expressed an opinion," the words "previous to his examination," and not applying to a present fixed belief.

4. The fact that the proposed juror swore that the opinion or prejudice which he had *at the time of the examination* was fixed and positive, and that the juror had *expressed such opinion*, and would require evidence, and even a good deal of evidence, for its removal, did not disqualify the juror, provided he could swear that he believed he could render a fair and impartial verdict in the case.

Judge Gary finally refused to allow the proposed jurors to be asked whether their opinion concerning the guilt or innocence of the defendants or their prejudice against them was such as would require evidence for its removal, even for the purpose of determining as to exercising a peremptory challenge.

5. Where proposed jurors admitted a prejudice or bias against Socialists, Anarchists or Communists, as a class, the judge refused to allow the defendants to ask questions as to whether that prejudice was such as to materially affect the credence they would accord to the evidence of the defendants, or as probable to affect them in determining the question of the guilt or innocence of the said defendants, if it should appear or be conceded that said defendants, or some of them, were Socialists, Anarchists or Communists; and refused to allow challenges for cause on account of any such prejudice or bias against such classes, and refused to allow this question to be asked, even as to determining upon a peremptory challenge.

The citizens summoned to serve on the jury (about one thousand) were almost without an exception wholesale dealers, board of trade gamblers, bankers, real estate agents and book-keepers and clerks of large business houses.

CHAPTER VI.

THE EVIDENCE FOR THE PROSECUTION.

The indictment called upon the defendants to answer to the specific charge of the murder of Officer M. J. Degan. It contained sixty-nine counts. In the technical language of the law the eight defendants, together with Rudolph Schnaubelt and William Seliger, were accused jointly of the act first with a bomb, second with a revolver, third with an unknown weapon; then *seriatim* each of the prisoners was charged in the same manner, the other nine being present, aiding, etc., and in another long series with not being present, but having aided, advised, etc.

Motion for separate trials having been refused and the jury empaneled, the trial began. State's Attorney Grinnell, in his opening address, took the position that there had been a conspiracy. He said:

"On May 3 everything was done that could be done to arouse the people to anarchy. The conspiracy was so large, the numbers so appalling, that it seems impossible to describe it. I believe at least thirty men should have been indicted for murder, and this would have been done had I known all the facts now in my possession at the time the grand jury was in session. The men who have incited this bloodshed have been picked out and should be blotted out.   *   *   *   *

"In breaking up the meeting Inspector Bonfield did the wisest thing he could have done. If he had waited until the next night the Socialists would have gained strength, and hundreds would have been killed instead of the seven that did fall. The action was the wisest thing ever done in this city. The courage and strength of the police saved the town. The inflammatory speeches of these people decided Inspector Bonfield that the meeting should be broken up. He formed his men in a court near the station and marched them north on Randolph street, their ranks filling the street from curb to curb. Fielden was speaking. Captain Ward alone of all those policemen had a revolver in his hand. He stepped forward in the usual manner, and ordered the people to disperse. At this command Fielden stepped from the wagon and said in a loud voice: "We are peaceable." At this remark, as though it was some secret signal, a man who had before been on the wagon, taking a bomb from his pocket, lit the fuse and threw it into the ranks of the police. Fielden, standing behind the wagon, opened fire and kept it up for several minutes, when he in turn disappeared. Fielden was the only one of all the men who had a spark of heroism in him. He stood his ground until he saw that any further opposition was useless, when he made his escape. The action of the police cannot be too highly commended. In all my examination of them I failed to find a man who ran. They stood and quietly awaited orders. Not a shot was fired by them until many of their comrades had fallen.

"I will try and show to you who threw the bomb, and I will prove to your satisfaction that Lingg made it. There never was a conspiracy yet where some conspirator did not divulge the secret. In this case the man was Seliger. I have yet to see the first man who will deny that a conspiracy existed.

"There are a great many counts in this case, but murder is the main one. It is not necessary to bring the bomb-thrower into court. Though none of these men, perhaps, threw the bomb personally, they aided and abetted the throwing of it, and are as responsible as the actual thrower."

On the 15th of July the testimony began. After the introduction of some maps and plans, INSPECTOR BONFIELD was sworn.

He testified that he was second in command on May 4. During that day had seen the circular calling the meeting and conversed with the mayor on the matter. At the Desplaines Street station there were all told about 180 men. Between 10 and 10:30 o'clock the order to march was given. Captain Ward and witness were at the head. Nearing the truck, where there was a person speaking, Captain Ward gave the statutory order to disperse, and added: "I command you and you to assist." Immediately Mr. Fielden, who was speaking, turned and said, "We are peaceable." Almost immediately after the bomb was thrown. At once firing from the front and both sides poured in. In a few moments the crowd was scattered in every direction.

On cross-examination he testified that he had been on the police force for ten years, part of which time he was a detective.

GODFRIED WALLER was next sworn. As will appear from the testimony, he stood in the role of an informer.

By trade a cabinetmaker; born in Switzerland and been in this country three years. Was a member of the "Lehr und Wehr Verein." "In the evening of the 3d of May I was at Grief's hall, 54 West Lake street; went there pursuant to a notice in the *Arbeiter-Zeitung*: "Y— come Monday night." This notice was a sign for a meeting of the armed section; called the meeting to order and was made chairman. There were about seventy or eighty men. Of the defendants there were only present Engel and Fischer.

THE EVIDENCE FOR THE PROSECUTION. 69

" There was talk about the men said to have been killed at McCormick's. Mr. Engel stated a resolution of a prior meeting as to what should be done, to the effect that if on account of the eight-hour strike there should be an encounter with the police they were to aid the men against them. He stated that the Northwest-Side group had resolved that in such a case they were to gather at certain meeting places, and the word "Ruhe" (translated as "quiet" or "rest"), published in the letter-box of the *Arbeiter-Zeitung*, should be the signal. A committee were to observe the city, and in case of conflict occurring bombs were to be thrown into the police stations."

Witness proposed a meeting of workingmen for Tuesday morning on Market square. Fischer said that was a mouse-trap and suggested the Haymarket and eight P. M., as there then would be more workingmen out. It was stated as the purpose of the meeting to cheer up the workingmen so that they might stand together in case of an attack. It was agreed that those present need not attend the meeting, save a committee to see and report if anything happened. Nothing was said as to what should be done in case the police attacked the meeting, though there had been discussion as to why police stations should be attacked *if* the police proved the aggressors.

" There was nothing said about the Haymarket. There was nothing expected that the police would get to the Haymarket, only if *strikers were attacked* we should strike down the police however we best could, with bombs or whatever would be at our disposition. The committee which was to be sent to the Haymarket was to be composed of one or two from each group. They should observe the movement, not only in Haymarket square, but in the different parts of the city. If a conflict happened in the daytime they should cause the publication of the word 'Ruhe.' If at night, they should report to the members personally at their homes. On the 4th of May we *did not understand ourselves* why the word 'Ruhe' was published. It should be inserted in the paper only if a downright revolution had occurred. Engel moved that the plan be adopted. The motion was seconded and I put it to vote."

Witness further testified that nothing was said on that evening " where dynamite or bombs or arms could be obtained." Admitted that six months before he had an eight-inch gas-pipe bomb, which was subsequently exploded in a hollow tree. Was present at a meeting the Sunday before on Emma street; of the defendants only Engel and Fischer were present. The same plan was discussed. "Somebody opposed this plan, as there were too few of us, and it would be better if we would place ourselves among the people and fight right in the midst of them. There was some opposition to this suggestion to be in the midst of the crowd, as we could not know who would be our neighbors; there might be a detective right near us, or some one else; Engel's plan was finally accepted."

I have given all the vital points in this testimony because upon this informer's word is mainly based the charge of a preconcerted plan and conspiracy. It will be remarked that he distinctly states that only two of the defendants were present, and that force was only to be resorted to in case of an unprovoked attack, or what they considered such, by the police upon the strikers. The cross-examination brought out a few additional facts.

He stated that none of the defendants belonged to the "Lehr und Wehr Verein" about the 4th of May. He had seen the call by the letter "Y" in the *Arbeiter-Zeitung* over a month previous. Neither Engel nor witnesses knew why the meeting was called. "*We* did not know for what purpose it was called. When more people arrived, I requested Engel to lay his plan again before the meeting. Engel stated both at the meeting on Sunday and at the Monday-night meeting that the plan proposed by him was to be *followed only* if the police should attack us; any time when we should be attacked by the police, we should defend ourselves.

" Nothing was said with reference to any action to be taken by us at the Haymarket. We were *not* to do anything at the Haymarket square. The plan was, we should not be present there at all; we did not think that the police would come to the Haymarket; for this reason *no* preparations were made for meeting a police attack there.

" * * * On the Haymarket, on my way to the meeting of the Furniture Workers' Union, I met Fischer; we were walking about some time. We once walked over to the Desplaines Street station; the police were mounting five or six patrol-wagons. I made the remark: 'I suppose they are getting ready to drive out to McCormick's, so that they might be out there early in the morning.' Fischer assented to my remark; that was all that was said about the police between us; nothing was said about preparations to meet an attack by the police.

" * * * I know I am indicted for conspiracy; I was arrested about two weeks after the 4th of May by two detectives, Stift and Whalen, and taken to East Chicago Avenue station; I saw there Capt. Schaack, and in the evening, Mr. Furthman (assistant state's attorney); I *was released* about half-past eight of the same day. No warrant was shown to me; I was never arrested *since* my indictment; I was ordered to come to the station four or five times; at every occasion had conversation with Furthman about the statements made here in court. I live now at 130 Sedgwick street, since one month; *Capt.*

THE EVIDENCE FOR THE PROSECUTION. 71

Shaack gave me $6.50 for the rent; whenever I used my time sitting in the station, I was paid for it; once we had to sit all day, and we were paid two dollars for that day. I was out on a strike, and Capt. Schaack gave my wife three times three dollars; he gave me twice before, five dollars each time. I have been at work for the last two weeks for Peterson; when I went there to commence work I was told that I was on the *black list*, and could not get work, and Capt. Schaack helped me to get the job. By the *black list*, I mean that the bosses put all those on a list who were in any way connected with the strike to obtain eight hour's work, and they were not to be employed any further. I know Spies by sight; I never had any conversation with him; I spoke to Mr. Neebe once a few words, at a meeting of the basket makers; I have no acquaintance whatever with Schwab, Parsons, Fielden or Lingg. I saw Lingg once making a speech."

Comment is unnecessary on the character of the witness as displayed under cross-examination, or on the generous disinterestedness of the police captain who so kindly nursed the willing informer. Engel, the former of the "plan," was at home and first heard of the occurrence from Waller himself, who says he "came to Engel's at about half-past ten," and in the words of a later witness, "came in and said he came from the Haymarket, and that 300 men were shot by the police and we ought to go down there and do something. Engel said whoever threw that bomb did a foolish thing; it was nonsense, and he didn't sympathize with such a butchery, and he told Waller he had better go home as quickly as possible; he said the policemen were just as good people; the revolution must grow out of the people, then the police and militia would throw away their arms and go with the people."

BERNARD SCHRADE followed Waller; he was also present at the Monday-night meeting; "We went down to the basement; nothing kept us back; when I got down the meeting was in order. Waller was presiding; there were about *thirty or thirty-five* people. The chairman stated the objects of the meeting; that so many men at the McCormick factory had been shot by the police; that a mass-meeting was to be held at the Haymarket square, and that we should be prepared, *in case the police go beyond their bounds*—attack us. I heard *nothing about assembling* in other parts of the city."

Witness was present at the Sunday-morning meeting on Emma street. "We talked there about the condition of the workingmen after the first of May, and the remark was made that it might not go off so easy after the first of May, if it should not, that they would help themselves and each other. It was said that if we were to get into a conflict with the police, we should mutually assist ourselves, and the members of the Northwestern group should meet at Wicker Park, in case it *should* get so far that the police would make an attack, and should defend themselves as much as possible, as well as any one could; *nothing was said about dynamite;* the word ' stuff ' was not used. Nothing was said about telegraph wires."

In relation to the " Lehr und Wehr Verein," witness said: " We had our military drills for pleasure; most of the members had been soldiers in the old country, and we were drilling here for fun—pleasure; we drilled once a week, at times." The signal "Y" was a signal for the " armed section" to meet at 54 Lake street. Did not hear anything said about the word " Ruhe " at the Monday night meeting.

" I know Spies, Parsons, Fielden, Neebe and Schwab only by sight, never had any business or conversation with any of them. Lingg and I belonged to the same Carpenters' Union, but we were not on terms of friendship; none of the defendants are members of the ' Lehr und Wehr Verein,' to my knowledge. I paid attention to all that was done while I was at the 54 West Lake Street meeting. I was at the Sunday meeting from half-past nine until half-past eleven. The discussion was, that *if* the police made an attack upon workingmen we would help the workingmen to resist it, and if the firemen helped, we would cut the hose. Nothing was said about dynamite or bombs at *any* of the meetings. *Nothing* was said about a meeting at any particular night to throw bombs. It was *not* agreed to throw bombs at the Haymarket meeting. While at the Haymarket I had no bomb; I don't know dynamite; I knew of no one who was going to take a bomb to that meeting. When I left the Haymarket everything was quiet; I did not anticipate any trouble; I had seen the signal 'Y' *before;* it was understood that the meetings were to be called by that kind of notice. I left the Haymarket meeting only on account of the approach of the storm. There were about two hundred people there when I left."

It will be seen by the above that the State's witness Schrade directly contradicts Waller as to the number present and subjects discussed at the Monday-evening meeting when the "conspiracy to destroy the city" was said to have been planned. In connection with the question asked Waller, whether he ever had any bombs, an interesting discussion arose between counsel which will explain the ground taken by the State and the court.

To the above question Mr. Foster of the defense objected. He held that the witness was not on trial, and that the fact that *he* might have had bombs was no evidence against the defendants on *their* trial for murder. Any bomb that the witness might have had had nothing to do with the case, unless it were traced to the man who threw it at the Haymarket. Mr. Foster also alluded to the fact that the witness in becoming an *informer* was evidently attempting to clear his own skirts by implicating his associates, and claimed that the witness had already shown that the two defendants who were present at that meeting could not have conspired to commit the particular crime charged in the indictment.

Mr. Ingham replied, saying that the theory of the State was that the defendants for two or three years had been engaged, as the leaders, in a gigantic conspiracy *against law and order*, of which the meeting on Monday night was but one step.

Mr. Foster asked: "If you show that some man threw one of these bombs without the knowledge, or authority, or approval of any of these defendants, is that murder?"

Mr. Ingham replied: "Under the law of the State of Illinois *it is* murder. The law of this state is strong enough to hang *every one* of these men."

This the court virtually sustained.

EDWARD J. STEELE, lieutenant of police, was in charge of a company at the Haymarket on the 4th of May. "When the command to halt was given I heard somebody say: 'Here comes the bloodhounds. You do your duty and we will do ours.'" Did not mean that the remark was made by the speaker from the wagon. "The word 'fire' was not given by anybody, but we began firing when they fired on us."

MARTIN QUINN, also a lieutenant in command on that night, testified to hearing about the same remark and that it did come from the speaker on the wagon. He says, further: "At that moment there was a bomb or shell fired into the rear, and when Ward had not quite finished his sentence there was a shot fired *from* the wagon by the man who was speaking at the time. It was Mr. Fielden. Just as he was going *down* he said: 'We are peaceable.' Some person had hold of his left leg. He reached back, and just when he was *going down* he fired right where the Inspector was, Captain Ward and Lieutenant Steele."

In this connection. recurring to Bonfield's testimony he stated that he and Captain Ward were not more than a few feet from the truck; that Fielden was facing him when he said in a loud voice: "We are peaceable." On cross-examination Bonfield said:

"Between my calling the halt and the explosion of the bomb I don't think it was a minute. As the captain finished, Fielden *stepped from* the truck and *faced us*, and stepping *on* the street, he turned to the sidewalk or curb, which is perhaps ten inches above the street and said: "We are peaceable." Within two or three seconds the explosion followed. When he stepped on the street *I could have reached out and touched him.*"

Yet Lieutenant Quinn, who admits that he was "within about *fifty feet* of where the speaker was," identifies Fielden as the man who fired *at* Bonfield twice before leaving the truck, all of which time Bonfield was close to him and facing him! Yet, "he fired a revolver right where" the Inspector was standing. We may dismiss him with his concluding remark: "I have done detective duty as an officer; am liable to be sent on that business at any moment."

JAMES P. STANTON, another lieutenant on duty that evening, was about four feet from where the bomb fell. "No shot was fired to my knowledge *before* the explosion of the bomb. I cannot swear from whom the firing began first, the police or the crowd."

H. F. KREUGER, police officer, also heard someone cry out: "Here they are now, the bloodhounds." He "should judge it was the speaker on the wagon; would not be positive, though. To the command by Ward I heard the man *on* the wagon respond: 'We are peaceable.' It was this man that spoke (pointing out Fielden.) He stood at the south end of the wagon." This is the *third* position in which Fielden was seen while saying three words! Kreuger further contradicts Quinn. He said: "He stepped down from the wagon and passed right to my right behind the wagon and in a moment the bomb fell behind me. *Then* I saw a pistol in his hand and he fired two shots at the column of police, taking cover *behind the wagon.*" He also added upon cross-examination: "At the time Fielden was down on the ground off the wagon, the bomb had not exploded. It was two or three seconds after. I did *not hear* any pistol fired before the bomb exploded. I don't know that Fielden fired from the wagon. I did *not see* the blaze of a pistol from the wagon before he got off. There was another *man in front of me*. Fielden was standing a little *north* of the south end of the wagon."

JOHN WESLER, an officer, was standing right behind Kreuger. After he had shot twice he "saw Mr. Fielden stand at the *middle* of the south end of the wagon, and I noticed before I got there a man who would not stand up, and who would shoot into the police and *get down* behind the wheel. I went up and saw Mr. Fielden was there, and he got up a second time and shot into the police, and he got down by the wheel of the wagon, and as he did I shot him and *he fell* under the wagon. Then *I ran* and left him."

At the date of trial this veracious witness was "on detective service." He admitted that he didn't "know at the time who this man was, that I shot at the wagon, I am positive *now* it was Fielden;" and further that he might have seen pictures of Fielden in the paper before identifying him!

PETER FOLEY followed. Another position was discovered for the ubiquitous Fielden by this brother *detective*. He saw "Wessler fire a shot at a man *lying* under the wagon; the man *was under* the wagon at the time the shot was fired." To be more precise he added: "The man at whom Wessler fired was *lying* under the body of the wagon, *between* the fore and hind wheels."

Whether Mr. Fielden was *on* the wagon, getting *down from* the wagon, on the *sidewalk*, back—*not quite behind* the wagon, in the *center* of the rear, or *under* the wagon when he was severally recognized, we need not concern ourselves, as no two agree. The wonder remains that Inspector Bonfield, who saw him descend in obedience to the order *before* the bomb was thrown, and to whom Mr. Fielden addressed the remark "We are peaceable" while within touching distance of each other, and who was admittedly the nearest witness, should have failed to discover the murderous weapon aimed "directly at him," simultaneously, from so many points of the compass!

Having settled Fielden's fate on the above evidence, Spies is implicated in the murder of Officer Degan by the introduction of the next witness, LUTHER MOULTON, of Grand Rapids, Mich. He announced himself as a patent solicitor and mechanical expert, and, through some occult cause, an officer in the Knights of Labor. He met August Spies in Grand Rapids on February 22, 1885, where he came to lecture. Though the seven other defendants objected, Mr. Moulton proceeded to unfold the following fearful tale:

"Spies was introduced to me as a prominent leader of the Socialists of Chicago by Mr. Tandler. Tandler requested me to introduce Spies at the meeting that was to follow that day. Spies stated that the organization which he represented was for the purpose of reorganizing society upon a more equitable basis, that the laboring man might have a better and a fairer division of the products of his labor. I remarked that the ballot-box and the legislation of the country were the proper means to resort to. He expressed no confidence in such methods, and that force and arms was the only way in which the result could be accomplished; that they were prepared for such a demonstration in Chicago and all the commercial centers of the country; that they had about three thousand men organized in Chicago; they had superior means of warfare; they would rapidly gain accession to their ranks, if they were successful, from the laboring men, to whom they would hold out inducements; demonstrations would be made, and laboring men would be idle in large numbers; they thought the country would fall in line, because they would be able to propagate their ideas rapidly among the country people and satisfy them that they were improving the condition of society. He thought there *might be* bloodshed, for that happened frequently in the case of revolution; that might be a punishable crime if it failed, but if a success it would be a revolution; George Washington would have been punished had he failed. *No details* were given in regard to the means or mode of warfare. I am quite certain the term 'explosives' was used in connection with arms, but nothing very definite. The conversation lasted about half an hour. * * * *I presided* at the meeting at which Spies spoke, and introduced him."

Upon this valuable piece of information connecting the eight defendants with the murder of Officer Degan, the cross-examination elicited the following:

"I first communicated this narrative to Mr. James H. Bonfield a few days ago at Grand Rapids. I was furnished with the means to come here by the Grand Rapids police."

Another man was also brought on to corroborate Mr. Moulton's terrible tale.

LIEUT. JAMES BOWLER did not recognize anybody firing. "I says to my men: 'Fire, and kill all you can.'" He fired nine shots. "Saw no one, either in the wagon or getting out of the wagon, do any firing. *I saw* Mr. Fielden coming off the wagon very plainly."

OFFICER L. C. BAUMANN thought he could swear he saw Fielden fire the historic shot *from the sidewalk*, right behind the hind wheel. "Saw him fire only once. There were a couple of hundred people there. The men in my company had broken ranks after that bombshell had exploded."

Q. How did you know it was Fielden then?

A. Well, *I simply asked* who that man was that fired the shot, and so they told me it was Fielden.

Q. Who told you it was Fielden that fired the shot?

A. Some of the officers. I have seen Fielden's picture in the paper."

OFFICER HANLEY also saw Fielden by one of the wheels of the truck *in the street*, with a revolver. He saw one shot go, and just as he found time to think of his revolver saw him rush for the alley.

MR. J. K. MAGIE then testified to attending a meeting where Spies and Fielden had spoken and advocated force. He had advocated the ballot, and incidentally mentioned that Spies alluded to him as "a political vagabond." Could not swear, notwithstanding, that either had used the word "dynamite."

THOMAS GRIEF, proprietor of 54 West Lake street, where the alleged "conspiracy" was planned, next took the stand. His saloon, on the ground floor, had been closed by the city since May 5. He rented the basement for a meeting on Monday, May 3, simply because his upper halls were all engaged. He had occasion to go down stairs to tap beer, and saw some twenty-five or thirty people there. The stairway leading from the saloon to the basement was open; no door to shut it off; there were no curtains before the windows; no attempt at concealment.

JOHN E. DOYLE, an officer injured at the meeting by a piece of the bomb, heard a man jump from the wagon and shout: "Now is your time, now is your time!" He was looking at the man and knows he did *not* shoot. He thought the man resembled Fielden.

OFFICER SPIERLING saw Fielden fire a shot from the *sidewalk, behind* the wagon, where he never could have reached the alley Officer Hanley saw him so distinctly rushing for. The only other noteworthy remark he offered was: "*After* he shot I paid no attention to him."

DETECTIVE JAMES BONFIELD followed, the same who unearthed the historian Moulton, of Grand Rapids. Was formerly bailiff and assistant jailer. Arrested Spies and Schwab on May 5. Returned to the *Arbeiter-Zeitung* office several times—three times. On some of his *later* visits was successful in finding "a small piece of fuse, a fulminating cap and a large double-action revolver. * * * I never saw the cap used for anything except dynamite and nitro-glycerine. *I have used it* in mines for that purpose." There was also paraded a box of empty Winchester rifle shells. On the evening of the 5th took some reporters down to interview Spies and Fielden, *while he listened.* In Fischer's house he had found an *empty* piece of gas-pipe about three or three and a half feet, which dangerous article was at once confiscated. "On my fourth visit I took away a lot of red flags and such stuff as that. * * Twenty or twenty-one compositors were arrested during that day. We had no search-warrant when any of these things were taken. We searched Spies and took the personal effects away from him. I took Mr. Spies, keys out of his pocket—everything I found, little slips of paper and everything I found. I had no warrant for anything of that kind. * * * I went down with the reporters about eight or nine o'clock. Spies, Schwab and Fielden were in separate cells. Spies said the action taken at the Haymarket was premature; it was done by a hot-head that could not wait long enough. I cannot use the words;

that is the sentiment and perhaps the words. Fielden said the police came up there to disperse them, and they had no business to. He *claimed* that they had a right to talk and say what they please under the Constitution, and they should not be interfered with. I don't think it was ever questioned that the meeting was a peaceable and quiet meeting. I don't think that he ever claimed that it was quiet or disorderly. The fulminating cap which I found did not look fresh and bright; it looked as though it might have laid there for a long while. When Chief of Police Ebersold came into the office at the central station he was quite excited, and talked to Spies and Schwab in German and made motions, and I got between them, and I told him this was not the time or place to act that way. I took the liberty to quiet him down a little. He used a word which I understood to *compare a man to a dog, or something lower.*"

Considerable time was then consumed in hearing testimony relative to the character of the crowd of strikers at McCormick s who were addressed by Mr. Spies on the 3d of May. Policemen and others gave evidence that while Mr. Spies was speaking some called out to go and kill the "damn scabs," but none stated that Spies was the man, but that it was a different man. None testified that Spies indorsed the cry or ceased speaking. The evident object of this testimony was to lead the jury to *infer* that but for Spies' speech that cry *might* not have been made.

Officer ENRIGHT stated that the police fired as soon as they heard shots but " could not state exactly whether the police had fired before I heard these shots." Further: " I personally fired five shots. The firing was pretty general from the men under my command. Some of my men were hit with rocks, *but not one of them shot.*"

CAPTAIN WARD, who gave the order to disperse at the Haymarket meeting, and who stood beside Inspector Bonfield when Fielden said: " We are peaceable," followed. He was close enough to the wagon to " almost touch it " and Fielden was facing him. " There was no pistol firing of any kind by anybody *before* the explosion of the bomb."

Officers testified to arresting Fischer and finding on him a revolver, a belt having " L. & W. V." on the buckle and containing a dirk. In excuse Mr. Fischer is said to have alleged that he carried arms because he often carried sums of money in returning home late at night.

In Fielden's house " no munitions of war of any kind " were to be found.

THEODORE FRICKE, business manager of the *Arbeiter-Zeitung,* was called by the State for the purpose of identifying the handwriting of "copy" found in the office. He testified that the manuscript of the word "Ruhe" was in Spies' handwriting. The call "Y" was in the handwriting of Mr. Rau. He readily identified the "Revenge circular" as from the pen of Mr. Spies. Editorial matter was identified as from Spies or Schwab. He narrated glibly to what "groups" of the International the several defendants belonged; some by knowledge, some by "guess." Established for the State the fact that Most's book on "Revolutionary Warfare" had been sold at their picnics and was at the office. Further, that Parsons and Fielden were often present at meetings where this book in German, of which neither could even read the title, was sold; though none of the defendants, it was elicited, had anything to do with the sale. After which grateful task he retired.

WILLIAM SELIGER, co-respondent with the defendants, and who secured his liberty by offering to turn State's evidence, now comes on the scene. His testimony is that of a man swearing to save his life, and who undoubtedly believed that immunity depended upon the character of his evidence against his former associates. He is a carpenter and Louis Lingg boarded with him. He was not at the Monday night meeting. In explanation of the "Y" call for armed men he said: "The armed men were divers ones, *all* the Socialistic organizations," of which there were several. On Tuesday he did not work at his trade, but did "diligently at some bombs." Lingg kept urging him on to more diligence. Three others were helping, and there were thirty, or forty or fifty bombs made that afternoon, which Lingg declared were going to be good fodder for the capitalists and the police, when they came to protect the capitalists; "nothing was said about *when* they wanted the bombs completed or ready."

In the evening he and Lingg filled a small trunk with bombs and carried it to Clybourn avenue, a long distance away from the Haymarket. He stated that Lingg *after* leaving the hall and his comrades there, expressed to him *alone* "that there should be made a disturbance everywhere on the North Side to keep the police from going over to the West Side. In front of the Larrabee Street station Lingg said it might be a beautiful thing if we would walk over and throw one or two bombs into the station. There were two policemen sitting in front of the station, and Lingg said that if the others came out these two couldn't do much. We could shoot these two down." After which brilliant suggestion, made *after* depositing his bombs, they went on and instead indulged in beer. He also testified that a little later Lingg saw a patrol wagon and becoming " quite wild, excited " wanted a match as he had none. Witness was *smoking a cigar*, and " jumped into a front opening before a store and lighted a match, as if I intended to light a cigar, so I could not give him a *light*," (!) After this demonstration of his *inability* to furnish a light the fellow bomb makers passed on. Lingg wanted to follow the wagon to see what had happened, thinking something might have happened on the West Side. (The Haymarket was on the West Side fully two miles distant.) Finally he went home with Seliger, arriving there at eleven o'clock, where Lingg *first saw the word* " *Ruhe* " in the columns of the *Arbeiter-Zeitung*, which he explained to his innocent fellow conspirator to mean "that everything was to go topsy turvy, that there was to be trouble."

Later they returned to the hall on Clybourn avenue, where there were several persons present, and perhaps owing to this circumstance, " did not speak with Lingg " there. After some further testimony relative to the purchase of more dynamite, and the manner of making bombs, witness was turned over to the defense for cross-examination, their motion to exclude this witness on behalf of all defendants other than Lingg having been overruled.

When first arrested he made a partial statement, " but not all that I have testified to-day." Made statements three times; "in the first statement I had not said much; I had done no work, *earned no money.*" Admitted receiving from Capt. Schaack once a dollar and a half, at another time five dollars. After he had made his third and fuller statement Capt. Schaack " told me that it would be *best* if I would tell the truth, and asked me whether I would tell the truth before the court, and I said yes." Upon further questioning he admitted that " it was not understood or agreed between me and other men who had the bombs that night at Clybourn avenue, that any one of us was to go to the Haymarket meeting. I know that Capt. Shaack paid my wife money at different times since my arrest; I don't know how much; I think $20 or $25. * * * I did not hear anything about an agreement that any of the bombs manufactured on the afternoon of May 4th were to be taken by anybody to the Haymarket." Did not know of a single bomb made for use at the Haymarket, nor who were expected to be there.

Mrs. Seliger affirmed her husband's testimony as to Lingg's " diligence " in the work of casting, filling and riveting bombs, using her cook stove to her great annoyance. She admitted telling all when locked up; that Capt. Schaack paid her rent besides giving money. Comment on this singular and self-contradictory story may well be deferred till we come to sum up the whole testimony.

A reporter named Williamson was introduced who had seen a public procession of Socialists in Chicago the year before, upon occasion of the grand banquet given at the opening of the new Board of Trade. With his own eyes he saw several red flags and banners there and actually beheld Parsons, Spies and Fielden in sympathy with and addressing the crowd. The point of the testimony was that the witness stated the speakers called the police bloodhounds and called upon the "mob to follow in an assault on Marshall Field's dry goods house and various clothing houses," etc. He called at the *Arbeiter-Zeitung* office to obtain a sensational interview and was fully gratified. Mr. Parsons and Mr. Spies gratified his love for the marvelous by exhibiting a veritable, yet solitary, "dynamite cartridge," or rather, "what they told me was" such. After exhibiting dynamite in the raw state, a coil of fuse and witnessing the explosion of a fulminating cap, all exhibited for the purpose of convincing a *stranger* and a *reporter* that "they were preparing for a fight for their rights" our credulous if veracious pencil pusher went down stairs, "where I met" two detectives, who of course would substantiate his terrible tale. Frequently during the winter months of 1884 and 1885 he attended their meetings and learned "that five cents' worth of dynamite carried around in the *vest pocket* would do more good than *all* the revolvers and pistols in the world." These meetings, he said, were always public. He heard proposals to sack clothing houses "at every single meeting," though he admitted that the "mob" gathered in halls averaged not "over twenty-five present," and always "quietly disposed." Yet even when only "ten men" were present the same proposal was invariably made. He admits that "both Parsons and Fielden knew me as a reporter at the time" of the first interview, on which occasion "there was nobody present!"

FRED. L. BUCK electrified the jury with an account of the explosive power of some dynamite, "which I received from the detectives' office."

Several police officers testified to hearing dire threats against the police in public meetings where all were free to go in. Officer Jones directly contradicted other witnesses as to the finding of the dynamite in the *Arbeiter-Zeitung* office; the advocate of seeing it found on the *second* and *third* floors being equally positive under oath.

Several detectives swore positively to finding dynamite, differing, however, as to its location.

JOHN J. RYAN, a retired army officer, attended several meetings and heard advice given to purchase rifles and dynamite for other purposes than "civilized warfare," as their objective aim was the police rather than foreign enemies. He admitted the "lake front meetings" were always public and a "policeman was usually around there."

Mr. Wilkinson, a city reporter, gave a thrilling description of Mr. Spies showing him a "czar bomb," and giving him a full description of how the revolution was to be inaugurated in the absence of leaders, and other tales, and he "wrote them up the first opportunity." He quoted Spies as saying that they had 9,000 bombs and a company of "tall men who could throw a five-pound bomb fifty paces." He added: "I did not believe all Spies said; I believed *about half* of it. The article written by me is wound up by the suggestion that when dressed to cold facts it was like a scare-crow flapping in the corn field; I did not write that; that was edited by some one who told me he did not *believe as much* of the matter as I did." Before Judge Gary, Spies' jokes became very solemn facts.

Franz Hein, a saloon-keeper, was sworn to connect Neebe with the conspiracy, which was done by stating that Neebe actually showed to him, on the evening of May 3, the "Revenge Circular." In speaking of the McCormick affair Neebe said: "It is a shame that police act that way, but may be the time comes that it goes the other way— that they get the chance, too." "He didn't *say* anything about the circular, he only showed it to me. He said: 'That is just printed now,' when he came in; was in five or ten minutes and went out."

At this stage the platform of the International Working Peoples' Association and John Most's "Science of Warfare" were submitted in translation, and Edward Olsen testified to their correctness. The defense objected to their introduction as evidence (1) because the platform had never been published editorially by the defendants; (2) that it had no connection with the death of Mr. Degan; (3) that Most's book had no relevancy to this case; (4) that the proper object of the trial is not to prove that certain men are Socialists or Anarchists, but who threw the bomb.

The State's attorney maintained that the platform was advocated by the defendants, and that Most's book was sold at their meetings, therefore they were admissible as evidence against them for the murder of Mr. Degan under the statutes. The court thereupon ruled as follows:

"I have no doubt but what it is competent. The circumstances may be significant or not, depending on the surroundings; whether it is significant or not it is for the jury to determine from the surroundings which come before them. Whether the defendants or any of them were intending to have a mob kill people, and were teaching them how to kill people, is a question which this jury is to find out from the evidence. And these two translations are admissible upon the investigation of that question."

THE EVIDENCE FOR THE PROSECUTION. 83

Whereupon the conservative middle-class jury were edified with the reading of the two translations in question by the prosecution, the reader losing no opportunity to give due emphasis to any part calculated to strike the jury and inflame them against the defendants.

GUSTAV LEHMANN was present at the meeting of Monday night on May 3, and testified that he got at the meeting late, but on suggestion stood at the door to see that those not interested should not remain and listen. He did not see Lingg at the meeting, but did afterwards, "*we had a little quarrel*." "Lingg came up to us from behind, on the sidewalk, and said to us, 'You are all oxen, fools!'" Lingg said, "if I wanted to know something I should come to 58 Clybourn avenue the next morning." At 3 o'clock the next day—May 4—he quit work and went to Lingg's, arriving there about 5 o'clock, remaining about ten minutes. "They did some work in the bed-room. I couldn't understand what they were doing. I did not work at anything. Lingg and Huebner had a cloth tied around their faces." At about 7 o'clock witness returned to Lingg's and found them "still busy in the bedroom," making fuse and caps. Although he "couldn't understand what they were doing," still, "that afternoon Lingg gave me a small hand-satchel, with a tin box in it, and three round bombs, and two coils of fuse and some caps." These he took home "to the woodshed, got up at three o'clock that night and carried them away to the prairie" and hid them; but "afterwards went to the prairie *with a detective* about May 19th or 20th to find the things that Lingg had given me."

He had attended in March a ball of the Carpenters' Union, where about ten dollars was realized from the sale of beer, which by resolution was handed over to Lingg with the instruction to buy dynamite with it and experiment with it to find out how it was used. He also presided over a meeting at which Engel spoke and made the "treasonable" suggestion that dynamite was cheaper than revolvers, and explained how it could be made a weapon. Said meeting "was a public, open-door meeting." Had seen the call "Y" before; was a member of the "armed section."

CLARENCE E. DRESSER, a reporter, was present when the demonstration was made against the festival upon the opening of the Board of Trade, which was intended, "in their language, to carry terror to the capitalistic heart. I asked Spies what was the object of the demonstration. He said, 'We ought to blow the institution up,' and made some reference to the character of the people that did business there." He also testified to hearing Parsons and Fielden denounce the capitalists, express a desire to see them "blown to hell," and a wish "that the workingmen rouse up and arm themselves and meet their oppressors, with weapons—meet them face to face, and consider that they were to be treated in the same manner."

Much of such testimony was introduced that space will not permit to give in full. In the opinion of the court it was legitimate to prove that the prisoners were opposed to the present order of society to establish that whoever threw the bomb *must* have acted upon their teaching, and consequently under the law they could be found guilty as conspirators, though they were ignorant of who did that act. At the Board of Trade demonstration some of the defendants gathered all the poor, unemployed "tramps," etc., they could collect and marched them through the city to show the degree of prosperity existing, which was being toasted in champagne within.

T. L. TREHORN, police officer, was on duty where said demonstration halted for speeches. He said: "Parsons characterized the Board of Trade as a *robbers' roost and den*; that they were reveling in the proceeds of the workingmen. He said: 'How many of my hearers could give twenty dollars for a supper to-night?' The invitations there *were twenty dollars,* I believe. He says, 'We will never gain anything by argument or words. The only way to convince these capitalists and robbers is to use the gun and dynamite.' Fielden said the Board of Trade was the largest gambling house in the world; that they were dabbling in money, the proceeds of the workingmen; that they raised the price of food to such an exorbitant price that they cannot live," etc., etc. Another detective told virtually the same story, and to witnessing the conversation between Spies and Williamson in which the latter was told a "ghost story" by Spies, and saw the dynamite, which "looked like red sand," and for all he knew might have been such.

MORIZ NEFF kept a saloon at 58 Clybourn avenue, where Seliger testified Lingg and he left a trunk of bombs. He said that back of the saloon was a hall. The North-Side group used to meet there. "On the night when the bomb was thrown I was at my saloon. Louis Lingg came in company with Seliger and another man whom I had not seen before. This stranger carried the satchel. It was a common bag, about a foot and a half long and six inches wide. He put it on the counter, after that on the floor. Lingg and Seliger were standing by, and Lingg asked me if some one had asked for him. That stranger, whose name I afterward found out to be Muensenberger, carried the satchel on his shoulder. That was ten or fifteen minutes after eight. I told Lingg that nobody had inquired after him. * * * I saw Lingg and Seliger again that night about eleven o'clock. Nobody had in the meantime inquired for Lingg. I saw Huebner there before

Lingg came. * * * Before Lingg and Seliger came back about eleven o'clock several individuals had come into the saloon. Lingg and Seliger dropped in a little later. They were all talking together. I didn't pay much attention to it. I heard one of them holloa out very loud, 'That's all your fault.' I heard them also say that the bomb had been thrown among the police and some of them had been killed; they came from the meeting." He also testified that Engel addressed a group in his hall in the preceding February. Engel wanted money for a new paper, *The Anarchist*, of which he was the editor, and gave a sketch of revolutionary history in the old country, and "stated that the nobility of France were only forced to give up their privileges by brute force; that the slaveholders in the South were compelled by force to liberate their slaves, and the present wage slavery would be done away with only by force, also; and he advised them to arm themselves, and if guns were too dear for them they should use cheaper weapons—dynamite, or anything they could get hold of to fight the enemy. To make bombs, anything that was hollow—in the shape of gas-pipes, would do."

Witness identified a copy of *The Anarchist*.

CHAPTER VII.

EVIDENCE FOR THE PROSECUTION.—(Con'd.)

On the 24th day of July the first witness called was GEORGE B. MILLER, a lieutenant in the Chicago fire department. He testified to finding three bombs under a plank sidewalk some indefinite time after May 4.

Next followed a lawyer who undertook to report the substance of a public speech by Fielden on the lake front, in which he understood the speaker to advocate the "equality of possession."

W. M. KNOX, one of the reporters who interviewed Spies on the night of May 5 in the presence of Detective Bonfield, said: "Spies asked us what the coroner's jury had done. We told him that they had held him to the grand jury, without bail, on the charge of murder. He said he didn't understand how they could do that; he had nothing to do with throwing the bomb; he did not want to go to the Haymarket meeting, and when he got there he didn't want to make a speech. He said he told Schwab so. He made a quieting speech; told the people that the time had not come for action; they should keep thoroughly organized and be prepared for the time when action should be necessary. He said he didn't know where the 'Revenge' circular was printed, neither where the circular calling the Haymarket meeting was printed; that some one had come to the office and showed him one of the latter circulars in the afternoon. He saw the sentence in the handbill calling upon workingmen to come armed to the meeting. He insisted that it should be taken out, and he had the man go and take it out. When the bomb exploded he went to Zepf's hall. The explosion of the bomb was a surprise to him; he thought the police had opened on the crowd with artillery. Some one there told him that a bomb had exploded. He stayed there a short time and then went home. He said he had a couple of giant-powder cartridges and some dynamite in the office for the purpose of showing them to reporters; that was all the dynamite in the office that he knew about. Schwab said he had written of late the greater part of the editorials, and that he had urged workingmen to arm, but never urged them to use dynamite. Fielden said he belonged to the American group, and that it met at the *Arbeiter-Zeitung* office on the night of May 4 for the purpose of organizing the sewing girls into a union. There he heard of the Haymarket meeting and went over there."

He said Spies said he could prove by a number of persons that he didn't want to go to the meeting, and disapproved of it. "I think Spies said: 'If I had known how the meeting would have resulted, I would have prevented it at all hazards.' Fielden said he didn't know anything about who threw the bomb; they all said that."

JOHN ASCHENBRENNER, the assistant foreman of the *Arbeiter-Zeitung*, under Fischer, testified to the setting up of the "Revenge" circular. On the morning of May 5, between eight and nine, Fischer said he had to go out. "Fischer said, I believe, that his wife was sick, and he went home. After coming back I found, while I looked for a shooting stick and mallet in the drawer underneath the stone that I was working at, a revolver and a belt of the L. & W. V. I asked him to take that away, so as not to get anybody into trouble who does not use any arms, as I was working at the place; and Mr. Fischer took the revolver and the belt and went off, and *while going down he was arrested* and taken back."

HERMANN PODEVA, a compositor on the *Arbeiter-Zeitung*, worked on the "Revenge" circular. The word "revenge" was not on the copy. He put in that word.

LAWRENCE HARDY, a reporter, attended a public meeting of McCormicks' employes on March 12th, at which Spies, Fielden and Parsons made speeches. Fielden is reported to have said: "We are told that we must attain our ends or aims by obeying law and order.

THE EVIDENCE FOR THE PROSECUTION.

Damn law and order. We have obeyed law and order long enough. The time has come for you men to strangle the law or the law will strangle you. What you should do is to organize, and march up the Black road and take possession of McCormick's factory; it belongs to you and not to him. You made it." Parsons called on workingmen "to assert their rights," and made the horrifying declaration that capitalists had " ground the workingmen under their heel and had robbed them for years past;" he also " abused the Pinkerton men and he advised them to get their rights, by force, in some way."

The most sensational feature of the day was the appearance on the stand of ANDREW C. JOHNSON, a detective on the Pinkerton force, who became a member of the "American Group" at "the instance of the detective agency, and made a report of what I heard and saw in writing." On February 22, 1885, at a meeting of the group, "Parsons stated that the reason the meeting had been called in that locality was to give the merchant princes that resided there an opportunity to attend and hear what the Communists had to say about the distribution of wealth. 'I want you all to unite together and throw off the yoke; we need no President, no congressmen, no police and no militia, and no judges. They are all leeches, sucking the blood of the poor, who have to support them all by their labor. I say to you rise one and all, and let us exterminate them all; woe to the police or militia whom they will send against us.' "

At a meeting on March 4, " a stranger present gave a lecture; he introduced Christianity. Spies said: ' We don't want Christianity in our meetings at all. We have told you so before.'" Nothing more sanguinary was reported on that occasion.

On March 22d, Spies spoke. " Previously a man named Bishop introduced a resolution of sympathy for a girl named Sorrel; the girl had been *assaulted by a master*; she had applied for a warrant which had been refused her on account of the high social standing of her master. Spies said what was the use of passing resolutions. ' We must act and revenge the girl. Here was a fine opportunity for some of our young men to go and shoot Wight.' That was the man whom this young girl was *said* to have been assaulted by." This was all the detective had to report of that meeting.

On March 29th, Fielden said: " A few explosives in the city of Chicago would help the work considerably; there is the new board of trade, a roost of thieves and robbers, we ought to commence by blowing that up." At the meeting of April 1, Spies " referred to a case of Martha Siedel, a girl who had preferred a charge of assault against the police sergeant, Patten. Spies said he had advised the girl to get a pistol and go and shoot the policeman. Fielden said that is what she ought to do."

On April 8th Parsons spoke, and referring to a strike at LaSalle, Ill., said that the next day "the authorities will probably send a train loaded with police and militia to shoot down the workingmen there." He proposed the following blood-curdling advice: "All you have got to do is to get some soap and place it on the rails and the train will be unable to move," and urged organization.

On April 19th Parsons offered a resolution of sympathy for Louis Reil and the half-breeds in the northwest.

In all the above cases I have given, somewhat condensed, *everything* that the detective could report of a "revolutionary character." It would be useless to encumber pages with a mere repetition of such reports. In the remainder only the most violent expressions of the defendants will be given.

On April 26th Parsons said: "I wish you all to consider the condition of the working classes, the cause of which are these institutions and government. I lived on snow-balls all last winter, but, by God, I will not do it this winter." Various remarks are reported in which the necessity of arming was urged.

On the 24th of August he was present where "a man armed with a long cavalry sword, dressed in a blue blouse, wearing a slouch hat, came into the room. He ordered all those present to fall in. He then called off certain names, and all those present answered to their names. He then inquired whether there were any new members who wished to join the military company. Myself and two others did so." Whereupon a drill took place. The remainder of this testimony is of the same character, identifying Parsons, Spies, Fielden and Schwab as frequently advocating the use of force and dynamite.

On the occasion of the drill "a man whose name I do not know, came into the room with two tin boxes, which he placed on the table. The drill instructor asked us to examine them, as they were the latest improved dynamite bomb. They were about in size and had the appearance of ordinary preserve fruit cans, the top part unscrewed; the inside of the cans were filled with a light brown mixture. There was also a small glass tube inserted in the center of the can. The tube was in connection with a screw, and it was explained that when the can was thrown against any hard substance it would explode. The inside of the glass tube was a liquid."

Upon cross-examination he stated: "I was a police officer at Lancastershire, England, for eight years, three years out of that a detective. I have been a detective ever since, pretty nearly.   *   *

THE EVIDENCE FOR THE PROSECUTION.   89

When I became a member of the American Group my antecedents were not inquired into. The group is open to anybody who has got ten cents and expresses a desires to come. I have sometimes seen reporters excluded from the meetings, but nobody else.   *   *   *
There was no ushers at the meetings, but I have seen some of the older members, when they saw strangers come, give up their own seats and ask them to sit down.   *   *   *   I have never heard in any of the meetings of an arrangement made or time fixed for the blowing up of the board of trade building, or any other building in the city of Chicago, or for the taking of the life of any one, or of the taking of any store in the city of Chicago. At the meeting on the night of the opening of the new board of trade no violence was proposed in any of the speeches that night; I heard of no proposal of violence of any kind. I heard Parsons when he first got up and stated the object of the meeting; I heard Fielden speak and Parsons when he replied, and I was there when the procession moved. Parsons said that there were the board of trade men sitting down to their twenty-dollar supper while the poor workingmen had to starve. I never heard either Parsons or Fielden or anybody else say they would go down there by force and eat of that twenty-dollar supper. I was listening there all the time."

WILLIAM H. FREEMAN, a reporter, testified to reporting speeches made at the lake-front meetings. On one occasion Parsons said, "that if the workingmen were driven to starvation they would unfurl the banner of liberty and equality and sweep everything before them, sweep away all their oppressors. He said it very emphatically and turned and shook his finger at the red banner that was hanging on the platform. He urged the workingmen there to take up arms and by that means right their wrongs. Spies spoke in German, which I do not understand. Fielden claimed that all aggregation and accumulation of property by individuals was wrong; that the workingmen had a direct interest in everything that was produced and that they could only be enabled to enjoy the fruits of their labor by the use of force."

Was present at the Haymarket meeting. "I remember Parsons alluding to Jay Gould, that he was a robber, and about his vast accumulations. Somebody in the crowd shouted out they would hang him or throw him in the lake. Parsons said: 'No, not yet,' if they did another Jay Gould would pop up in his place like a jack in the box. They must overturn the whole system by which Jay Gould was able to secure the vast amount of money and power that he had secured, and the way to do that was to use force, and he said, 'To arms! To arms!'

a number of times during his remarks. The crowd applauded from time to time the utterances of the speakers.

"Fielden discussed legislation and congress. Martin Foran had stated that no legislation could be enacted that could benefit the workingman; from that it was clear that it was impossible for the workingman to obtain any sort of redress through legislation. They ought not to be fools enough to send such men as Martin Foran to congress to legislate for them, when they admitted that there was no possibility of doing anything that would redound any benefit to the workingman. He compared the revolution proposed by the workingmen to the revolution which established the government of this country, and that it was equally as proper. He spoke of the law and of the oppressive acts of capital which injured the workingmen, as being the result of the law, and urged his hearers to overthrow the law, to kill it, stab it, to throttle it. Those are about the last words I remember before the arrival of the police. The police came up very quietly, and, standing between the two wagons, I had no knowledge that they were on the ground until the command to disperse was given. After hearing that I stepped at once onto the sidewalk and started to go south towards the police, and before I reached the south end of the wagon the bomb was exploded. The explosion made a great noise, but I saw no light or fire. Immediately after the explosion the firing began, and I simply crouched *behind* the wagon for a moment or two, and then went towards the alley. (I saw that there was no firing from there.) * * * I crouched behind the speakers' wagon. I was almost *alone* in the space behind that wagon. I don't know where the firing began first. * * *

" I was within eight or ten feet of Fielden. I did not hear Fielden say: 'There come the bloodhounds now,' or anything of that kind. I did not hear him say: 'Now you do your duty and I will mine.' I know of nothing to prevent my hearing that remark if Mr. Fielden had said it in a loud tone of voice before I was aware of the presence of the police. * * * I saw no shots fired from the wagon. I did not see Mr. Fielden shoot as he jumped off the wagon. After the bomb exploded the firing began. Who was firing? I don't know, except I presume the officers were. I saw the flashes near the police, where the police were at that time."

JOSEPH GRUENHUT, inspector of the health department, was present at the interview between Wilkinson and Spies. Mr. Wilkinson asked how many members belonged to the military societies of organized trade and labor unions. Spies said there were many thousand; that these organizations were open to everybody, and at meetings people were asked to become members, but their names would not be known because they would be numbered, and they didn't keep any record of names. Mr. Spies laid some toothpicks on the table so as to show the position of armed men on tops of houses, on street corners, and how they could keep a company of militia or police in check by the use of dynamite bombs. The conversation was carried on in a conversational tone, half joking.

"At the time of the conversation, and the discussion over the toothpicks there, no date was fixed when there was going to begin trouble in Chicago. I didn't hear in that conversation anything about an attack to be made on the 1st of May." " Parsons and Spies, during conversations within twelve months before the bomb was thrown, said that arming meant the use of dynamite bombs by individuals; all men should individually self-help, as against a squad of policemen or company of militia, so that they need not be an army."

Dr. F. H. Newman identified a nut and some fragments of metal taken from wounded officers.

M. E. Dickson, a reporter, testified to conversations with some of the defendants at a meeting on Twelfth street. " Mr. Parsons made a speech, during which he said that the degradation of labor was brought about by what was known as the rights of private property," etc. Schwab " said that the gap between the rich and poor was growing wider; that, although despotism in Russia had endeavored to suppress Nihilism by executing some and sending others to Siberia, but Nihilism was still growing. * * * That freedom in the United States was a farce, and in Illinois was literally unknown; that both of the political parties were corrupt, and what was needed here was a bloody revolution which would right their wrongs. Spies said in German that the workingmen should revolt at once; he had been accused of giving this advice before, it was true, and he was proud of it; that wage-slavery could only be abolished through powder and ball."

" Parsons said to me that when the social revolution came, it would be better for all men, it would place every man on an equality. He pictured me personally as a wage-slave, referring to my position as a newspaper reporter, and that all reforms had to be brought about through revolution, and bloodshed could not be avoided. Parsons never expressed any distinct proposal to inaugurate the revolution at any particular time, or by the use of any particular force. He simply spoke of the social revolution as *the inevitable* future."

Paul C. Hull, a reporter, was confident that on the evening of Haymarket meeting, "the firing began from the crowd before the police fired." " I saw arching through the air the sparks of the burning fuse; according to my recollection, it seemed to come from about fifteen or twenty feet *south* of Crane's alley, flying over the third division of police and falling between the second and third. It seemed to throw to the ground the second and third division of police. At almost the same instant there was a rattling of shots that came from both sides of the street and not from the police."

WHITING ALLEN, a reporter, was also present at the Haymarket meeting. Parsons "mentioned the name of Jay Gould; there were cries from the crowd: 'Hang Jay Gould, throw him into the lake,' and so on. He said, '*No, no,* that would not do any good. If you would hang Jay Gould now, there would be another and perhaps a hundred up tomorrow. It don't do any good to hang one man; you have to kill them all, or get rid of them all.' Then he went on to say that it was not the individual, but the system; that the government should be destroyed."

CHARLES R. TUTTLE, a reporter, was at the Haymarket meeting, in company with the preceding witness. " One man, I believe the same one who had spoken when he referred to Gould, stuck up his hand with a revolver in it and said: 'We will shoot the devil,' or some such expression, and I saw two others sticking up their hands, near to him, who made similar expressions, and had what I took to be at the time, revolvers."

EDWARD COSGROVE, a detective, was present at the Haymarket meeting. "I reported at the station from time to time what was going on at the meeting."

TIMOTHY McKEOUGH, also " on the detective force." Both testified to seeing Schwab at the meeting in the early portion of the evening. " Later I heard Mr. Parsons say, taking off his hat in one hand: 'To arms! to arms! to arms!' Then I went over to Desplaines street station and reported to Inspector Bonfield. When I came back Fielden was speaking. He criticised Martin Foran, the congressman that was elected by the working people. Speaking about the law, he says the law was for the capitalists. Yesterday when their brothers demanded their rights at McCormick's the law came out and shot them down. When Mr. McCormick closed his door against them for demanding their rights the law did not protect them. If they loved their wives, their children, they should take the law, kill it, stab it, throttle it, or it would throttle them. That appeared to make the crowd near the wagon more excited, *and I made another report* to Inspector Bonfield."

EDGAR E. OWENS, a reporter, was on duty at the meeting. He met Mr. Parsons early in the evening and " asked him where the meeting was to be held; he said he didn't know anything about the meeting. I asked him whether he was going to speak. He said no, he was going over to the South Side. Mrs. Parsons and some children came up just then and Parsons stopped a car and slapped me familiarly upon the back, and asked me if I was armed, and I said: 'No. have you any dynamite about you?' He laughed, and Mrs Parsons said: 'He is a very dangerous looking man, isn't he?' * * * I believe the bomb exploded about ten minutes after ten o'clock. I heard the explosion of the bomb and pistol shots almost simultaneously with the outcry." Did not see Schwab there after 8:30.

Mr. Heinemann was recalled. Heard no shots before the explosion of the bomb. "Almost instantly after it shots were heard: I could not say whether the first shots came from the police or the crowd. Spies started out by saying that the meeting was intended to be a peaceable one. It was not called to raise a disturbance, and then gave his version of the affair at McCormick's the day before."

Louis Haas, detective, recalled to testify that Fielden, on the approach of the police, made this remark: "Here comes the bloodhounds; now, men, do your duty and I'll do mine." Upon cross-examination he stated that he was a witness at the coroner's inquest on May 5, and "did *not* say in my testimony there anything about this alleged remark of Fielden's."

G. P. English, reporter; was at the Haymarket meeting. Took short-hand notes; "had a note book and a short pencil in my overcoat pocket, and made notes in the pocket. My notes are correct; some of them I can read, some I can't."

His synopsis of Spies' and Parsons' remarks present no marked differences from what they admit to have said. Concerning Fielden's speech, the first he had written out was: "There are premonitions of danger, all know it. The press say the Anarchists will sneak away; we are not going to. If we continue to be robbed it will not be long before we will be murdered. There is no security for the working classes under the present social system. A few individuals control the means of living and hold the workingmen in a vice. Everybody does not know that. Those who know it are tired of it, and know the others will get tired of it, too. They are determined to end it and will end it, and there is no power in the land that will prevent them. Congressman Foran says the laborer can get nothing from legislation. He also said that the laborers can get some relief from the present conditions when the rich man knew it was unsafe for him to live in a community where there are dissatisfied workingmen, for they would solve the labor problem. I don't know whether you are democrats or republicans, but whichever you are, you worship at the shrine of heaven. John Brown, Jefferson, Washington, Patrick Henry and Hopkins said to the people, the law is your enemy. We are rebels against it. The law is only framed for those who are your enslavers. (A voice: 'That is true.') Men in their blind rage attacked McCormick's factory and were shot down by the law in cold blood, in the city of Chicago, in the protection of property. Those men were going to do some damage to a certain person's interest who was a large property owner, therefore the law came to his defense and not the workingman's defense, when he, McCormick, attacked him and his living. There is the difference. The law makes no distinctions. A million men hold all the property in this country. The law has no use for the other fifty-four millions. (A voice: 'Right enough.') You have nothing more to do with the law except to lay hands on it and throttle it until it makes its last kick. It turns your brothers out on the wayside and has degraded them until they have lost the last vestige of humanity, and they are mere things and animals. Keep your eye upon it, throttle it, kill it, stab it, do everything you can to wound it—to impede its progress. Remember, before trusting them to do anything for yourself, prepare to do it yourself. Don't turn over your business to anybody else. No man deserves anything unless he is man enough to make an effort to lift himself from oppression."

Then there was an interruption on account of some storm-clouds; everybody started to go away. Mr. Parsons suggested that they adjourn over to Zepf's hall. Fielden said no, the people were trying to get information, and he would go on. And he went on:

"Is it not a fact that we have no choice as to our existence, for we can't dictate what our labor is worth? He that has to obey the will of another is a slave. Can we do anything except by the strong arm of resistance? The Socialists are not going to declare war; but I tell you war has been declared on us; and I ask you to get hold of anything that will help you to resist the onslaught of the enemy and the usurper. The skirmish lines have met. People have been shot. Men, women and children have not been spared by the capitalists and minions of private capital. It has no mercy—so ought you. You are called upon to defend yourselves, your lives, your future. What matters it whether you kill yourselves with work to get a little relief, or die on the battlefield resisting the enemy? What is the difference? Any animal, however loathesome, will resist when stepped upon. Are men less than snails or worms? I have some resistance in me; I know that you have, too; you have been robbed and you will be starved into a worse condition."

"That is all I have. At that time some one alongside of me asked if police were coming. I was facing the northeast, looked down the street and saw a file of police about the middle of Randolph street."

Upon cross-examination witness made the following important statements:

"I thought the speeches they made that night were a *little milder* than I heard them make for years. I didn't hear any of them say or advise that they were going to use force that night. Before I went to the meeting my instructions from the *Tribune* office was *to take only the most incendiary parts of the speeches.* I did not hear Mr. Fielden say: 'There come the bloodhounds now; you do your duty and I'll do mine.' I heard nothing of that import at all."

M. M. THOMPSON, " employed in the dry-goods business of Marshall Field & Co.," the merchant princes, was at the meeting. He testified to seeing Mr. Schwab about eight o'clock. He "saw Spies get up on the wagon and he asked for Parsons. Parsons didn't respond. He then got down and Schwab and Spies walked into the alley at Crane Brothers', near which the wagon was situated. The first word I heard between Schwab and Spies was 'pistols,' the next word was 'police.' I think I heard 'police' twice, or 'pistols' twice. I then walked just a little nearer the edge of the alley, and just then Spies said: 'Do you think one is enough, or hadn't we better go and get more?' I could hear no answer to that. They then walked out of the alley and south on Desplaines street, and west on the north side of Randolph to Halsted, and cut across the street and went over to the southwest corner and was there about three minutes; came out of the crowd again and came back. On the way back, as they neared Union street, I heard the word 'police' again. Just then I went past them and Schwab said: 'Now, if they come we will give it to them.' Spies replied he thought they were afraid to bother with them. They came on and before they got up near the wagon they met a third party, and they bunched right together there, south of the alley, and appeared to get right in a huddle, and there was something passed between Spies and the third man; what it was I could not say. This here (indicating picture of Schnaubelt) is, I think, the third man."

Certainly most positive and damaging evidence, if true. Bearing in mind that both Schwab and Spies are Germans, and that Schwab at that time talked but broken English, let us follow the cross-examination. He had never seen any of the defendants before that night. "When I saw Spies and Schwab go into the alley there was *a crowd* there. I couldn't see down the alley unless I turned my face to it. I was right around the corner of the alley, within three feet, probably, at the farthest, and I moved down to within half a foot. I did not look down the alley, only when they came out of the alley I did look. The conversation between Spies and Schwab *was in English.* I do not understand German. I didn't hear any words between 'police' and 'pistols.' They were in there probably two or three minutes. * * * I cannot say that I knew Mr. Schwab's voice at that time. I only knew Mr. Spies' voice from what I heard him ask on the wagon. Spies was the one who used the words 'pistols' and 'police.' *I did not see him* when he said it. I could not see him without putting my head around the corner. They went out of my sight when they went into the alley." When they came out and walked two blocks west to Halsted " I trailed after them all the time, part of the time beside of them, part of the time ahead and past them, but all the time close to them. There was nobody else following them besides me." He testified to this conversation before the coroner's jury. Had seen picture of Schnaubelt before. "I think Mr. Furthman showed it to me about a week ago."

Comment on this remarkable account of persistently following two Germans who were totally unknown to witness, who were discussing conspiracy in a language they were not in the habit of using in ordinary conversation, will be deferred till after the testimony for the defense is placed before the reader.

AUGUST HUEN, printer, set up the German part of the circular calling the meeting. He "saw the boss take out the line, 'Workingmen, come armed and appear in full force.'"

A detective testified to finding dynamite, or "a kind of yellowish, greasy sawdust," at the *Arbeiter-Zeitung* office. It was in a bag, wrapped in brown paper, lying on a closet shelf.

HUGH HUME, a reporter, saw "Mr. Fielden and other defendants in the sweat-box" at the central station on the night of May 5. Had a conversation with Spies, in which Spies "said to me that the people had reached a condition where they were ready to do any violence, and he had advocated violence of that kind; it was necessary to bring about the revolution the Socialists wanted. He said he had advocated the use of dynamite. I asked him if he was in favor of killing police officers with dynamite. He hesitated a little, and then said the police represented the capitalists and were enemies of theirs, and when you have an enemy he has got to be removed. This is the gist of what he said. Spies said he didn't know anything about the bomb having exploded until afterwards; he had heard a noise that resembled the sound of a cannon, and thought the police were firing over the heads of the people to frighten them.

THE EVIDENCE FOR THE PROSECUTION.

"I had a little talk with Mr. Fielden. He was suffering somewhat from his wound. When I asked him how the Haymarket affair accorded with his ideas of Socialism, he said: 'You are on dangerous ground now. There is an argument, though, that we have, that is to the effect that if you cannot do a thing peaceably it has got to be done by force.' Something to that effect."

The conversation was not confidential; several detectives were present. "Spies saw me write down his answers. He knew I wanted the interview for publication." Remembered that Spies said: "I thought I would not be at the meeting, but finally went when the people who got up the circular promised to take out the words 'with arms.' He also said the throwing of the bomb was wrong. In answer to the question: 'Do you consider the work of Tuesday night as a victory?'" witness said that Spies answered, "No, it was disgusting." Witness further stated, "Schwab speaks English somewhat *laboriously*."

HARRY L. GILMER was called, and as his testimony contains the most direct evidence against Spies, and was the one most relied on by the prosecution, considerable space must be given to it. He was a painter by trade. He arrived at the meeting that night about a quarter to ten o'clock. Took his position at the corner of the alley and near the wagon.

"I was standing in the alley, looking around for a few minutes; noticed parties in conversation right across the alley. Somebody in front of me, on the edge of the sidewalk, said: 'Here comes the police.' There was a sort of rush to see the police come up. There was a man came from the wagon down to the parties that were standing on the south side of the alley; he lit a match and touched it off, something or another. The fuse commenced to fizzle, and he give it a couple of steps forward and tossed it over into the street. I knew the man by sight who threw the fizzing thing into the street. I have seen him several times at meetings at one place and another in the city. I do not know his name. He was a man about *five feet ten inches high*; somewhat full-chested, and had a light sandy beard, not very long; he was full-faced; his eyes somewhat back in his head; judging from his appearance he would probably weigh 180 pounds. My impression is his hat was dark brown or black. This here (indicating photograph of Schnaubelt) is the man who threw the bomb out of the alley. There were four or five standing together in the group. This here (pointing to Spies) is the man who came from the wagon towards the group. That man over there (pointing at defendant Fischer) was one of the parties."

98   THE EVIDENCE FOR THE PROSECUTION.

Upon cross-examination witness said he had been at the trial several times during the previous two weeks. He told a reporter of having seen the match lighted and the bomb thrown; that was on May 6. He "was in the neighborhood of where Fielden talked for about fifteen minutes," but could not remember anything Fielden said. Communicated his information to Mr. Bonfield on the 6th or 7th. The wagon had low side-boards. Was positive that Spies lighted the bomb and Schnaubelt threw it *from the alley*. Thinks he saw Schwab. Was as positive Fischer was there as that it was Schnaubelt who threw the bomb.

"I did not run at the time of the shooting. I did not move at all. I stood right at the mouth of the alley. There were no bullets coming in around my locality in the alley." Up to the evening of May 6th he talked with several about the riot; stated he was there, but told no one that he had seen the bomb lighted and thrown. "The man who threw the bomb was about five feet and eight, ten or nine inches high." Admitted having "received some money two or three times from Detective Bonfield. I did not tell to any person at any time, except the officers that I mentioned, that I saw the act of lighting the bomb accomplished. Neither Mr. Grinnell or Bonfield, or any officer, told me to keep silent in regard to the matter. I am six feet three in height. I could pretty near *see right over the head* of the fellow who threw the bomb."

On presenting the testimony for the defense it will be seen:

First. Gilmer was impeached by ten persons, from among the most respectable classes of the community, some of them large property holders, coming forward and swearing that they were acquainted with his general reputation for truth and veracity among his neighbors, these being persons who had lived in the same house with him, or in the same immediate locality, and swearing, without hesitation, that his reputation for truth and veracity was bad, and that they would not believe him under oath. It is true that counterproof was introduced, including a number of citizens of Iowa and of Chicago; but not one of all these had ever lived in the same neighborhood with Gilmer, or had ever conversed about his reputation with those who did so live in his immediate vicinity, nor did they know where Gilmer lived at any time.

Second. It appears upon the testimony of three or four witnesses that Fischer, at the time of the explosion of the bomb, was in Zepf's hall, sitting at one of the tables in company with Mr. Wandry, who was one of the witnesses.

Third. It is shown upon the testimony of several that Spies did

THE EVIDENCE FOR THE PROSECUTION 99

not leave the wagon and go to the alley in question at all, but was on the wagon at the time the order to disperse was given, and had just dismounted from the wagon to the pavement when the bomb exploded.

Fourth. It is proved by officers, reporters and several other witnesses that the bomb was, in fact, thrown not from the alley at all, but from a point on the sidewalk from fifteen to twenty feet south of the alley. One witness, Burnett, states that he was alongside of the man who threw the bomb, and this was the story Burnett told the day after the meeting as well as under oath. The testimony is overwhelming to this fact.

Fifth. It is shown by the testimony of Mr. Graham, a reporter for *The Times*, that on the day after the Haymarket affair he had a conversation with Gilmer, in which Gilmer stated to him that he saw the man light the fuse *and throw* the bomb, and that he believed he could recognize the man if he were to see him again. That nothing whatever was said by Gilmer about any other man participating in the act. Gilmer swore positively that he knew Spies' face well, having frequently heard him at meetings, and from that knowledge recognized him. Yet in the conversation with Graham on the afternoon of the 5th of May, he never alluded directly or indirectly to Spies as participating in throwing or lighting the bomb.

Sixth. Schnaubelt is shown to have been six feet two or three inches in height and not present at the time of the explosion.

Seventh. In his opening address Mr. Grinnell himself used the following language: "At that moment *a man*, who had a moment before been on the wagon, *lighted the bomb and threw it* into the police."

It is perhaps sufficient to say in conclusion, that so completely and overwhelmingly was Gilmer impeached, contradicted and discredited that the State did not ask a single instruction to the jury, based upon the belief by them that Schnaubelt threw the bomb.

Officers testified to finding an apparatus or "blasting machine" at Engel's house, which Engel stated had been left there by another man. The machine, or furnace, was new; never had fire in it or been used.

HERMAN SCHUTTLER, police officer, narrated the story of the arrest of Lingg. That Lingg on being accosted jumped back and drew a revolver and half cocked it, and both struggled together for the possession of it. Another officer came to his companion's rescue and Lingg was ironed, demanding of them to shoot and kill him. In his trunk there was found "a small lead bomb in a stocking" and in another stocking a revolver. The accompanying officer testified to finding four bombs instead of one.

Dr. John B. Murphy, surgeon at the County Hospital, testified as to the nature of the wounds inflicted on the officers at considerable length. Objection was entered as not material to the issue; overruled. Clothing worn by the wounded officers on the night of the 4th was offered in evidence, evidently for the purpose of working on the feeling of the jurors.

Capt. Michael Schaack, of the fifth police precinct, was sworn. Talked with Lingg after his arrest; he admitted being at the Monday-night meeting. "He said he had made some bombs to use them himself. He said he had reason for being down on the police, they had clubbed him out at McCormick's. He said he was down on capitalists, and found fault with the police for taking the part of the capitalists. If the capitalists turned out the militia and the police force with their gattling guns, they couldn't do anything with revolvers, and therefore they had adopted these bombs and dynamite. He said he had learned to make bombs in scientific books of warfare published by Most of New York. He had got his dynamite on Lake street. He said the bombs they found in his place were all he made."

He said Mrs. Engel called at the station; she said to Engel: "Do you see what trouble you got yourself into?" That Engel answered: "Mama, I can't help it." "I told him why he didn't stop that nonsense, and he said: 'I promised my wife so many times that I would stop this Anarchism or Socialism business. But I can't stop it. What is in me has got to come out. I can't help it, that I am so gifted with eloquence. It is a curse. It has been a curse to a good many other men, a good many men have suffered already for the same cause, and I am willing to suffer and will stand it like a man.'" He testified to experiments made with the dynamite found in Lingg's room, which Lingg had bought in open market, showing its terrible effectiveness as a destructive agency, for the edification of the jury.

Witnesses testified to finding cans filled with dynamite underneath a sidewalk, three miles from the Haymarket, and surgeons gave testimony to the ghastly nature of bomb wounds.

Charles B. Prouty, manager in a gun store told of the heinous offense committed by Engel, calling at the store, buying a pistol and inquiring the price for "perhaps one or two hundred." Later Engel said "they had found something else for a little less money that would answer the purpose."

Another dealer in guns said Mr. Parsons had visited his store and inquired the price of "a quantity of revolvers — I think forty or fifty. * * * He did not purchase any."

W. S. Haines, professor of chemistry in Rush Medical College,

THE EVIDENCE FOR THE PROSECUTION.

made a chemical examination of pieces of metal said to have been taken from Officer Degan, and also pieces of metal said to have been connected with Lingg and with Spies, and found in all about the same proportion of tin, antimony, zinc and iron. He said finally: "In a mixture of the ordinary commercial tin and the ordinary commercial lead you would find traces of antimony, zinc and iron. I do not think they they would have been added to the substances I examined. They probably came in as impurities in both the two constituents." The amount of tin varied from $1\frac{6}{10}$ to $2\frac{1}{2}$ per cent. The remainder was lead. Divested of learned technicality the bombs said to have been made by Lingg, that given by Spies to the reporter, Wilkinson, and that found on the Haymarket were all made of lead, but differed from commercial lead in containing slight traces of tin.

Officers testified to knowing Officer Degan and to his death.

DETECTIVE BONFIELD testified to finding about forty banners at the office of the *Arbeiter-Zeitung*, containing such inscriptions as these: " Every government is a conspiracy against the people;" " Down with all law." They were duly paraded before the jury.

The prosecution here rested its case.

Counsel for defendants moved the court to send the jury from the court-room while they would present and urge on behalf of the defendant Neebe the motion that the jury be instructed to find a verdict of not guilty as to said Neebe. The court refused; thereupon a motion was made that the court instruct the jury to find a verdict of not guilty for Neebe. Counsel for the defense argued the motion at some length; the attorneys for the State remained quiet. During the discussion the following expressions were made by the court:

THE COURT.—There are other things. I won't respect them, however, unless you want me to call your attention to the things that are in my mind so you can argue the question to me.

MR. SALOMON.—It is proper your Honor should state that.

THE COURT.—There is testimony from which the State will be permitted to urge upon this jury that he (Neebe) presided at meetings at which some of the speeches were made, urging the killing of people. Is there not evidence in the case from which the State will be permitted to urge upon the jury that he, *without* being an active man in the *Arbeiter-Zeitung, yet was interested in it*, and it was published with his co-operation and assent? What inference can they urge upon this jury from the testimony, that when the officers went there, he replied that he supposed that in the absence of Spies and Schwab he was in charge? * * * Whether he had anything to do with the dissemination of advice to commit murder, is, I think, a debatable question which the jury ought to pass upon; whether the *Arbeiter-Zeitung* was published with his aid or not.

Mr. Black.—There is not a particle of testimony—I desire your Honor to call attention if you can, or the gentlemen on the other side, to call attention to any evidence in this case—that shows it was published with his aid.

The Court.—There have been witnesses who said he was *frequently seen there* * * * and that when Spies and Schwab were arrested and in custody, *then* he took charge of it.

Mr. Black.—Certainly; what does that prove?

The Court.—It proves that he had some control. * * * Why he took control of it is a matter you must debate—whether he did it at the request of Spies or Schwab or took possession because he was next in command, or why he took it, I shall not undertake to say.

The Court.—If it depended upon prior knowledge and participation at the Haymarket meeting, the question would be quite different, but if there is *general* advice to commit murder, the time and occasion not being foreseen, the adviser is guilty when it is committed."

After full argument the court overruled the above motion on behalf of the defendant Neebe, to which counsel for defendants excepted. But, in the language of the court, "when Spies and Schwab were arrested and in custody, *then* he took charge" of the *Arbeiter-Zeitung*, was sufficient to secure a sentence of fifteen years at hard labor from a jury, the majority of whom admitted that they entertained " a prejudice against Socialists, Anarchists and Communists."

CHAPTER VIII.

ARGUMENT FOR THE DEFENSE.

On Saturday, July 31, forty days after the trial began, the evidence for the State closed and Mr. Salomon opened the case for the defendants as follows:

It is a usual thing in all important cases, especially in criminal cases, after the selection of a jury, for the counsel to express their opinion, individually or collectively, to the jury, and it seems to me in this instance it is most proper for me to say to you, gentlemen, that sitting here for a number of weeks as you have, patiently listening to the evidence that has been introduced so far by the State, and in the

ARGUMENT FOR THE DEFENSE. 103

manner of your selection and while waiting for the evidence to be introduced, you have each and all of you shown admirable patience and judgment. You have proven yourselves in my eyes and in my judgment, willing, patient and able to listen to the evidence in this case and decide it upon its merits. It is therefore almost unnecessary for me to beg of you a further continuance of that faithful canvass and consideration that you have already shown. We expect it and feel that you will bestow it. This, gentlemen of the jury, as you have heard said often in your presence, is no common case. It is no ordinary case, both from the nature of the crime that is charged and from the number of defendants whom it is sought to hold responsible for the commission of the crime. It has been stated to you by Mr. Grinnell, the state's attorney, in his opening—and he said it for the first time—that this was a trial of Anarchy and of Socialism and for the life of Anarchy and of Socialism. We have steadily refused, and we still refuse to believe that any man on this jury will be willing to convict any of these defendants either because he may be an Anarchist or a Socialist. Every question put to you both by the defense and by the prosecution in this case tended and its purpose was, and it was said under your obligation of oaths as jurors, to ascertain whether or not these defendants are guilty of the crime that is charged against them. The state's attorney detailed to you the proof which he expected to introduce in this case, and he stated that he told you all fully and frankly. I ask you, gentlemen of the jury, whether the state's attorney did make a full, free and frank statement of what he was going to prove? If he had followed out his proof and statement of proof, I feel satisfied, and I hope to convince you that the law is, that this prosecution could not be maintained.

Mr. Grinnell failed to state to you that he had a person by whom he could prove who threw the bomb, and he never expected to make this proof until he found that without this proof he was unable to maintain this prosecution against these defendants; and it was as this case neared the prosecution end of it that the prosecution suddenly changed their front and produced a professional tramp and a professional liar, as we will show you, to prove that one of these defendants was connected with the throwing of it. They then recognized, as we claimed and now claim, that that is the only way they can maintain their case here. It needs, I hope, gentlemen, no apology from me for the manner in which I shall present this case of the defendants to you. This burden, this duty towards our clients has devolved upon me, and, gentlemen, I shall endeavor to fully and fairly state to you what these defendants rely upon, and when the proof is made as I shall state it to you upon which they will rely for an acquittal, you will acquit them. Now, gentlemen, I desire to call your attention to what these defendants on trial are charged with. As I told you a moment ago, they are not charged with Anarchy; they are not charged with Socialism; they are not charged with the fact that Anarchy and Socialism is dangerous or beneficial to the community; but, according to the law under which we are now acting, a charge specific in its nature must be made against them, and that alone, must be sustained, and it is the duty of the jury to weigh the evidence as it bears upon that charge; and upon no other point can they pay attention to it. Now, gentlemen, the charge here is shown by this indictment. This is the accusation. This is what the case involves, and upon this the defendants and the prosecution must either stand or fall. This indictment is for the murder of Mathias J. Degan. It is charged that each one of these defendants committed the crime, each defendant individually; and it is charged in a number of different ways. Now, I desire to call your attention to the law governing this indictment and to read it to you; and I am presenting the law to you now, gentlemen, so that you can understand how we view this case and how the evidence is affected by what the law is. The section of the law under which this indictment is framed is as follows:

"Murder is the unlawful killing of a human being in the peace "of the people with malice aforethought, either expressed or implied. "The unlawful killing may be perpetrated by poisoning, striking, "stabbing, shooting, etc., or by any other of the various forms or "means by which human nature may be overcome and death thereby "occasioned. Express malice is that deliberate intention unlawfully "to take away the life of a fellow-creature which is manifested by "external circumstances capable of proof. Malice shall be implied "when no considerable provocation appears, or when all the circum- "stances of the killing show an abandoned and malignant heart."

Now, it is not claimed that any of these defendants did what the statute, which I have just read, said they must do or what the proof must show they have done before they can be held; but it is sought by the following provision to hold them accessory. Section 274 of the Revised Statutes, Chapter 38:

"An accessory is he who stands by and aids, abets or assists, or "who not being present aiding, abetting or assisting, hath advised, "encouraged, aided or abetted the perpetration of the crime. He who "thus aids, abets, assists, advises, or encourages shall be considered "as principal, and punished accordingly."

Section 275 says:

"Every such accessory, when a crime is committed within or without this State by his aid or procurement in this State, may be indicted and convicted at the same time as the principal, or before, or after his conviction, and whether the principal is convicted or amenable to justice or not, and punished as principal."

The specific crime which was committed, and which, I expect to show you the law says, no matter whether these defendants advised generally the use of dynamite in the purpose which they claimed to carry out, and sought to carry out, yet if none of these defendants advised the throwing of that bomb at the Haymarket, they can not be held responsible for the action of others at other times and other places. What does the evidence introduced here tend to show? It may occur to some of you, gentlemen, to ask: "What, then, can these defendants preach the use of dynamite? May they be allowed to go on and urge people to overturn the present government and the present condition of society without being held responsible for it and without punishment? Is there no law to which these people can be subjected and punished if they do this thing?" There is, gentlemen, but it is not and never has been murder, and if they are amenable, as the evidence introduced by the prosecution tends to show, it is under another and a different law, and no attempt on the part of the prosecution to jump the wide chasm which separates these two offenses can be successful unless it is done out of pure hatred, malice, ill-will, or because of prejudice. The law protects every citizen. It punishes every guilty man, and according to the measure of his crime; no more and no less. If a man be guilty of conspiracy, or if he be guilty of treason, he is liable to punishment for that offense, and not for a higher one. This is what the people of the State of Illinois have said, and that is their law. That is what they want enforced, and that is what I stand here for as the advocate of these defendants. I claim for them, and for the entire people of this State, that the law shall be applied as it is found, and as they have directed it to be enforced. Now, what is the statute on conspiracy, of which these defendants may be guilty, if they are guilty of anything? It reads:

"If two or more persons conspire and agree together with a fraudulent and malicious intent to injure the person, character, business, or property of another, or to obtain money on other property by false pretenses, or to do any illegal act injurious to the public trade, health, morals, police, or administration of public justice, or to prevent competition in the letting of any contract by the State or the authorities of any county, city, town, or village, or to induce any "person not to enter into said competition, or to commit any felony, "they shall be deemed guilty of a conspiracy; and every such of- "fender, and every person convicted of conspiracy at common law, "shall be imprisoned in the penitentiary not exceeding three years, or "fined not exceeding $1,000."

The next section is as follows:

"That if two or more persons conspire either to commit any "offense against the State of Illinois or any county, incorporated city, "etc., in any manner, or for any purpose, and one or more of such "parties do any act to effect the object of the conspiracy, all parties "to such conspiracy shall be liable to a penalty of not less than $100 "and not more than $5,000, and to be imprisoned either in the peni- "tentiary or the county jail for any period not exceeding two years. "The time and place of the confinement and the amount of the fine "to be determined by the jury trying the cause."

Gentlemen, the state's attorney's opening statement to you, the proof in this case, with the exception of Gilmer's testimony, shows and shows only that the State has a case within those sections which I have last read to you, and no other, if they have a case against them at all. Now, gentlemen, I have read to you the section of the statute relating to accessories. As I have told you before, it is only the perpetrator and the abettor in the perpetration of a crime who, under the decision of almost every supreme court in the United States and in England, can be held.

[Mr. Salomon here quoted from Wharton's Criminal Law and also read from reports of various cases corroborative of his argument.]

Now, gentlemen, that is one theory of this case, and this law must be applied to each and every one of these defendants who was absent from that meeting, unless it is shown by the prosecution that they were connected with the bomb throwing, and we shall endeavor to show you that they knew nothing of the throwing of the bomb. Those defendants who are present, however, might be held under this indictment if you believe from the evidence that the object of the meeting and those present was to use force and violence against the police. Then all who took part knowingly in that meeting can be held liable as being present there *if* the proof shows that the meeting itself was an unlawful one and that its purpose was unlawful; that its purpose was to kill the police—to aggressively kill the police; and when I say aggressively I mean that the defendants willfully attacked them, because, if the defendants, or any of them, were unlawfully attacked, then, of course, they had a right to defend themselves.

Now, gentlemen, I don't care to read to you any more authorities than those I have referred you to. That view of the law that they must be proven to be accessories to the crime is the one point only upon which the prosecution can sustain their case, and is the only one upon which this case must proceed according to our view. Now, these defendants are not criminals; they are not robbers; they are not burglars; they are not common thieves; they descend to no small criminal act. On the contrary, this evidence shows conclusively that they are men of broad feelings of humanity, that their only desire has been and their lives have been consecrated to the betterment of their fellow-men. They have not sought to take the life of any man, of any individual, to maliciously kill or destroy any person, nor have they sought to deprive any man of his property for their own benefit. They have not sought to get McCormick's property for themselves; they have not sought to get Marshall Field's property for themselves; and to deprive Marshall Field of it feloniously, but they have endeavored and labored to establish a different social system. It is true they have adopted means, or *wanted* to adopt means that were not approved of by all mankind. It is true that their methods were dangerous, perhaps, but then they should have been stopped at their inception. We shall expect to prove to you, gentlemen, that these men have stood by the man who has the least friends; that they have endeavored to better the condition of the laboring men. The laboring men have few friends enough. They have no means without the combination and assistance of their fellow-men to better their condition, and it was to further that purpose and to raise them above constant labor and constant toil and constant worry and constant fret, and to have their fellow-men act and be as human beings and not as animals, that these defendants have consecrated their lives and energies. If it was in pursuance of that, wrought up perhaps through frequent failures and through the constant force exercised against them, that they came to the conclusion that it was necessary for them to use force against force, we know not, and we do not expect to prove nor to deny that these defendants advocated the use of force, nor do we now intend to apologize for anything they have said, nor to excuse their acts. It is neither the place nor the time for counsel in this case nor of the gentlemen of the jury to either excuse the acts of these defendants nor to encourage them. With that we have here nothing to do. Our object is simply to show that these defendants are not guilty of the murder with which they are charged in this indictment. But the issue is forced upon us to say whether it was right or wrong, and whether they had the right to advocate the bettering of their fellow-men. As Mr. Grinnell said, he wanted to hang Socialism and Anarchy; but twelve men nor twelve hundred nor twelve thousand can stamp out Anarchy nor root out Socialism, no more than they can democracy or republicanism, that lie within the heart and within the head. Under our forms of government every man has the right to believe and the right to express his thoughts, whether they be inimical to the present institutions or whether they favor them; but if that man, no matter what he advocates or who he be, whether democrat, republican, Socialist or Anarchist, kill and destroy human life deliberately and feloniously, that man, whether high or low, is amenable to criminal justice, and must be punished for his crime, and for no other.

Now, what was the object of these defendants, as they are charged, in being so bloodthirsty? Their purpose was to change society, to bring into force and effect their Socialistic and Anarchistic ideas. Were they right or were they wrong, or have we nothing to do with it? As I told you, they had the right to express their ideas. They had the right. They had the right to gain converts, to make Anarchists and Socialists, but whether Socialism or Anarchy shall be established never rested with those defendants, never rested in a can of dynamite or in a dynamite bomb. It rests with the great mass of people, with the people of Chicago, of Illinois, of the United States, of the world. If they, the people, want Anarchy, want Socialism, if they want democracy or republicanism, they can and they will inaugurate it. But the people also will allow a little toleration of views. Now, these defendants claim that Socialism is a progressive social science, and it will be a part of the proof which you will have to determine. Must the world stand as we found it when we were born, or have we a right to show our fellow-men a better way, a nobler life, a better condition. That is what these defendants claim, if they are forced beyond the issue in this case. We find that the government is constantly progressing, endeavoring to institute reforms and new movements. We find that it is for the betterment of commerce that there should be a time for every district in the United States, and they inaugurate an eastern time, a central time, and a western time. The country thinks it is for the best. They endeavor to establish a uniform dollar in every community in the United States. The country thinks it is for the best. Many of you, gentlemen, fought for this Union and liberated the slave because you thought you had a right to fight. You had to take life in freeing those slaves, and many lives were lost, and it was because you thought it was right, as men living among men, to do that act. You recognized the fact that slavery should go under, and that no man should own another. You fought in the Rebellion because there were men who held and controlled other men, and these defendants talked because they thought that there were white slaves and white men who were under the control of their bosses. In furtherance of that plan what have these defendants done? Have they murdered many people? What was their plan when they counseled dynamite? They intended to use dynamite in furtherance of the general revolution; never, never against any individual. We will show you that it was their purpose, as the proof, I think, partly shows already, that when a general revolution or a general strike was inaugurated, when they were attacked, that then, in fact, while carrying out the purposes of that strike or that revolution, that then they should use dynamite, and not until then. If it is unlawful to conspire to carry out that thing, these men must be held for that thing. We shall show you that these men, in carrying out their plan for the bettering of the condition of the workingmen, inaugurated the eight-hour movement; they inaugurated the early-closing movement; they inaugurated every movement that tended to alleviate the condition of the workingman and allow him a greater time to his family for mutual benefit. That is what these defendants set up for a defense. That is what they claim was their right to do, and that is what they claim they did do, and *they did nothing more.*

Now, gentlemen, we don't say that we desire to go into this proof, because we think it has nothing to do with this case, if our theory is correct, but if we are forced to show why they did these things it is simply to convince you that their objects were not for robbery, not for stealing, not to gain property for themselves, and not to maliciously or willfully destroy any man's good name or his property interests.

We expect to show you, further, that these defendants never conspired, nor any one of them, to take the life of any single individual at any time or any place; that they never conspired or plotted to take at this time or at any other time the life of Mathias Degan or any number of policemen, except in self-defense while carrying out their original purpose. We expect, further, to show you that on the night of the 4th of May these defendants had assembled peaceably, that its purpose was peaceable, that its objects were peaceable, that they delivered the same harangue as before, that the crowd listened, and that not a single act transpired there previous to the coming of the policemen by which any man in the audience could be held amenable to law. They assembled, there, gentlemen, under the provision of our Constitution, to exercise the right of free speech, to discuss the situation of the workingmen, to discuss the eight-hour question. They assembled there to incidentally discuss what they deemed outrages at McCormick's. No man expected that a bomb would be thrown; no man expected that any one would be injured at that meeting, but while some of these defendants were there and while this meeting was peaceably in progress, the police, with a devilish design, as we expect to prove, came down upon that body with their revolvers in their hands and pockets, ready for immediate use, intending to destroy the life of every man that stood upon that market square. That seems terrible, gentlemen, but that is the information which we have and which we expect to show you. We expect to show you, further, gentlemen, that the crowd did not fire, that not a single person fired a single shot at the police officers. We expect to show you that Mr. Fielden did not have on that night and never had in his life a revolver; that he did not fire, and that that portion of the testimony here is wrong. We expect to show you, further, gentlemen, that the witness Gilmer, who testified to having seen Spies light the match which caused the destruction coming from the bomb, is a professional and constitutional liar; that no man in the city of Chicago who knows him will believe him under oath, and, indeed, I might almost say that it would scarcely need even a witness to show the falsity of his testimony, because it seems to me that it must fall of its own weight. We expect to show you, gentlemen, that Thompson was greatly mistaken; that on that night Schwab never saw or talked with Mr. Spies; that he was at the Haymarket early in the evening, but that he left before the meeting began and before he saw Mr. Spies on that evening at all. We expect to show that Mr. Parsons, so far from thinking anything wrong, and Fischer, were quietly seated at Zepf's hall, drinking, perhaps, a glass of beer at the time the bomb exploded, and that it was as great a surprise to them as it was to any of you. We expect to show you that Engel was at home at the time the bomb exploded, and that he knew nothing about it. With the whereabouts of Lingg you are already familiar. It may seem strange why he was manufacturing bombs. The answer to that is, he had a right to have his house full of dynamite. He had a right to have weapons of all descriptions upon his premises, and until he used them, or advised their use, and they were used in pursuance of his advice, he is not liable any more than the man who commits numerous burglaries, the man who commits numerous thefts, who walks the streets is liable to arrest and punishment only when he commits an act which makes him amenable to law.

    I did not expect to address you concerning Mr. Neebe, and it is unnecessary for me to make much comment on that, but will show you that Mr. Neebe did not know of this meeting, that he was not present, that he was in no manner connected with it, and there is no proof to show that he was. We will also prove to you, gentlemen, that Mr. Fielden did not go down the alley, as some of the witnesses for the

State have testified, but that he went down Desplaines street to Randolph, and up Randolph, as, indeed, if my memory serves me right, the statements made by Mr. Fielden immediately after the occurrence already sufficiently show.

Now, gentlemen, in conclusion, as I stated to you a moment ago, we do not intend to defend against Socialism, we do not intend to defend against Anarchism, we expect to be held responsible for that only which we have done, and to be held in the manner pointed out by law. Under the charge upon which these defendants are held under this indictment, we shall prove to you, and I hope to your entire satisfaction, that a case has not been made out against them. Whether they be Socialists or whether they be Anarchists we hope will not influence any one of you, gentlemen. Whatever they may have preached, or whatever they may have said, or whatever may have been their object, if it was not connected with the throwing of the bomb it is your sworn duty to acquit them. We expect to make all this proof, and we expect such a result. Gentlemen, I thank you.

CHAPTER IX.

TESTIMONY FOR THE DEFENSE.

On the morning of Monday, August 2, the defense placed its first witness on the stand in the person of CARTER H. HARRISON, Mayor of Chicago. We have already alluded to his testimony in part. He said that on the morning of the 4th he " received information of the issuance of a circular of a peculiar character," calling the Haymarket meeting. He directed the chief of police that if anything should be said at that meeting " that might call out a recurrence of such proceedings as at McCormick's factory, the meeting should be dispersed. I believed that it was better for myself to be there and disperse the meeting myself instead of leaving it to any policeman." He heard Spies' speech " and all of Mr. Parsons up to the time I left, with the exception of about five or ten minutes, during which I went over to the station. When I judged that Mr. Parsons was looking towards the close of his speech I went over to the station, spoke to Captain Bonfield and determined to go home, but instead of going immediately I went back to hear a little more; staid there about five minutes longer and then left. Within about twenty minutes from the time that I left the meeting I heard the sound of the explosion of the bomb at my house.

"I did in fact take no action at the meeting about dispersing it. There were occasional replies from the audience as 'shoot him,' 'hang him,' or the like, but I do not think from the directions in which they came, here and there and around, that there were more than two or three hundred actual sympathizers with the speakers. Several times cries of 'hang him,' would come from a boy in the outskirts, and the crowd would laugh. I felt that a majority of the crowd were idle spectators, and the replies nearly as much what might be called 'guying' as absolute applause. Some of the replies were evidently bitter; they came from immediately around the stand. The audience numbered from 800 to 1,000. The people in attendance, so far as I could see before the speaking commenced, were apparently laborers and mechanics, and the majority of them not English-speaking people, mostly Germans. There was no suggestion made by either of the speakers for the immediate use of force or violence toward any person that night; if there had been I should have dispersed them at once.
* * * When I went to the station during Parson's speech, I stated to Captain Bonfield that I thought the speeches were about over; that *nothing had occurred yet or looked likely to occur to require interference*, and that he had better issue orders to his reserves at the other stations to go home, * * * I don't remember hearing Parsons call 'To arms! To arms! To arms!'"

BARTON SIMONSON, born in Chicago, and traveling salesman for seven years. On May 4, "after supper, I went to the Haymarket meeting. In the afternoon I had received a copy of the circular calling the Haymarket meeting. This (producing circular) is the copy of the circular I received." It *did not* contain the line "Workingmen, arm yourself and appear in full force."

"I reached the Haymarket about 7:30. I found no meeting there. I walked around among the crowd, which was scattered over the Haymarket, then I went to the Desplaines Street station and shook hands with Captain Ward, whom I knew. He introduced me to Inspector Bonfield and I had a conversation with him. Later on I went back and remained throughout the whole meeting until the bomb had exploded. The speakers were northeast of me in front of Crane Brothers' building, a few feet north of the alley. I remember the alley particularly. As far as I remember Spies' speech, he said: 'Please come to order. This meeting is not called to incite any riot.'" Witness then gave a synopsis of the speech, which in no wise differs from that previously given as written out by Spies.

He thought Mr. Parsons did say "To arms, to arms," but in what connection could not remember. "Somebody in the crowd said 'shoot' or 'hang Gould,' and he says, 'No, a great many will jump up and take his place. What Socialism aims at is not the death of individuals, but of the system.'

"Fielden spoke very loud, and as I had never attended a Socialist meeting before in my life, I thought they were a little wild. Fielden spoke about a Congressman from Ohio who had been elected by the workingmen and confessed that no legislation could be enacted in favor of the workingmen; consequently he said there was no use trying to do anything by legislation. After he had talked a while a dark cloud with cold wind came from the north. Many people had left before, but when that cloud came a great many people left. Somebody said, 'Let's adjourn'—to some place—I can't remember the name of the place. Fielden said he was about through, there was no need of adjourning. He said two or three times, 'Now, in conclusion,' or something like that, and I became impatient. Then I heard a commotion and a good deal of noise in the audience, and somebody said, 'police.' I looked south and saw a line of police. The police moved along until the front of the column got about up to the speaker's wagon. I heard somebody near the wagon say something about dispersing. I saw some persons upon the wagon. I could not tell who they were. About the time somebody was giving that command to disperse, I distinctly heard two words coming from the vicinity of the wagon or from the wagon. I don't know who uttered them. The words were, 'peaceable meeting.' That was a few seconds before the explosion of the bomb. I did not hear any such exclamation as, 'Here come the bloodhounds of the police; you do your duty and I'll do mine,' from the locality of the wagon or from Mr. Fielden. I heard nothing of the sort that night. At the time the bomb exploded I was still in my position upon the stairs. There was no pistol firing by any person upon the wagon before the bomb exploded. No pistol shots anywhere before the explosion of the bomb.

"Just after the command to disperse had been given, I saw a lighted fuse, or something—I didn't know what it was at the time—come up from a point *twenty feet south* of the south line of Crane's alley, from about the center of the sidewalk on the east side of the street, from behind some boxes. I am positive it was *not* thrown from the alley. I first noticed it about six or seven feet in the air, a little above a man's head. It went in a northwest course and up about fifteen feet from the ground, and fell about the middle of the street. The explosion followed almost immediately. Something of a cloud of smoke followed the explosion. After the bomb exploded there was pistol shooting. From my position I could distinctly see the flashes of the pistols. My head was about fifteen feet above the ground. There might have been fifty to one hundred and fifty pistol shots. They proceeded from about the center of where the police were. I did not observe either the flashes of the pistol shot or hear the report of any shots from the crowd upon the police prior to the firing by the police. The police were not only shooting at the crowd, but I noticed several of them shoot just as they happened to throw their arms. I concluded that my position was possibly more dangerous than down in the crowd, and then I ran down to the foot of the stairs, ran west on the sidewalk on Randolph street a short distance, and then in the road. A crowd was running in the same direction. I had to jump over a man lying down, and I saw another man fall in front of me about 150 to 200 feet west of Desplaines street. I took hold of his arm and wanted to help him, but the firing was so lively behind me that I just left go and ran. I was in the rear of the crowd running west, the police still behind us. There were no shots from the direction to which I was running.

"I am not and never have been a member of any Socialistic party or association. Walking through the crowd before the meeting, I noticed that the meeting was composed principally of ordinary workingmen, mechanics, etc. The audience listened and once in while there would be yells of 'Shoot him,' 'Hang him.' The violent ones seemed to be in the vicinity of the wagon. My impression is that some were making fun of the meeting. I noticed no demonstration of violence, no fighting or anything of that kind on the part of the crowd.

"I heard about half a dozen or perhaps a few more of such expressions as 'Hang him' or 'Shoot him,' from the audience. I did not find any difference in the bearing of the crowd during Fielden's speech from what it was during Parsons' or Spies'. In the course of the conversation with Capt. Bonfield at the station before the meeting that night, I asked him about the trouble in the southwestern part of the city. He says: 'The trouble there is that these'—whether he used the word Socialist or strikers, I don't know—'get their women and children mixed up with them and around them and in front of them, and we can't get at them. I would like to get 3,000 of them in a crowd without their women and children'—and to the best of my recollection he added—'and I will make short work of them.' I noticed a few women and children at the bottom of the steps where I was."

Upon cross-examination this graphic and evidently truthful narration was not weakened in the least. Among other things he added in confirmation the following: "The firing began from the police, right in the center of the street. I did not see a single shot fired from the crowd on either side of the street. I don't know what became of the men on the wagon. I was not looking at the wagon all the time, but was looking over the scene in general. If you get up on a place as high as I was, and it was dark, you could see every flash; the flashes show themselves when they are out of the revolvers, on a dark night. The scene impressed itself so upon me, that now, looking back, I see it as I did then. Looking at where the bomb exploded, I could not help looking towards the wagon, too."

The witness went to the meeting out of mere curiosity to see what Socialist meetings were, and no subsequent witness could in any manner affect his character as an exemplary citizen and Christian gentleman.

JOHN FERGUSON, a resident of Chicago for seventeen years and engaged in the business of cloak-making. His testimony was straightforward and pertinent as to the character of the meeting. On May 4th he happened to be passing through an adjoining street with an acquaintance, " and noticing something of a crowd further south on Desplaines street we walked down to it. Some gentleman was speaking in broken English. My acquaintance told me he believed it was Spies. I stopped about ten minutes and listened to his speech. Then we walked down Desplaines street about half way to the station, and passed Carter Harrison and two gentlemen with him. I turned around and went back, expecting to hear one of Carter's speeches. Spies was still speaking, but finished in a few minutes, and Mr. Parsons made a speech of about thirty or thirty-five minutes. Then Mr. Harrison went away, and I turned to go away, and, meeting an acquaintance, stopped and conversed with him for a few minutes. I then listened to about fifteen minutes more of Mr. Parsons' speech from the crossing of Randolph street. During his speech, when he mentioned Jay Gould's name, somebody said, ' Throw him in the lake,' and a man almost in front of me took his pipe from his mouth and hollered out, ' Hang him.' Parsons replied that would do no good, a dozen more Jay Goulds would spring up in his place. ' Socialism aims not at the life of individuals, but at the system.' I didn't hear any other responses from the crowd than those I mentioned.

" After Parsons concluded another gentleman got up and began speaking about Congressman Foran. After a few minutes I saw quite a storm cloud come up. Some one interrupted the speaker with the remark: ' There is a prospect of immediate storm, and those of you who wish to continue the meeting can adjourn to '—some hall, I don't remember the name of it; but the speaker, resuming, said: ' I havn't but two or three words more to say, and then you can go home.' I walked away from the meeting, across Randolph street to the southwest corner. There I saw the police rush out from the station in a body; they whirled into the street and came down very rapidly towards us; the gentleman in command of the police was swinging his arm and told them to hurry up. After they had passed us we turned to walk south towards the station and we heard a slight report, something like breaking boards, or like slapping a brick down on the pavement. We turned, and we had just about faced around, looking at the crowd, when we saw a fire flying out about six or eight feet above the heads of the heads of the crowd and falling down pretty near the center of the street. It was all dark for almost a second, perhaps, and then there was a deafening roar, then almost instantly we saw flashes from towards the middle of the street, south of Randolph on Desplaines, and heard reports. That side of the street where the crowd was was dark; at that time there did not appear to be any light there. Then we hurried away. I did not see any flashes from either side of the street. The crowd was very orderly, as orderly as I ever saw anywhere in the street.

"It could not have been longer than five minutes from the time Fielden said that we will be through in a short time that the police marched down the street. I am not a Socialist, nor an Anarchist, nor a Communist; I don't know anything about what those terms mean."

LUDWIG ZELLER was the next witness. Went to the meeting after ten o'clock, stopping because attracted by the crowd. Shortly after he saw the police marching towards them. He was standing by the lamp post near Crane's alley. "When they passed me I heard the command of the captain; heard no reply from anybody on the wagon or near the wagon. I turned and went south to Randolph street, and in turning I saw a light go through the air about six, or eight, or ten feet *south of the lamp*. It went in a northwesternly direction, right into the middle of the police; then I heard an explosion and shooting. * * * The shots came from the center of the street."

Witness was present at a meeting of the Central Labor Union on Sunday, May 2d, as a delegate from the Cigar Makers' Union, No. 15. "The delegates of the Lumber-Shovers' Union at that meeting requested me to send a speaker to a meeting of the Lumber-Shovers' Union to be held on Monday, May 3d, at the Black road; they wanted a good speaker, who could keep the meeting *quiet and orderly*. In the afternoon of the same day we had another meeting of the Central Labor Union, at which Mr. Spies was present as a reporter of the *Arbeiter-Zeitung*, and I told him personally to go out to the meeting and speak in the name of the Central Labor Union. * * * I did not notice any firing back from the crowd at the police."

Upon cross-examination he said:

"I am not an Anarchist; I am a Socialist. I was standing about five or six feet *south* of that alley. I saw the fuse about eight or ten feet *south of me*. * * * There was an express wagon about ten or twelve feet south of the alley. I can't remember any boxes there, there were so many men standing around me; and I was only a few minutes there."

CARL RICHTER, in the leather business, was at the meeting, and particular attention is called to his testimony in connection with the evidence of Thompson that Spies and Schwab conversed in the alley. He said:

"I was standing at the mouth of Crane's alley when the meeting was opened. Mr. Spies was on the wagon, a little *north* of the alley, and asked, 'Is Parsons here?' or something like that. After that Spies left the wagon. I did not notice in what direction he went. About five or ten minutes later Spies was on the wagon again, and commenced his speech. During all the time Spies was away I was standing right there at the alley. There was nothing to prevent my seeing whoever went in the alley." He was slightly acquainted with Mr. Spies, but no tie of relationship or friendship connected them. "I never saw this gentleman (indicating Schwab) before in my life, to my knowledge. I did not see Mr. Spies or Mr. Schwab go into the mouth of the alley at the mouth of which I was standing. There were not many people around me at the time, may be ten people in my immediate neighborhood."

The meeting was quite orderly. Witness was not a Socialist, a Communist, nor an Anarchist, nor connected with any of their organizations. Saw no firing from the crowd. Heard all the speaking, but did not hear the police called bloodhounds or any remark referring to them. Saw no change in the demeanor of the crowd during Fielden's speech from what it had been.

FRIEDRICH LIEBEL also gave testimony directly opposite to that of Gilmer and Thompson. He was standing on the southeast corner of the alley, the previous witness being about in the center of the mouth of the alley. Is a carpenter. Heard Spies ask for Parsons and saw him leave the wagon. Did not leave his position while Spies was about. Had frequently heard him speak and therefore knew his face. Did not see Schwab that night. Did not see Spies go towards the alley and the gas lamp was lighted.

As to the direction from which the bomb proceeded, he directly contradicts Gilmers' tale. When the police came he was a few feet south of the alley, the wagon being a few feet north of it. "After I heard the captain's command I went south (that is, still further from the alley), tried to get out of the crowd, partly I was shoved, partly I shoved myself. The next thing I observed was a light which I took at the time for the stump of a cigar, about midway between the alley and the corner of Randolph street (still further south), over the east sidewalk, about four feet over my head. It went in a northwesternly direction. After that I heard shots coming from west of me, from the direction of the police. I didn't see any of the people on the sidewalk return the fire. I heard the explosion of the bomb and the revolver shots so near together that I can't say which was first. A great many shots came from behind me while I was running on Randolph street. I did not notice anybody in front of me shoot back."

Witness never belonged to any Socialistic group, armed or otherwise.

The reader will bear in mind that the burden of Gilmer's evidence was that Spies lit the fuse and Schnaubelt threw the bomb *from the mouth of the alley,* Fischer being present. Thompson was called to prove that Spies and Schwab talked about "pistol" and "police" in the alley, and inferentially about bombs. We have seen them both flatly contradicted by fair and unbiased witnesses. But the counter-proof is by no means exhausted.

DR. JAMES D. TAYLOR, physician by profession, came to this country from England forty-four years ago and is seventy-six years old. On the night of May 4th he was at the Haymarket meeting and stood close to the *north* side of Crane's alley. It will be remembered that Richter stood at about the center and Liebel on the south side of the alley, all three of them on the sidewalk of Desplaines street, thus giving them all a full view of the entrance to the alley. He was there twenty minutes before the speaking began and remained there till the storm of bullets suggested other thoughts. The tail end of the wagon was about four feet from where he stood on the curbstone. "What particularly struck me in Spies' speech was his reply to some persons who said 'Hang Jay Gould.' Spies said: 'You had better shut up and go home and learn more about what you ought to know before you begin talking about hanging anybody. We are not here for that purpose.' * * *

" I saw the police come up. The front rank was on line with me. I could have touched the first man with my arm. They went up to within about six feet from the wagon. I heard one of them say; 'I command you in the name of the State of Illinois to disperse.' Mr.

Fielden was on the wagon or just about coming down from the wagon at that time. When the police came up I noticed those south of the alley began to disperse. Just before that I heard Mr. Fielden say, 'We have talked long enough and it is time to disperse.' Fielden spoke in his ordinary tone.

"I heard the explosion of the bomb. I heard no pistol shot prior to it. I saw Fielden get down from the wagon. I saw him *after* the bomb exploded. I heard Fielden reply to the command to disperse: 'We are peaceable,' while he was still on the wagon. I did not see Fielden draw a revolver and shoot in the direction of the police; I never saw anything of the kind. He came down from the wagon nearest to the police; he was only a few feet distant from me at the time. I watched him as long as I could, but finally looking in the direction in which he had been standing, he wasn't there. I did not see him use a pistol on or off the wagon.

"I saw the bomb in the air, as near as I could judge twenty to forty feet south of the alley, and the man who threw it stood beyond a number of boxes. These boxes were about five or six feet elevated one on the other, on the sidewalk, south of the lamp-post. I revisited the ground the next morning and saw the boxes there. * * * *

"The pistol firing and the explosion of the bomb seemed to me almost simultaneous. The pistol firing came from the direction where the police were. I did not see any pistol-firing from the crowd upon the police; I went up to Crane's alley behind other people going into the same alley. When I revisited the ground the next morning I noticed bullet marks on the wall of Crane's building, which form the north side of Crane's alley. I could not find one bullet mark on the wall of the south side of the alley. I examined a telegraph pole on the west side of Desplaines street north of Crane's alley. I noticed that all the perforations were on the south side of that telegraph pole. I did not find one pistol shot or fresh mark upon the north side of that telegraph pole."

Yet Gilmer said he remained quietly during the shooting "right at the mouth of the alley; and after it was all over I backed out the alley, took a car and went home!" Dr. Taylor further said: "After I got into the alley I took a zigzag course to get out of the way of pistol shots" which were being fired into and down the alley. On cross-examination he said Fielden could not have pulled out a revolver before he left the scene without witness seeing it. "A good many bullets came into the alley." He went south afterwards on Desplaines street and for two blocks distant had to dodge in several places as "the police were shooting all the way down. They shot down Randolph street, they shot on Madison street, two blocks south of Randolph street. I took refuge in the court of St. Dennis Hotel. There was one policeman who passed me saying, 'God damn you, you shall go to hell,' and away he blazed at the people going on Madison street. I heard him shoot about three times. * * * I believe in organized government: I believe in the oath in courts of justice, but I believe a man ought to speak the truth even if there was no oath. I know nothing about the armed section of the American group. I never advocated the use of force; I never handled any dynamite bombs."

Next follows some testimonials as to the character of Mr. Gilmer.

L. C. MOSES, a grocer, sixty-four years of age. " I know Harry Gilmer, who I understand was a witness in this case, since he came into the neighborhood, between six and seven months ago. I know his general reputation for truth and veracity in the neighborhood in which he resides. It is very bad, I should judge. I should not believe him under oath." He said that he wouldn't trust Gilmer a dollar; but why he would not believe him was not on that account, but from information received from people who boarded where he did.

MRS. B. P. LEE knew Gilmer. Had always heard that his reputation for veracity was bad and that he was not to be believed under oath. Had heard this before Gilmer's name appeared in the case as a witness.

FRANK STENNER was called to testify in Fielden's behalf. He is a machinist and attended the meeting because he had read the circular calling it. He was four or six feet from the speaker's wagon. He heard Fielden say: " We are peaceable," or something like that, but that afterwards Fielden said " all right " and got down from the wagon on the west side. " As soon as the bomb was thrown the policemen shot. I didn't see anybody except the police shoot." He laid down for safety on the steps of Crane Brothers' factory. " I remained there a few minutes, a policeman came and arrested me. From reading the paper I guess the policeman's name was Foley. When I was in the cell Officer Wessler came to me, showed me a revolver and said, ' It is your revolver.' When I was examined before the justice of the peace, Wessler said to the judge, he had seen me on the steps of Crane Brothers; there was a shot from that place and he guessed I was the man that shot. That revolver was found by Officer Foley, about *fifty feet from the wagon* while I was in his custody. He said three shots were out and two were in." Foley swore that he picked up this pistol while "going by the wagon." Witness further said the crowd was peaceably inclined; while some cried "Hang him," others

TESTIMONY FOR THE DEFENSE. 121

called "rats." "When Parsons was talking one man who stood by my side said, 'You are a liar.'"

"There was no shot fired from the wagon before the bomb exploded. I was looking at Fielden when he got off the wagon." He was held as a "suspect" under arrest for three weeks, but discharged upon examination.

JOSEPH GUTSCHER, a shoemaker, was also at the meeting, and standing on the west side of Desplaines street, across from the speakers' wagon. He also testified to the fact that the police did all the shooting. "I was shot myself in the back and in the leg. There were three other men near me who were shot. One of them received three shots. The police took me to the station *and locked me up for two weeks.*" Nothing appears to show the witness was in sympathy with the social heretics to whom he was listening, he stating, in fact, that living half a block distant he went "because I saw many people go there." After being confined in the station for two weeks, with two bullets in him, for the crime of being there, he was removed to the hospital, where he remained one week.

FRANK RAAB, a baker, was casually passing, and seeing the crowd, stopped. Had no acquaintance with any of the defendants; although a Socialist, belongs to no organization. Was present when the bomb was thrown, but "saw no fire go through the air from the mouth of the alley."

"I did not see any shooting from the audience at the police either before I started to run or when I was running. Lots of men were falling down while I was running. I jumped over three or four. *After* I turned the corner a man fell before me and another behind me, and I jumped and sort of caught my foot and fell down into the basement. I stayed there two or three minutes; then went out and the police were still shooting, not very much, however. I went across the street, where there is a saloon on the corner, and there I saw a citizen shot right through his hand." Cross-examination only brought out the fact that he was not a reader of any Socialistic paper, and had never even seen the *Arbeiter-Zeitung*.

JOHN O. BRIXEY had known Gilmer since 1880; had lived in the same neighborhood with him in 1880 and 1881, and again "some time last year. I was then living where I am living now, and Gilmer lived next door to me. I think I know his general reputation for truth and veracity among his neighbors. It is bad. I don't think I could believe him under oath." Had heard his reputation discussed as far back as 1880. "It was a kind of a general thing to discuss Gilmer's truthfulness and veracity." Testified reluctantly.

JOHN GARRICK, ex-chief deputy-sheriff, was slightly acquainted with Harry L. Gilmer. Had first met him in 1881, "when he was a tenant of mine. I am acquainted with his general reputation for truth and veracity among his neighbors and acquaintances where he resides. His reputation is very bad, as far as I heard. I should hate to believe him under oath; *I could not.*" Had "seen him associate with very questionable characters, both men and women." Got rid of him as a tenant as quickly as possible.

WILLIAM URBAN, compositor at the *Arbeiter-Zeitung* since 1879; a member of the Central Labor Union; knows Mr. Spies. Witness corroborated Mr. Zeller that Spies was selected to speak at the Lumber-Shovers' Union, near McCormick's factory, on May 3. "Mr. Spies said he was very busy, and if he could go out to the Black road the next day he would do so." It was not of his own inclination that Spies went.

Was at the Haymarket. Mr. Parsons was speaking from the wagon when he arrived, a few feet north of the alley. Heard Parsons propose an adjournment and Fielden reply that he would "only talk a few minutes longer." When the police came he was on the corner of the alley, near the lamp-post. "Captain Ward stepped forward and said, 'In the name,' etc., and I saw two or three policemen four or five feet behind the captain have something shining in their hands. I guess it was revolvers. Then I looked around and saw something like a firecracker in the air, then I heard a deep noise and shooting. It seemed to me all these noises came at once. This fire that looked to me like a fire-cracker must have started about fifteen to eighteen feet *south* of the lamp-post, at Crane's alley. It went awfully fast, made a kind of circle," etc. He ran toward Randolph street, but "fell over a pile of people lying there and couldn't get any further," so jumped over a railing into an area-way. Saw none of the citizens return the fire of the police. Neither heard Mr. Fielden nor any one else refer to the police as "bloodhounds."

WILLIAM GLEESON; not a Socialist, Communist nor Anarchist. Was at the Haymarket meeting with witness Ferguson. "Parsons was speaking when I arrived at the meeting. I remember his making some comments as to Gould. Some person in the audience cried out, 'Hang him!' Parsons replied something to the effect that Socialism or Socialists did not want any one killed; they wanted the system killed that created and encouraged such men as Gould. In this connection he deprecated the abusing of scabs by trade unionists, stating that they were only parasites on the body politic. He told the story about the fleas and the dog, and said that while the trade unions were going to kill off the fleas, which he compared with the scabs, Socialists wanted to kill the dog—which was the system that created these scabs." While standing on the southwest corner of Randolph street with Ferguson, "we suddenly saw a number of policemen rush out of the alley that led down to the police station, coming on and forming along the street, and they were so impetuous that one of the young lieutenants, I presume he was in command, ran five or six feet in advance of his column and was shouting and hurrying them up to be quick, and rallying them, as it were, to advance quicker than they were doing. They advanced very quickly, I should say between a run and a walk." Instantaneously with the bomb the shooting began, and came from the center of the street.

WILLIAM SAHL, blacksmith; in sympathy with the Socialists, but not an Anarchist. Heard Spies ask for Parsons from the wagon, and saw him get down and walk with two or three other persons in a southwesterly direction. Knows Mr. Schwab and that he was not one of those accompanying Spies; did not see him on the wagon. Did not see Mr. Schwab around that place at any time that night. Never belonged to any group.

EBERHARDT HIERSEMENZEL, painter, testified that all the shots came from the police. "I only saw that everyone wanted to get away to save himself. I did not see any of the citizens have in their possession any revolvers or weapons of any kind." When he ran he saw several lying prostrate and others near him fell, and he fell over them and injured his knee.

CONRAD MESSER, cabinet-maker, stood by the wagon when the police came and heard Fielden respond, "We are peaceable." Saw Fielden get down. "I saw Fielden all that time. He had no pistol in his hand. I didn't see him fire one shot. I saw no citizen shoot there. The firing came from the police. I am not a Socialist. I do not belong to any group of Anarchists or armed section."

AUGUST KRUMM, woodworker and machinist, gave important testimony. He was neither Socialist, Communist nor Anarchist. Don't think he ever saw any of the defendants before that night. Arrived at the meeting about a quarter of nine. Knew nothing about the meeting, and being down town stopped merely out of curiosity. A Mr. Albright was with him. "I stood close to the north wall of Crane Brothers' building, right at the corner of Crane's alley. Remained there all the evening. Later in the evening Albright and myself went back a little ways into the alley. He gave me a pipe of tobacco. *I lit a match and lighted his pipe and mine.* When we went back to the corner I saw the police coming up, and one man walked up to the wagon. Shortly after that I heard a shot fired from the direction where the police stood, from the south. Right after the bomb exploded. I didn't see any shot fired from the wagon. While we were lighting our pipes in the alley, and while we were at the corner, I did not see any one enter the alley. We went back into the alley to light our pipes because there was a kind of draft on the sidewalk." Saw the bomb in the air, "something like a burnt-out match," coming from a point about twenty feet south of the alley. "It could not have started from the mouth of the alley." He knew none of the speakers; thought it was Spies who spoke last, but, asked to point him out, promptly indicated Fielden. A long and searching cross-examination failed to shake his testimony.

ROBERT LINDINGER was at the meeting with Carl Richter, and standing with him at the mouth of Crane's alley when Spies asked for Parsons and got down from the wagon. Did not see Spies approach him and never saw Schwab before in his life. Stayed there till the close and heard Fielden reply something containing the word "peaceable." Heard no one refer to the police as "bloodhounds." Saw no pistol in Fielden's hand when he got down. "I did not see anybody in the crowd fire a shot. I saw shots when I last looked at the wagon from where the police were standing. I did not see anybody on the sidewalk shoot back at the police. I am no Socialist." Witness was a member of the Knights of Labor and belonged to no other organization."

WILLIAM ALBRIGHT, who was with Krumm in the alley, corroborated his companion's testimony as to the lighting of the pipe and "as I came out I saw the police coming." Was not a Socialist, but was a Knight of Labor. His testimony was essentially the same as that of Krumm's.

GEORGE KOEHLER testified to the police doing the shooting and to the bomb starting from south of the alley.

THEODORE WEIMELDT, canvasser, was at the meeting. Saw the circular on the street and it did not contain the words, "Workingmen, arm yourselves and appear in full force." On his way to the meeting had a conversation with Mr. Kelly, the bailiff of the police station, whom he had known for four or five years. The State objected to the next question, which was:

Q. I will ask you what Mr. Kelly said, if anything, in regard to trouble that might be expected that night?

The court sustained the objection, but witness stated that *after the conversation* he concluded not to stay and went directly home.

FREDERICK C. GROH, carpenter, was at the meeting in April where Engel spoke. Mr. Engel never spoke at those meetings but once. They were Carpenters'-union meetings. "I didn't hear Mr. Engel say in his speech anything in regard to saving money to buy revolvers. He said he wanted all workingmen to join the union. I did not hear him say anything about getting revolvers to shoot policemen down. Am secretary of the union."

AUGUST KRAUSE, carpenter, was chairman of the meeting where Engel spoke, and corroborated the previous witness.

WILLIAM RADTKE keeps a saloon at 888 Clybourn avenue, in the suburbs. "On the night of May 4 last, I saw Mr. Schwab in my saloon about fifteen or twenty minutes after nine. He stayed there about ten minutes. Then I saw him go over to the prairie and make a speech."

DIEDRICH BEHRENS lived in the same vicinity. "I remember to have seen the defendant Schwab, on the night of May 4 last, in Schilling's saloon, on the corner of Clybourn and Ashland avenues, between a quarter-past ten and half-past ten."

CHARLES HEIDERKREUGER, eighteen years of age, while passing the meeting stopped. Stood by the corner of the wagon; was suddenly pushed, and looking up saw the police sixteen or twenty feet away from him and the crowd already running. He threw himself on his face for safety; saw no arms in the crowd. "When I laid myself down officers got around me; I wanted to get away. I got up and went towards the officers, wanted to go home; one of the officers stopped me, told me to hold up my hands, which I did, *and he hit me with his club*, arrested me, and I was taken to the station and locked up."

JOSEPH SCHWINDT, shoemaker, was at the meeting; "stood ten or twelve feet south of the wagon, between the lamp-post and the boxes on the sidewalk, at the time the police came up, facing the police." Saw no one shoot except the police.

M. D. MALKOFF, reporter, attended a meeting of the Furniture Workers' Union at Zepf's Hall on the evening of May 4. At the time of the explosion was standing down stairs in the saloon with Mr. Allen. "I saw Parsons at Zepf's Hall from five to ten minutes before the explosion of the bomb. He was sitting at the window, north of the entrance door, in company with Mrs. Parsons and Mrs. Holmes. The saloon was pretty crowded at that time." Although nearly a block distant witness heard "the bullets rattling on the walls."

WM. A. PATTERSON, printer, was a member of the American Group, and in response to an "ad" in the *News* attended a meeting of the group at 107 Fifth avenue on the evening of May 4. There were present Parsons, Fielden, Schwab and others. "The business of the meeting was to organize the working-women of Chicago. There was a call at the telephone. I believe they wanted a speaker at Deering (Clybourn avenue), and a young man, a clerk in the office, answered." Mr. Schwab's name was mentioned and he was sent. Shortly before they adjourned "a gentleman came in and said that speakers were wanted at the Haymarket." Never heard of the word "Ruhe" nor knew its meaning; cannot read German. "The children of Mrs. Parsons were present at the meeting."

JOHN HOLLOWAY, expressman, on May 4 was walking on Desplaines street with a friend; looked at the patrol wagons near the station and was roughly accosted by some one.

Q. State what you saw and heard there.

Objected to.

MR. SALOMON.—I wish to show by this witness that he was told at the station by persons connected with the same that before twelve o'clock at night blood would flow pretty freely, or words to that effect.

Judge Gary sustained the objection. The witness, however, went and stood near the alley until "the police came up and charged the meeting to disperse." Heard Fielden say, "We are peaceable." "I was looking at the speaker up to the time he was spoken to by one of the policemen, and listened to him. My hearing and eyesight are pretty good. I did not hear anybody at any time that night say, 'Here come the bloodhounds,' nothing of the sort took place." There were no shots from the direction of the wagon; they came from the center of the street. Saw no one have weapons. "*I am sure* that nothing came out of the alley while I stood there." The bomb came from the south. "Have never had anything to do with any Socialistic group," and knew none of the speakers.

HENRY LINDMEYER, mason, calcimined the *Arbeiter-Zeitung* rooms from May 2 to the 5th. It will be remembered that Officers Duffy and Marks testified to finding a greasy bag containing dynamite on a closet shelf there on May 5th. Witness the same morning, missing a brush, searched the closet and the shelf. "I found no bundle, no large package, no dynamite on the shelf. Saw no indication of greasiness there." He had previously calcimined the closet. His clothes were on that shelf. "There was no grease on there, else I wouldn't have put my clothes there." The closet was on the third floor.

A very suspicious circumstance regarding the finding of this dynamite is the fact that while the detectives Haas and Marks swear positively that this alleged find was captured *on the third floor* of that building, Officer Duffy, who was the first of these witnesses, swears just as positively that it was found *on the second floor* of the building. Duffy located the room where the stuff was found, *first,* as being on the first floor of the *Arbeiter-Zeitung* office; *second*, as on the second floor of the building; *third*, as two floors below the type-setting room, and, *fourth*, as being one floor below the third floor. *All* these locations refer to the second floor of the building. The only evidence produced came from men for years in the detective service, trained to *produce* evidence.

EDWARD LEHNERT, engineer, saw Schnaubelt at the Haymarket meeting about ten o'clock, and conversed with him.

Q. What was the conversation?

Objected to by the State.

MR. ZEISLER.—We offer to show by this witness that Schnaubelt stated to Lehnert that he did not understand English, that he had expected a German speaker would be present, that no one was present who spoke German except Spies, that Spies had already made an English speech, and that he did not want to stay any longer, and asked Lehnert if he would go along; that Lehnert thereupon said he did not go in the same direction, and that then Schnaubelt went away with another party. We have been able to trace Schnaubelt only a short distance on his way home. We offer this conversation with Lehnert for the purpose of explaining Mr. Schnaubelt's movements after meeting Lehnert."

Ruled out by the court.

Witness, however, stated that he saw Schnaubelt leave with a Mr. Krueger. Saw the bomb rise south of the alley.

WILLIAM SNYDER, born in New York, was on the wagon with the speakers. Was first at the meeting of the American Group to organize the sewing girls and acted as chairman. Knew nothing of the meeting till he saw notice in the paper. Was on the wagon when the police came; "they were marching up very fast." He helped Fielden down and just then they heard the explosion of the bomb. "Fielden did not shoot; *he would have killed me if he had shot;* I was south of him." They separated at the alley into which witness ran. "Fielden did not, after getting out of the wagon, stand on the sidewalk between the wheels of the wagon and fire at the police or in the direction of the police. I had my hand right on him a while, until we reached the mouth of the alley." Heard no shooting except on the part of the police. Never heard of the word "Ruhe;" cannot read German; was of Yankee descent. Never saw any dynamite. Left a note under Mrs. Parsons' door on May 6 which was found by detectives. Was thereupon arrested without a warrant and was still in confinement.

THOMAS BROWN, of the American Group, also arrested with Snyder as a "suspect," was at the meeting, and went with Parsons to Zepf's

Hall, where they were when the bomb exploded. "I saw Fischer there." Never knew the meaning of the word "Ruhe;" does not read German. Was not armed that night and never carried arms in his life.

HENRY W. SPIES, cigar manufacturer, brother of defendant August Spies. Accompanied his brother to the Haymarket meeting. When they got off the wagon before the meeting opened "we went in a south-westerly direction," or nearly the opposite direction of the alley. Schwab was not there. They walked one block only, it was not two, as Thompson alleged. "August was not out of my sight or out of my hearing at any time of that walk. I was right behind him all the time. I never heard my brother and Schnaubelt talk in English. I don't believe Schnaubelt can speak English." His account of the meeting and speeches is similar to that heretofore given. He saw Fielden get off the wagon.

"I told my brother to get off and reached my hand over to help him jump. He took my hand, and in fact got down on the side of the wagon, pretty near the middle of it. Just at that time the explosion took place. I asked him what it was, he said 'They got a gatling-gun down there,' and at the same time as he jumped, somebody jumped behind him with a weapon, right by his back, and I grabbed it, and in warding of the pistol from my brother I was shot." A man named Legner was present. All the firing came from the center of the street. There was no firing back. Never carried arms. Was arrested on May 6.

AUGUST KRUEGER, to whom Lehnert referred, testified that he left the Haymarket with Schnaubelt about ten o'clock. After going some blocks they separated. On his way home witness stopped at Engel's house, reaching it about 10:15. Engel was at home. Later Waller came and informed them "that three hundred men were shot by the police and we ought to go down there and do something. Engel said whoever threw the bomb did a foolish thing; it was nonsense, and he didn't sympathize with such butchery, and he told Waller he had better go home as quick as possible; he said the policemen were just as good people; the revolution must grow out of the people."

JOHN F. WALDO, printer, attended the meeting of the American Group at 107 Fifth avenue, on the evening of May 4. Corroborated testimony as to telephone message for Schwab to go out to Deering. Did not know anything about the word "Ruhe;" does not understand German. The "armed group" never had arms. Was at the Haymarket and shot in the leg; "the ball went in from behind while I was running. I was not armed that night; I never carried a revolver in my life; I did not see any revolvers in the audience. Schwab left after receiving the message."

JOHN M. FLEMING, M.D., surgeon, performed service on the wounded at the Desplaines street station. Took a bullet from the knee of an officer named Kreuger. Asked what conversation ensued, and the State objected.

MR. FOSTER—We propose to prove by this witness that at the time the officer asked to see the bullet it was handed to him, and that he at once recognized it and said, "that came from the police revolver."

Judge Gary sustained the objection.

On being shown a regulation bullet the witness thought it was the same. Other bullets extracted were of the same appearance.

OTTO WANDRAY was at the Haymarket and met Fischer there. When Fielden was speaking they left and went to Zepf's hall, where they were together sitting at a table when the bomb exploded. Saw Parsons there.

EDWARD PREUSSER lives near Deering's factory. "Not a Socialist, Anarchist or Communist." In response to a request from a committee he telephoned for a speaker, suggesting Spies. Spies, he was answered, could not attend, "and I said, 'I don't suppose it makes any difference which one.'" Later he was informed that Mr. Schwab was on his way. Went to meet Mr. Schwab on the car. Met him about half-past nine. They then went to Radtke's saloon, 888 Clybourn avenue and then to the prairie meeting. After the meeting they went to Schilling's and had lunch and beer. From there to the Haymarket is nearly an hour's ride.

Other witnesses testified to hearing Schwab's speech. Another saw him leave the Haymarket on a car before the speaking began. The next, from five years' acquaintance with Gilmer, "would not believe him under oath."

HENRY WITT, a member of the Lumber-Shovers' Union, heard Mr. Spies speak on May 3. Witness had made the request for a speaker and Mr. Spies had been sent. They had nothing to do with McCormick's factory; were not employed there. When some, three hundred to four hundred, left on hearing McCormick's bell ring, Spies advised them to remain, as they had no connection with McCormick's; he continued to speak fifteen minutes longer. Witness was not a Socialist. "When McCormick's bell rang Spies said the people should not go to McCormicks, as they had no interest in the McCormick factory; they should remain there quietly; he did not go to McCormick's himself." There were between six and seven thousand present.

Three other witnesses corroborated the above testimony.

WILLIAM MURPHY, cooper, was at the Haymarket on the wagon with the speakers when the police came up. Before the order to disperse was given no one else had got off. Saw no revolvers around him in the crowd and heard no threat. Got up on the wagon to look for a friend, and while looking the police came and the bomb was thrown. Had been there five or ten minutes. Was not a Socialist.

JOHANN GRUENEBERG, a friend of Fischer. On May 4 he went from the *Arbeiter-Zeitung* office to get the Haymarket circulars. At Fischer's order he went back " and gave the printer the order to leave out the line 'Workingmen, arm yourselves,' etc., from the English as well as the German part." He ordered those already printed to be suppressed. Fischer gave him the order in the presence of Spies and Schwab.

Under cross-examination several questions were asked having no bearing upon his direct examination, for instance, as to where a certain group drilled, to which the defense objected. Whereupon the court gave the following remarkable ruling:

THE COURT—You have put this witness upon the stand for the purpose of showing a thing was taken out a particular circular; whether he has told that thing *as it occurred depends* in some degree upon what his associations, feelings, inclinations, biases are in reference to the whole business.

MR. BLACK—Whether he has told the truth in regard to that depends upon his bias and inclinations?

THE COURT—*Whether it is to be believed.* I don't mean whether he has told the truth.

In other words, it may be the truth, but by permitting an irregular cross-examination, the State may lead the jury to disbelieve it!

Two other witnesses, business men, knew Gilmer and "would not believe him under oath."

ADOLPH TENNES was at the Haymarket. Had no knowledge of Socialism and never saw Spies or Parsons before. Was four or five feet from the wagon when the police came. When he started to run Spies and Fielden were not yet off the wagon. The explosion and firing followed immediately.

MARTIN BECHTEL, brewer, knew Oscar Neebe since March. Was chairman of a meeting of brewers at which Neebe spoke on May 3. Afterwards he went with Neebe to Hein's saloon, nobody being with them. He saw none of the "Revenge circulars" in Neebe's hands or on the tables, thus directly contradicting Hein.

Reporter HEINEMAN, recalled, testified to meeting Mr. and Mrs. Parsons and two little children about half-past seven on the evening of May 4.

LIZZIE MAY HOLMES, assistant editor of the *Alarm*, was present at the American Group on Tuesday evening, May 4, "called to consider the organization of the sewing girls, the working girls in the city." She arrived late with Mr. and Mrs. Parsons, and Schwab was no longer there. Some one came in and requested speakers at the Haymarket. They walked over; subsequently went to Zepf's Hall with Mr. and Mrs. Parsons and Mr. Brown. Mr. Parsons remained there till after the explosion of the bomb. Also saw Mr. Fischer there. Never heard of the word "Ruhe" till after this trial began; knew nothing about anticipated trouble at the Haymarket. Was arrested on the 5th of May as a "suspect" and confined until the Saturday following. Was an Anarchist. "The word Anarchy, from its definition, means 'no coercion;' it really means self-government. I should consider it perfect liberty to live according to natural laws as distinguished from compulsory laws; that is the kind of Anarchist I am. I don't understand Anarchy, and I didn't teach it in my articles, as having reference to force or dynamite. The theory of Anarchy is opposed to all idea of force or coercion."

SAMUEL FIELDEN followed. On the 4th of May he was engaged, as a teamster, in hauling stone. When he got home in the evening and read the evening paper he saw an announcement of a meeting of the American Group. As he was the treasurer he attended. Remembered the telephone request for a speaker at the Deering meeting to which Schwab responded. Paid out five dollars for hand bills for the purpose of calling sewing girls together. During the meeting a request for speakers came from the Haymarket meeting to which witness and Parsons responded. "1 did not wish to speak, but Mr. Spies urged me and I spoke about twenty minutes. Then I went on to state that under such circumstances (referring to Congressman Foran's declaration) the only way in which the working people could get any satisfaction from the gradually decreasing opportunities for their living—the only thing they could do with the law was to 'throttle it.' I used that word in a figurative sense. I said they should throttle it because it was an expensive article to them and could do them no good."

Witness gave a summary of his speech and a detailed account of its close. When Captain Ward commanded them to disperse, he responded that the meeting was a peaceable one "in a very conciliatory tone of voice, and he very angrily and defiantly retorted that he commanded it to disperse, and called, as I understood, upon the police to disperse it. Just as he turned around in that angry mood, I said, 'All right, we will go,' and jumped from the wagon and jumped to the sidewalk." Then the explosion followed. He ran to Randolph street and turned east, but on his way received a shot in the leg. "I had no revolver with me on the night of May 4. I never had a revolver in my life. I never fired at any person in my life." Never heard of the word "Ruhe" or its significance until some days after his arrest. Knew nothing of the Haymarket meeting until he was informed that evening that speakers were wanted there. Never heard of the Monday night meeting at 54 West Lake street till he read of the alleged conspiracy in the papers. Remembers the detective, Johnson, but never had any conversation with him as alleged; knew long before that he was a detective. "The American Group was open to everybody."

Under cross-examination witness was required to answer questions having no reference to his direct examination, thus making him a direct witness for the State against himself, which the court sustained, such as the organization of groups, his connection with the *Alarm*, etc. Knowing his innocence, he had expected to be discharged by the coroner's jury. He was engaged to speak elsewhere on the night of May 4, but only yielded to urgent solicitation when he went to the Haymarket. His remarks were all in a general sense; had no idea of violence from any one that night.

ERNST NIENDORF presided over a meeting of the Carpenter's Union at Zepf's Hall, on Monday evening, May 3, at which defendant Lingg was present; he was there early; made a report at nine o'clock and had the floor two or three times later. The meeting lasted till eleven o'clock, and Lingg was there till the close.

This was the evening of the alleged conspiracy at 54 West Lake street. Another member of the union testified to Lingg's presence at Zepf's Hall the entire evening.

HENRY SCHULTZ, of Wisconsin, strayed into the Haymarket meeting while visiting Chicago. Is not a Socialist, and knew none of the defendants at that time. When the bomb exploded he ran north to Lake street, where he saw the police clubbing two men they had down in the gutter. When the cloud came up most of the audience and all "the women and children left." Heard the speaker say he would get through in a few minutes.

JOSEPH BACH attended the meeting of the American group and corroborated previous testimony as to Schwab going to Deering, and the rest going, by request, to the Haymarket. When the police came he was standing on an elevated platform where he could look over the heads of the crowd. Heard the command to disperse and saw Fielden getting off the wagon and Spies making his way to the sidewalk. Pistol shots all seemed to come from the center of the street, where the police were. The bomb did not come from the alley. When the police came the crowd had thinned out fully one-half. Fielden was about concluding.

MAX MITLACHER, brother-in-law to the previous witness, was present throughout the meeting with Bach and corroborated his testimony.

S. T. INGRAM, nineteen years old; working for Crane Brothers, near where the meeting of May 4 was held. Received on that day a circular, which he still had. It was produced and did *not* contain the line, "Workingmen, arm yourselves," etc. Saw Spies when he inquired for Parsons, and saw him get down from the wagon on its south side, but not go to the alley. When the cloud came up the witness left; stopped at Zepf's Hall and identified Mr. Parsons as being there. Returned to the meeting; was there when the police came and saw Fielden jump from the wagon. "After the explosion of the bomb I stepped back against the wall to keep from getting killed. There was a great deal of shooting going on then; most of it seemed to come from the policemen, from the center of the street. I did not see anybody where I stood have a revolver or speak about a revolver. My hearing and eyesight are good, and were so on that night. I saw no citizen or person dressed in citizens' clothes use a revolver. It was a very peaceable meeting. I heard nobody say that night, at any time, 'Here come the bloodhounds; do your duty and I'll do mine.' If Mr. Fielden had said those words I would have heard them. I am sure he did not utter those words." No shots were fired from or near the wagon.

After another witness, a business man, had sworn that Gilmer's reputation for truth and veracity was *nil*, an important witness was called.

JOHN BERNETT, a candymaker; "not a Socialist, Communist nor Anarchist." Was at the Haymarket meeting, between thirty-five and forty feet *south* of Crane's alley.

"I saw the bomb in the air. I saw the man who threw it; *he was right in front of me*. It went west and a little bit north. The man who threw it was about my size, maybe a little bit bigger, and I think he had a moustache. I think he had no chin beard." Witness was five feet nine inches in height. On being shown Schnaubelt's photograph witness promptly said that it was not the man, and that he had previously so informed the state's attorney. The same story he had told right after the occurrence.

MICHEL SCHWAB. When called by telephone to go to Deering to speak on the evening of May 4, he walked over to the Haymarket to see if he could get Mr. Spies to go, but did not see him and immediately took a car and left. He spoke at Deering, as testified to by Preusser and others. He returned home about eleven o'clock. He at no time that evening saw Mr. Spies, or entered Crane's alley for any purpose.

AUGUST VINCENT THEODORE SPIES testified at some length. Had been an editor on the *Arbeiter-Zeitung* since 1880. On the evening of Sunday, May 2, he attended a meeting of the Central Labor Union at 54 West Lake street, in the capacity of a reporter. While there he was invited to address the Lumber-Shovers' Union the following day. He did not know until his arrival at the meeting that it was in the immediate neighborhood of McCormick's factory.

"Having spoken two or three times almost every day for the preceding two or three weeks I was almost prostrated, and spoke very calmly, and told the people, who in my judgment were not of a very high intellectual grade, to stand together and to enforce their demands at all hazards, otherwise the single bosses would one by one defeat them. While I was speaking I heard somebody in the rear, probably a hundred feet away from me, cry out something in a language which I didn't understand—perhaps Bohemian or Polish. After the meeting I was told that this man had called upon them to follow him up to McCormick's. I should judge about two hundred persons standing a little ways apart from the main body detached themselves and went away. I didn't know where they were going, until, probably five minutes later, I heard firing." Shortly afterward, having finished his business, he went up to McCormick's to see what was going on. "When I came up there on this prairie, right in front of McCormick's I saw a policeman run after and fire at people who were fleeing, running away."

Not being able to do anything he returned to the place of the meeting, and thence back to the city. 'The same evening I wrote the report of the meeting which appeared in the *Arbeiter-Zeitung* of the next day. Immediately after I came to the office I wrote the so-called ' Revenge' circular, except the heading 'Revenge.' At the time I wrote it I believed the statement that six workingmen had been killed that afternoon at McCormick's. I wrote at first that two had been killed, and after seeing the report in the five-o'clock *News* I changed the two to six, based upon the information contained in the *News*. I believe 2,500 copies of that circular were printed, but not more than half of them distributed, for I saw quite a lot of them in the office of the *Arbeiter-Zeitung* on the morning I was arrested. At the time I wrote it I was still laboring under the excitement of the scene and the hour. I was very indignant.

On May 4 I was performing my regular duties at the *Arbeiter-Zeitung*. A little before nine in the forenoon I was invited to address a meeting at the Haymarket that evening. That was the first I heard of it. I had no part in calling the meeting. I put the announcement of the meeting into the *Arbeiter-Zeitung* at the request of a man who invited me to speak. The *Arbeiter-Zeitung* is an afternoon daily paper, and appears at two o'clock. About eleven o'clock a circular calling the Haymarket meeting was handed to me to be inserted in the *Arbeiter-Zeitung*, containing the line, 'Workingmen, arm yourselves and appear in full force.' I said to the man who brought the circular that if that was the meeting which I had been invited to address, I certainly should not speak there on account of that line. He stated that the circular had not been distributed, and I told him if that was the case and if he would take out that line it would be all right. Mr. Fischer was called down at that time, and he sent the man back to the printing-office to have the line taken out. I struck out the line myself before I handed it to the compositor to put it in the *Arbeiter-Zeitung*. The man who brought the circular to me and took it back with the line stricken out was on the stand here—Grueneberg, I believe is his name."

When he walked down to the Haymarket that evening with his brother Henry he expected to address the meeting in German. Finding no other speakers there he opened the meeting. When he asked for Parsons some one told him that Parsons had been seen shortly before at the corner of Halsted and Randolph, two blocks west. He told him to go and call him. "He left and stayed quite a while, and I left the wagon myself, and in the company of my brother Henry, one Legner and Schnaubelt, whom I had just met, went up the street to find Parsons. Schwab was not with me at that time or at any time during that evening. Schnaubelt told me that I had been wanted at Deering, but as I had not been at hand Schwab had gone out there. After I left the wagon I did not go to the mouth of Crane's alley. I did not even know at the time that there was an alley there at all. I did not enter the alley with Schwab; had no conversation with him there in which I referred to pistols and police, and Schwab asked whether one would be enough, etc., nor anything of that kind; neither did I have that conversation with anybody else. I left the wagon and moved in a southwesterly direction obliquely across the street to the corner of the street. From there I went in company with those I mentioned up on Randolph street (west), beyond Union and pretty near Halsted street, but seeing only a few people, probably twenty or twenty-five, standing there scattered, and not seeing Parsons, we returned, walking on the north side of Randolph street, as we had in going down. I went on the wagon and addressed the meeting. I had no conversation with Schwab at or about the crossing of Union street in which we spoke about being ready for them and that they are afraid to come. I had no such conversation with any one. I don't remember exactly of what we were speaking, but Schnaubelt and I, as we walked along, were conversing in German. I have known Schnaubelt for about two years. I think he has not been in the country more than two years. *He cannot speak any English at all.* I never had an English conversation with him, and I don't know of anybody who ever attempted to carry on a conversation with Schnaubelt in English."

He then gave a sketch of his remarks that evening, substantially as already given, which is uncontradicted by the evidence of others. On seeing Mr. Parsons present, and being fatigued, he stopped and introduced Mr. Parsons. When Parsons had concluded, the hour being late, he asked Mr. Fielden to say a few words in conclusion and then adjourn. When the police came the meeting was almost as well as adjourned, there being only about 200 left. The appearance of the weather was so threatening that most of the people left. His brother and Legner helped him to alight from the truck upon hearing Capt. Ward's summons to disperse. Distinctly heard Fielden respond that the meeting was a peaceable one. On reaching the ground he heard the explosion and thought it was a cannon. "Fielden did not draw a revolver and fire from the wagon upon the police or in their direction. I did not, before the explosion of the bomb, leave my position upon the wagon, go into the alley, strike a match and light a bomb in the hands of Rudolph Schnaubelt. Schnaubelt is about six feet three inches tall, I should judge, of large frame and large body.

Q. What is the usual language in which you carried on conversations with Schwab?

To this question Mr. Grinnell objected and was sustained by Judge Gary.

He remembered the witness Wilkinson, a reporter, who came to interview him. Among other things "he asked whether I had ever seen or possessed any bombs? I said yes, I had had at the office for probably three years four bomb-shells; two of them had been left at the office in my absence, by a man who wanted to know if it was a good construction; the other two were left with me one day by some man who came, I think, from Cleveland or New York, and was going to New Zealand from here. I used to show those shells to newspaper reporters, and I showed one to Mr. Wilkinson and allowed him to take it along and show it to Mr. Stone; I never asked him for it since. * * *

"Talking about the riot drill that had been shortly before held on the lake front, and about the sensational reports published by the papers in regard to the armed organizations of Socialists, I told him that it was an open secret that some 3,000 Socialists in Chicago were armed; I told him that the arming of these people, meaning not only Socialists but workingmen in general, began right after the strike of 1877, when the police attacked workingmen at their meetings, killed some and wounded others; that they were of the opinion that if they would enjoy the rights of the constitution, they should defend them too, if necessary; that it was a known fact that these men had paraded the streets, as many as 1,500 strong at a time, with their rifles; so that there was nothing new in that, and I could not see why they talked so much about it. And I said that I thought they were still arming and I wished that every workingman was well armed.

"Then we were speaking generally on modern warfare. Wilkinson was of the opinion that the militia and the police could easily defeat any effort on the part of the populace, by force, could easily quell a riot. I differed from him. I told him that the views the *bourgeoise* took of their military and police was exactly the same as the nobility took, some centuries ago as to their own armament, and that gunpowder had come to the relief of the oppressed masses and had done away with aristocracy very quickly; that the iron armor of the nobility was penetrated by a leaden bullet just as easily as the blouse of the peasant; that dynamite, like gunpowder, had an equalizing, leveling tendency, that the two were children of the same parent, that dynamite would eventually break down the aristocracy of this age and make the principles of democracy a reality. I stated that it had been attempted by such men as General Sheridan and others, to play havoc with an organized body of military or police by the use of dynamite, and it would be an easy thing to do it. It was a kind of disputing dialogue which we carried on. He asked me if I anticipated any trouble, and I said I did. He asked me if the Anarchists and Socialists were going to make a revolution. Of course I made fun of that; told him that revolutions were not made by individuals or conspirators, but were simply the logic of events resting in the condition of things."

Witness then proceeded to illustrate how the militia could be effectively resisted by the use of fire-arms and dynamite in case the contingency should arise. "I knew he wanted a sensational article for publication in the *News*, but there was no particular reference to Chicago, or any fighting on our part. The topic of the conversation was that a fight was inevitable, and that it might take place in the near future, and what might and could be done in such an event; it was a general discussion of the possibilities of street warfare under modern science."

Admitted having written the word "Ruhe" for insertion in the *Arbeiter-Zeitung* on May 4. He was in the habit of receiving announcements from labor organizations and unions, and on that day received a letter in German which read: "Mr. Editor, please insert in the letter box the word 'Ruhe' in prominent letters." Accordingly he had done so. "The manuscript which is evidence is in my handwriting. At the time I wrote the word and sent it up to be put in the paper, I did not know of any import whatever attached to it. My attention was next called to it a little after three o'clock in the afternoon. Balthazar Rau, an advertising agent of the *Arbeiter-Zeitung*, came and asked me if the word 'Ruhe' was in the *Arbeiter-Zeitung*. I had myself forgotten about it, and took a copy of the paper and found it there. He asked me if I knew what it meant; I said I did not. He said there was a rumor that the armed sections had held a meeting the night before, and had resolved to put in that word as a signal for the armed sections to keep themselves in readiness in case the police should precipitate a riot, to come to the assistance of the attacked. I sent for Fischer, who had invited me to speak at the meeting that evening, and asked him if that word had any reference to that meeting. He said none whatever, that it was merely a signal for the boys, for those who were armed, to keep their powder dry, in case they might be called upon to fight within the next few days. I told Rau that it was a very silly thing, or at least there was not much rational sense in that, and asked him if he knew how it could be managed that this nonsense would be stopped, how it could be undone; and Rau said he knew some persons who had something to say in the armed organizations, and I told him to go and tell them that the word was put in by mistake. I was not a member of any armed section; I have not been for six years.

"I know absolutely nothing about the package of dynamite which was exhibited here in court and was claimed to have been found in a closet in the *Arbeiter-Zeitung* building; I never saw it before it was produced here in court."

When arrested he was attending to his usual work in the office. When taken to the police headquarters they were received by the superintendent, who accosted them as follows: "You dirty, Dutch sons of bitches, you dirty hounds, you rascals, we will choke you, we will kill you," forgetting in his rage that he was himself a German. "Then they jumped upon us, tore us from one end to the other, went through our pockets, took my money and everything I had. I never said anything."

Under cross-examination he was interrogated at length upon matters which did not appear in his direct examination, which, notwithstanding every objection, were uniformly admitted by the court, and thus converted into a witness for the prosecution against himself. For instance, he was made to identify a postal card from Johann Most, and admit having received it, though he had never carried on any correspondence with Most. As to the phrase, "the social revolution," sometimes used in his articles, he always meant by it the evolutionary process, or changes from one system to another, which takes place in society. "I wrote the 'Revenge circular,' everything except the word 'Revenge.' I wrote the line, 'Workingmen, to arms!' When I wrote it I thought it was proper; I don't think so now. I wrote it to arouse the working people who are stupid and ignorant to a consciousness of the condition they were in, not to submit to such brutal treatment as that by which they had been shot down at McCormick's the previous day. I wanted them not to attend meetings under such circumstances unless they could resist. I did not want them to do anything in particular. That I called them to arms is a phrase, probably an extravagance. I did intend that they should arm themselves, and it would be well for them if they were all armed. I called upon them to arm themselves, not for the purpose of resisting lawfully constituted author-. ities of the city and county, in case they should meet with opposition from them, but for the purpose of resisting the unlawful attacks of the police or the unconstitutional and unlawful demands of any organization, whether police, militia or any other."

The letter from Most, not referred to in the direct examination, which was taken from the *Arbeiter-Zeitung* office without warrant, and had no reference to the case, and certainly none to the other defendants, was then offered in evidence by the State. Objection thereto was made, but, as usual, unavailingly. The letter was translated, and appears on the record as follows:

"N. Y., 1884.

"DEAR SPIES:—Are you sure that the letter from the Hocking Valley was not written by a detective? In a week I will go to Pittsburgh, and I have an inclination to go also to Hocking Valley. For the present I send you some printed matter. There Sch. 'H' also existed but on paper. I told you this some months ago. On the other hand I am in a condition to furnish 'medicine,' and the 'genuine' article at that. Directions for use are probably not needed with these people. Moreover, they were recently published in the "Fr." The appliances I can also send. Now, if you consider the address of Buchtell thoroughly reliable I will ship twenty or twenty-five pounds. But how? Is there an express line to the place, or is there another way possible? Don't forget to put yourself into communication with Drury in reference to the English organ. He will surely work with you much and well. Such a paper is more necessary than *The Truth*. This, indeed, is getting more miserable and confused from issue to issue, and in general is whistling from the last hole. Enclosed is a fly-leaf which recently appeared at Emden and is, perhaps, adapted for reprint. Greeting to Schwab, Rau and you. Yours, JOHANN MOST.

"P. S.—To Buchtell I will, of course, write only in general terms."

The postal card which was offered by the State in evidence where eight lives were in jeopardy, read as follows:

'L. S. (presumably, Dear Spies):—I had scarcely mailed my letter yesterday when the telegraph brought news from H. M. One does not know whether to rejoice over that or not. The advance is in itself elevating. Sad is the circumstance that it will remain local, and therefore might not have a result. At any rate, these people make a better impression than the foolish voters on this and the other side of the ocean. Greetings and a shake. Yours, "J. M."

ALBERT R. PARSONS was called. Caused a notice calling for a meeting of the American group on the evening of May 4 to be inserted in the *Daily News* of that evening. "In the evening I left my house in company with Mrs. Holmes, my wife and two children about eight o'clock; we walked from home until we got to Randolph and Halsted streets. There I met two reporters that I had seen frequently at workingmen's meetings. One of them was a *Times* reporter whose name I don't know; the other was Mr. Heinemann of the *Tribune*."

Taking the car, they proceeded to 107 Fifth avenue, where, as all witnesses agree, the only topic of discussion was how best to organize the sewing women of Chicago. While there some one came and said there was a large body of people at the Haymarket and no one to address them but Mr. Spies, and witness and Mr. Fielden were urged to go there. He had returned from Cincinnati, Ohio, that morning, and knew nothing of that meeting.

After his speech he mounted another wagon where his wife and Mrs. Holmes were seated and remained about ten minutes, when a sudden coolness in the atmosphere attracted his attention. "I looked up and observed white clouds rolling over from the north, and as I didn't want the ladies to get wet I went onto the speakers' wagon and said: 'Mr. Fielden, permit me to interrupt you a moment.' 'Certainly,' he said. And I said, 'Gentlemen, it appears as though it would rain; it is getting late, we might as well adjourn anyway, but if you desire to continue the meeting longer we can adjourn to Zepf's Hall, on the corner near by.' Some one in the audience said, 'No, we can't, it is occupied by a meeting of the Furniture Workers.' With that I looked and saw the lights through the windows of the hall and said nothing further. Mr. Fielden remarked that it did not matter, he had only a few more words to say."

Witness then went back to where the ladies were, and, as did the larger portion of the crowd, at once left the meeting. The speaking having made him somewhat hoarse, they, with a friend, Mr. Brown, went to Zepf's Hall to get a glass of beer. While there he also saw Mr. Fischer seated at one of the tables. Anxious to go home and get rest, he looked out to see if the meeting had not closed, and "all at once I saw an illumination. It lit up the whole street, followed instantly by a deafening roar, and almost simultaneously volleys of shots followed, every flash of which it seemed I could see. The best comparison I can make, in my mind, is that it was as though a hundred men held in their hands repeating revolvers and fired them as rapidly as possible until they were all gone. That was the first volley. Then there were occasional shots, and one or two bullets whistled near the door and struck the sign. I was transfixed. Mrs. Parsons did not move. In a moment two or three men rushed breathlessly in at the door. That broke the apparent charm that was on us by the occurrence in the street, and with that I called upon my wife and Mrs. Holmes to come with me to the rear of the saloon."

Witness then proceeded to recapitulate for the benefit of the jury the points of his speech of that evening, as given in preceding pages. In the course of his speech he said: "In the light of these facts and of your inalienable right to life, liberty and the pursuit of happiness, it behooves you, as you love your wives and children, and if you would not see them perish of want and hunger, yourselves killed or cut down in the streets, Americans—in the interest of your liberty and independence, to arm, to arm, to arm yourselves." A voice said, "We are ready now." Parsons responded, "You are not."

Several witnesses having said that he used the expression "To arms! to arms! to arms!" corroboration of this statement is essential, and it is not wanting. It was a very natural mistake for persons in the audience, not listening closely and not taking notes of the speech, to have received that erroneous impression. The reader will remember the testimony of Mr. English, a reporter for the *Tribune*, from whose notes we have given Mr. Fielden's speech. We have reserved Mr. English's testimony to bring in in connection with this point. His notes are identically the same, containing also the same interruption and reply. And Mr. English says positively that when Parsons said " to arms " he said it " in his ordinary way of talking. I did not notice any difference in him when he said that." He says further that this expression followed shortly an utterance of Parsons in the following language : " *I am not here for the purpose of* inciting anybody, but to speak out, to tell the facts as they exist, even though it shall cost me my life before morning."

The short-hand notes of Mr. English are surely more reliable than the testimony of other witnesses testifying merely from recollection. And further, bear in mind the fact that Mr. English was under instructions to report only " the most inflammatory utterances," and that his entire notes of Parsons' speech would not make here even one page of print; showing that he found scarcely anything to report under his instructions. There is not a single point in the speech as delivered before the jury that conflicts with the few notes that Mr. English took, a plain indication that it was a moderate utterance for the time and place. Certainly there was nothing in that speech which in the remotest degree incited immediate violence, or indicated in any manner that the speaker contemplated any immediate outbreak on the part of his audience or any portion of it, a fact still further sustained by Mayor Harrison's testimony as to its nature.

Under cross-examination he said that for the past two years he had been editor for the *Alarm*, for which he received eight dollars per week. He made no mention of dynamite that evening ; admitted being a Socialist and an Anarchist, as he understood those terms.

W. A. S. GRAHAM, the reporter of the *Times* who talked with Gilmer on the 5th of May about the bomb, testified to that fact. The conversation was in the corridor of the City Hall, just outside the police headquarters. " He said to me in that conversation, at the time and place referred to, that he saw the man light the fuse *and throw* the bomb, and added ' I think I could identify *him* if I saw him.' I asked him what kind of looking man he was, and Gilmer said : 'He was a man of medium height, and I think he had whiskers, and wore a slouch hat, *but his back was turned to me.*' And to the best of my recollection Gilmer said the man had dark clothes. He said nothing about *anybody else* in that connection.

"I had this conversation about four o'clock in the afternoon of May 5. I talked with him about three or four minutes."

At this point the defense rested and by agreement the following articles were read to the jury:

For the State an extract from the *Alarm*, which, as epitomized, read as fellows:

"THE RIGHT TO BEAR ARMS.

"After the conspiracy of the workingmen, [which expression did not appear in the *Alarm*,] the working classes in 1877, the breaking up of the meeting on Market square, the brutal attack upon a gathering of furniture-workers in Vorwart Turner Hall, the murder of Tessmann and the general clubbing or shooting down of peaceably inclined wageworkers, the proletarians organized the Lehr und Wehr Verein, which in about a year and a half had grown to a membership of about one thousand. This was regarded by the capitalists as a menace, and they procured the passage of the militia law, under which it became an offense for any body of men, other than those authorized by the governor, to assemble with arms, drill or parade the streets. The members of the Lehr und Wehr Verein, mostly Socialists, who believed in the ballot, made up a test case to determine the constitutionality of this act, rejecting the counsel of the extremists. Judge Barnum held the law to be unconstitutional—an appeal was taken—and the Supreme court upset this decision and held the law constitutional. Thereupon the Lehr und Wehr Verein applied to the Supreme Court of the United States, which, within a few days, affirmed the decision of the Supreme Court of the State. Do we need to comment on this?

"That militia law has its uses. Where there was before a military body, publicly organized, whose strength could be easily ascertained now there exists an organization whose numbers cannot be estimated, and a network of destructive agencies of modern military character that will defy suppression."

The defendants submitted and read to the jury Victor Hugo's well-known "address to the Rich and Poor," containing language far more startling; an article from the *Alarm* by Parsons defining Anarchy, as follows:

"ANARCHY *vs.* GOVERNMENT.

'Anarchy, from the Greek, meaning no government, is the denial of the right of coercion—the abrogation of statute law, a constitution by means of which man governs his fellow man. In behalf of government it is argued that man is wicked and must be restrained, and therefore government is necessary. The free society which Anarchy would establish proceeds upon the theory that under natural law men could not but act right, since none would be protected in wrong doing.

"Under government we see the standard of right and wrong regulated by enactments. One portion of society dictating to the other and exacting service. Anarchy teaches that law is to be discovered, not manufactured, and that conformity to natural law means happiness; disregard thereof, misery. The form of government is immaterial. Anarchy denies the right of one man to rule another, and to the shibboleth, 'The greatest good to the greatest number' answers, 'The greatest good *to all.*' Under Anarchy arbitration would take the place of courts; asylums of prisons; voluntary co-operation of wage-slavery. Exchange of equivalents would take the place of the system of competition and modern commerce. The workshops would belong to the workers, the tools to the toilers, the product to the producers, while the means of existence would become the heritage of the race. Occupation and use would be the sole title. But under government natural law is set aside by statutory enactment. Natural law is self-enforcing—statutory law requires the paraphernalia of courts, jail, police and armies to its enforcement."

The following incendiary language of John Stuart Mill was quoted to the jury from the *Alarm*:

"If, therefore, the choice were to be made between Communism, with all its chances, and the present state of society, with all its sufferings and injustice; if the institution of private property necessarily carries with it as a consequence that the produce of labor should be apportioned, as we now see it, almost in an inverse ratio to the labor—the largest portion to those whose work is almost nominal, and so on, in a descending scale, the remuneration dwindling as the work grows harder and more disagreeable, and until the most exhausting and fatiguing bodily labor cannot count with certainty on being able to earn the necessaries of life; if this or Communism were the alternative, all the difficulties, great or small, of Communism would be as dust in the balance."

There was also submitted another extract from the *Alarm*, being a passage from a discourse delivered in New York by the Rev. Dr. Rylance, in which he indulged in the following expressions:

"FORCIBLE GOSPEL.

"Patronizing talk was of no use as a remedy for existing evils. Workingmen were not to be won over by mere potent eloquence. It was no use telling a man that if he were industrious and saved his money he might become a capitalist himself, when, in many cases, the amount he received as wages was barely sufficient for a mere existence. The tyranny of capital was fast becoming as bad as European despotism. He contrasted the squalid tenements and crowded neighborhoods in which the working people were huddled together with the stately residences of those who lived in luxury from the results of labor, and maintained that poverty was not the result of ignorance, and that wealth was the result of co-operation of labor and capital. The present condition of capital was founded on force and not on knowledge."

The State then proceeded to introduce rebutting evidence.

CAPTAIN BONFIELD, recalled, admitted having a conversation with Mr. Simonson on the night of May 4, but denied having made the assertion that he "would like to get a crowd of three thousand without the women and children, and in that case make short work of them."

RICHARD S. TUTHILL, a lawyer, would believe Harry L. Gilmer under oath from what he knew of him. Admitted that Gilmer had never been to his house or any place of entertainment with him; never knew where he lived nor his neighbors, nor even investigated his character.

CHARLES A. DIBBLE, a lawyer, knew Gilmer and would believe him under oath. Admitted that he didn't know where Gilmer lived for three years past; Gilmer was never at witness' house; had met him at picnics, but had never introduced his family or anybody to him; having never heard anything against him supposed his reputation good; their meetings were casual.

JOHN STEELE, painter, knew Gilmer for six or seven years; would believe him under oath. Admitted that they had never worked together, never knew where Gilmer lived or of his neighbors' opinion as to his character. Witness had marched with Gilmer in a military company and seen him at balls, but "I never introduced Gilmer to my wife or to my daughter, or to anybody, or to any of my acquaintance."

Other witnesses were called who testified to the same effect. Some had met Gilmer in the militia at their regular drill, but didn't know anything of his habits, whether married or single, or where he lived.

Witness from Des Moines swore to the reputation of Gilmer as good while residing there.

EX-JUDGE COLE, while willing to believe him under oath, had known nothing about him since 1879. Though knowing him in Des Moines, had never invited him to his house. He had occasionally employed Gilmer by the day, " paid him, and with that our associations substantially terminated."

Others for whom he had worked as a painter doing odd jobs were equally ignorant of Gilmer's habits. He had worked in their houses and nothing was missing; never heard his character disputed and consequently never investigated it; knew him as a mechanic and not as an associate or friend. It appeared, however, that he had served as a special policeman while living there. In Chicago he was a member of the Veteran Police Patrol, and employed as police patrolman in strikes.

JOHN L. MANNING, lawyer and manager of the Veterans' Police Patrol, said in reference to Gilmer: " I employed him on the occasion of a strike on the Wabash road. I did not have him on the 4th of May; I had him on the night of the 7th, 8th and 9th of May; he was a special deputy sheriff under the management of our officers on the Wabash road; his duties were simply to guard the property. I only know Gilmer from that occasion and from meeting him at the Veteran Club; I recommended him a great many times for employment as a member of the club. I don't know anything about his reputation for truth and veracity in the neighborhood in which he lived."

As a sample of the testimony brought to sustain the character of Gilmer we will quote from the last witness brought forward:

C. F. SCHAEFER, of Des Moines, Iowa. Had been a policeman there for nearly nine years; knew Gilmer and would believe him under oath. Under cross-examination witness said:

" I got acquainted with Gilmer in 1876, about the time he went on the police force as *special officer* on the occasion of the Centennial. He was on the force off and on, when we needed any officer. He seemed to be busy at work in the city, and when we called him for assistance he generally went to work. I don't know where Gilmer lived in 1876, but I knew where his wife died; that was about nine blocks from where I lived. I never visited at his house nor he at mine, except that he did a job of painting for me. I did not inquire around his associates in the neighborhood where he resided, or within several blocks around his house, about his reputation. I don't know anything about what he did since he went away from Des Moines."

EDWARD FURTHMAN testified that John Bernett told him on the 6th or 7th of May that the bomb was thrown from ten to fifteen feet *south* of the alley. Another witness said that he was engaged in the fish business on the corner of Desplaines and Randolph streets, and that he had some fish boxes on the sidewalk on the evening of May 4.

Fourteen police officers then followed and swore that on the evening in question they had nothing " bright and shining " in their hands before the bomb was thrown, whereupon the case rested.

CHAPTER X.

REVIEW OF THE EVIDENCE.

The position taken by the State may be summed up briefly as follows:

They contended that the death of Degan was murder, resulting from a conspiracy, a conspiracy in which all of the defendants were held to be accessory; that its general object and design was the overthrow of the existing social order and of the constituted authorities of the law, by force. This premise being assumed they proceeded to lay down the law of conspiracy, to wit:

1. Where there is a conspiracy to do an unlawful act, which naturally or probably involves the use of force or violence, the act of each conspirator done in furtherance of the common design is the act of all. If murder results, all are guilty of murder; and that, too, although the conspirator who does the act cannot be identified; and

2. Even though the particular act may not have been arranged for, or the means of its perpetration, provided the act was the natural result of the conspiracy and was perpetrated in furtherance of this common design; whether the act was the act of a member of the conspiracy, whether it was done in furtherance of the common design, is a question for the evidence to determine.

As to the competency of the evidence the prosecution held that:

1. Any act or declaration of any of the defendants tending to prove the conspiracy, or the connection of that defendant with it, whether made during the existence of the conspiracy or after its completion, is admissible against him.

2. That the conspiracy having been established *in the opinion of the trial judge*, any act or declaration of any member of the conspiracy, though he may not be a party defendant, in furtherance of the conspiracy, is evidence against all the conspirators on trial.

3. That the conspiracy *per se* may be established in the first instance by evidence having no relation to the defendants. It may be shown by acts of different persons at different times and places and by any circumstances which tend to prove it.

It is admitted that neither of the defendants on trial actually threw the bomb, that the language used in their writings and speeches was general in its character and not specifically directed to any particular person to do any particular act, but that the law of accessories was sufficient to convict them of murder, even though that party was unknown. To sum up the whole spirit of the prosecution without doing them any injustice we might say that the defendants were tried for being *social heretics,* for long and persistent invective against social conditions, for prominence as "leaders."

Judge Gary gave the following illustration of the law:

" Suppose that the leaders of the radical temperance men should for a long period of time, by speeches and publications, declare that there was no hope of stopping the evils of the liquor traffic except by blowing up saloons and killing saloonkeepers; that it was useless to expect any reform by legislation; that no prohibition laws or high license laws, or any other laws, would have any effect in their estimation, and that therefore they must blow up the saloons and kill the saloonkeepers, and justify that course of conduct. Suppose, further, that in addition to all this teaching they had further taught the means by which saloons could be blown up and saloonkeepers killed, advising how to manufacture dynamite, the easiest mode of making bombs, how to throw them and declaring that their use against the saloonkeepers and the saloons was the only remedy and the only way to reach the end desired by the radical temperance men. Then supposing these same *leaders* called a meeting in front of the saloon at 54 West Lake street, Chicago, and spoke denouncing the liquor traffic and denouncing the saloons and the saloonkeepers, indulging in figures and facts about the liquor traffic, and one would say, ' If you are ready to do anything, do it without making any idle threats,' and another speaker says, 'throttle,' 'kill,' ' stab ' the saloon busines, ' or it will kill, throttle and stab you ;' and then while that speaking is going on some unknown man out of the crowd, with a bomb of the manufacture and design of the temperance men, explodes No. 54 West Lake street and kills the occupant of the house. Can there be any doubt that such *leaders,* so talking, so encouraging, so advising, would be guilty of murder ?"

Without entering into any discussion of the exactness of the parallel, would it not have been still more so if the learned jurist had further " supposed " that the suppositious meeting had been invaded by 180 armed and drilled saloonkeepers with the avowed intent to disperse the assemblage by force ?

We have given at some length the position taken by the prosecution. Does the evidence sustain it? Let us first take into consideration the character of the Haymarket meeting itself, as shown by the record.

The Haymarket, so called, is a widening of Randolph street between Desplaines and Halsted streets, extending a distance of two blocks. The territory was sufficiently large for the holding of an immense meeting, and the evidence shows that when it was called a very large attendance was expected. This expectation was not realized. Only here and there small groups of men gathered on the Haymarket square, and the speakers were late in arriving. At the hour named, 7:30 in the evening, no one was upon the ground to call the people together or to open the meeting. There is no contradiction of the testimony as to these points. It is proved alike by the witnesses for the State and for the defense, that no move was made toward calling to order the meeting itself until August Spies, looking around for a suitable rostrum from which to address the crowd, selected the truck wagon which he found standing close to the edge of the sidewalk on Desplaines street, and directly in front of the steps leading up to the door entering into the Crane Bros'. manufacturing establishment. The end of the wagon was some six or eight feet, or more, north of the north line of the Crane Bros'. alley. This is a short alley, as shown by the diagram, which enters the block from Desplaines street towards the east upon the south line of Crane Bros'. building, and extends about halfway through the block, then makes a junction with another short alley extending out from the point of junction southward to Randolph street. This alley is a perfect trap rather than a means of escape, as all egress from it could be stopped by a handful of men at the Randolph street exit.

Having selected the wagon Mr. Spies mounted it about half-past eight o'clock and inquired for Parsons. Parsons not responding, Spies dismounted from the wagon and went in search of him, being absent, as estimated by the different witnesses, from five to ten minutes, and returning again, mounted the wagon and commenced to speak. He spoke about twenty minutes. As soon as Parsons and Fielden arrived Spies brought his remarks to a close and introduced Parsons. Parsons did not commence to speak until about nine o'clock; he spoke from three-quarters of an hour to an hour. At the end of Parsons' speech Fielden was introduced. He spoke about fifteen minutes; and at about ten minutes past ten o'clock, when he was about concluding, his speech was interrupted by the arrival of the police, the order to disperse, and the subsequent explosion of the bomb.

From its beginning to its close, the meeting was as orderly as any ordinary out-door meeting. Mr. English, the *Tribune* reporter and present private secretary to Mayor Roche, says: "It was a peaceable and quiet meeting for an out-door meeting. I didn't see any turbulence. I was there all the time."

Mayor Harrison's testimony was equally explicit. He estimated the audience at one time to be from 800 to 1,000; but when the cloud, threatening rain, came up "there was not one-fourth of the crowd that had been there during the evening, listening to the speakers at that time. When I went to the station, during Parsons' speech, I stated to Capt. Bonfield that I thought the speeches were about over; *that nothing had occurred yet, or looked likely to occur, to require interference*, and that he had better issue orders to his reserves at the other stations to go home."

While alarmed lest the meeting might be a covert plan to attack McCormick's, yet in listening to the speeches he concluded it was not an organization to destroy property that night, and went home.

This was the testimony of the chief executive officer of the city, who was there upon the ground, charged with the duty of preserving the peace and preventing violence. Did the meeting change its character in the twenty minutes intervening between the mayor's departure and the ordering out of the police? All witnesses agree that the audience was rapidly thinning out, that Fielden had twice said "in conclusion," that no resistance was given to the approach of the police or crowd sufficient to impede their progress. As to the character of this movement of the police, the testimony of the officers themselves shows that the order to fall in was given urgently; there was no halting of the head of the column until the complete column was formed; the head of the column moved without halting at a rapid march, so that those who came later out of the station and formed the second and third companies of the column were compelled to proceed almost if not quite at a double quick in order to get their position in the line, and that they did not, in fact, gain that position until the head of the column had reached the position of the halt. This appears from the testimony of Lieutenant Stanton, Ferguson and Gleeson.

No explanation is given by any of the officers in charge of the force that night of this singular haste. The reader will bear in mind, however, that both Holloway and Weimeldt when on the stand were prepared to testify that they had been informed at the station that blood would flow before midnight, and that Judge Gary refused to permit them to do so. Here was in process of dissolution a meeting from which no violence or danger was apprehended before. Captain Bonfield says that he was in receipt of constant information from this meeting. We are therefore warranted in saying that when he ordered his men to fall

REVIEW OF THE EVIDENCE.

in he must have known that the meeting was about to break up and the people to go home; that he knew up to the time of the latest advices received by him that no proposal to do any unlawful act had been advanced, and no turbulent or lawless character had been developed in the meeting itself. Substantially all the witnesses concur in saying that the meeting was more enthusiastic and responsive while Parsons spoke than when Fielden spoke, a position vouched for by the fact that those present were wearied of their long standing in the cold street.

When Captain Ward ordered the meeting to disperse he turned at once to the bystanders and said: "And I call upon you and you to assist." To assist in what? In dispersing a meeting that was refusing to peacefully disperse upon command? Was it a riotous or unlawful assemblage of citizens? Did it in any way menace the peace and dignity of "the people of the State of Illinois?" Nothing of the kind. No resistance was attempted by the speakers, unless it was Fielden's exclamation of surprise, "We are peaceable." When the order to disperse was given no reasonable and proper opportunity for compliance was given, or a moment allowed to see whether it would not be complied with, but there was an immediate call upon the bystanders to assist in the forcible dispersion of a meeting that was confessedly quiet, orderly, peaceable, small in numbers, and upon the very eve of voluntary dispersion.

Where were the alleged conspirators? Upon the arrival of the police Spies and Fielden alone were present. Parsons and Fischer had left and were in Zepf's Hall. Schwab was at Deering. Engel, Lingg and Neebe were quietly sitting in their own homes. The order for dispersion was given but a minute before the bomb exploded.

Gilmer swore that he saw Spies get down from the wagon, come into Crane's alley with Fischer and Schnaubelt, and saw him light the bomb that was *thrown from the alley*. The improbabilities of this story are:

1. He made no outcry.
2. He did not tell of this to any one, although the same evening and a few moments afterward he had different conversations about the meeting, and talked with people in the street car going home
3. He would not be positive he ever even told Bonfield he saw the fuse lighted.
4. He was not called before the coroner's jury the next day, nor before the grand jury, where there were full investigations, notwithstanding before the grand jury met he had talked with the prosecuting officer in reference to what he knew.
5. He told Grinnell these facts (?) Sunday morning after the Hay-

market meeting on Tuesday evening, but didn't tell him he knew the parties.

6. The prosecuting attorney, Mr. Grinnell, in his opening speech, said he had a witness who saw *a man* light *and* throw the bomb, instead of two men, as Gilmer subsequently swore.

Gilmer stated that he only told Mr. Grinnell that he believed he could identify the person who threw the bomb if he saw him. He admitted to having received unknown sums of money from time to time from the prosecution. Witness was six feet three inches in height and could nearly see right over the head of the man who threw the bomb. The testimony absolutely demolishes this "evidence," and in asking instructions the prosecution virtually abandoned it. The record shows that Gilmer's testimony did not fit Schnaubelt, whose photograph he identified as that of the bomb-thrower, probably because he was absent, for Schnaubelt was of equal heighth, and witnesses swore that he left the meeting before the police arrived. That Spies did not leave the wagon—and therefore could not have been in the alley before the bomb was thrown—is abundantly proven.

AUGUST SPIES.

1. August Spies himself so testifies. He says that his brother Henry and Ernst Legner helped him down; that just as they reached the sidewalk the bomb exploded. They were pushed by the fleeing crowd to the north, away from the alley, which was ten feet south and east, and went to Zepf's Hall, three-quarters of a block north.

2. Spies gave the same account when first arrested.

3. Henry Spies testifies that when the police commanded the meeting to disperse his brother August was still on the wagon and he assisted him to alight; that almost immediately afterward he was himself shot in warding off a pistol-shot from his brother, and there was no shooting by anybody, as the whole case shows, until after the bomb exploded.

4. Ernst Legner, who knew all these facts and assisted Spies from the wagon, was a witness before the grand jury and his name was indorsed as one of the witnesses for the State on the indictment, but for some unknown reason was not produced, nor have his whereabouts been since ascertained. We claim, therefore, that it follows as an irresistible conclusion that Ernst Legner, when under oath, gave substantially the same account as to Spies being on the wagon when the police came up and his helping Spies from the wagon, that was given by Spies to Bonfield after his arrest. Therefore, when the case was put together afterward Legner's testimony was adverse to the new theory advanced

REVIEW OF THE EVIDENCE. 153

by Thompson and Gilmer, and he was not only left out as a witness on the trial, but *mysteriously disappeared from the city!*

5. That Spies *was seen* to get down from the wagon after the order of dispersal was given by Joseph Bach, Max Mitlacher, Sleeper T. Ingram, Conrad Messer, August Krumm, William Albright, William Murphy, Adolph Tennes and Samuel Fielden.

It is thus demonstrated by a conclusive preponderance of testimony that Mr. Spies did not leave the wagon until the order to disperse had been given. It is therefore impossible that he should have stood on the sidewalk at the side of the wagon in conversation with somebody before Gilmer went into the alley. The fact is, Gilmer said on his direct examination that Spies came down from the wagon into the alley and lighted the bomb. But upon cross-examination he stated that at the time Spies came into the alley he, Gilmer, was standing *about twelve or fourteen feet* from the mouth of the alley, and was forced to admit that it was physically impossible for him to have looked around the corner and seen the wagon from that point. Finding himself thus cornered, he said Spies did not get down off the wagon, but came from toward the wagon, where he had seen him standing on the sidewalk, before he (Gilmer) went into the alley. We have already shown by abundant testimony that Gilmer could not have seen Spies in the alley at all, as he remained on the wagon.

As to the McCormick meeting the State signally failed to identify Spies with the riot, and the defense showed clearly that his mission there was a peaceable one. This is uncontradicted and appears from the testimony of Zeller, Urban, Witt, Breest, Schlavin, and Pfeiffer.

Spies swears that he had no idea, when he was invited, of any relationship of McCormick's employes to that meeting, or that the locality of the proposed meeting was in the neighborhood of McCormick's factory. Besides, it is shown, without contradiction, that the lumbershovers whom Spies was addressing had absolutely no connection with the factory or employes of McCormick. While having no weight as regards the other defendants even if proven, its complete failure in reference to Spies himself shows that its only effect was to inflame the jury against Spies and his associates as dangerous labor agitators.

In regard to the "Revenge circular" but little need be said. But twenty-five hundred were printed, of which not more than half were distributed. Mr. Spies admits that he wrote it under a high degree of excitement. His testimony is manly and straightforward, but no evidence was brought to show that Spies had any connection with armed groups of workingmen. Not one word can be found in the circular itself which in any way relates to the Haymarket meeting, or to the throwing of the bomb thereat. There is no evidence whatever that the party who threw the bomb ever read the circular, even heard of it or even was influenced or induced by it to commit the act charged in the indictment. Its being permitted to be introduced in evidence and read to the jury as evidence against all defendants was characteristic of the rulings of the court.

The Haymarket circular, it will be remembered, was said to contain these words: "Workingmen, arm yourselves, and appear in full force!" It is a matter of record that Mr. Spies ordered that line stricken out. His reasons for doing so he stated as follows: "I objected to that principally because I thought it was ridiculous to put a phrase in which would prevent people from attending the meeting; another reason was that there was some excitement at the time, and a call for arms like that might have caused trouble between the police and the attendants of that meeting." It is not shown that any containing that line were distributed, while it appears that those which witnesses received on the street, some of which were presented in court did *not* contain the line in question. This is established by the testimony of Grueneberg, who carried the message to the printers, and of Heun who set up the type. Further, in the *Arbeiter-Zeitung* of that date the circular appeared without the line in question.

The signal "Ruhe." It appears from the testimony that on this, *and previous occasions*, it had been determined by the armed groups, in certain contingencies the word "Ruhe" should appear in the *Arbeiter-Zeitung* as a signal for certain meetings by those present.

Theodore Fricke identified the manuscript of the word "Ruhe" as in Spies' handwriting, as well as a lot of other manuscript, but there is no evidence tending to show that Spies knew the significance of the word. This will be considered further when we come to the examination of the alleged Monday-night conspiracy.

MICHEL SCHWAB.

The incriminating evidence added by the State against Mr. Schwab is alone that of M. M. Thompson. It is a matter of record that Mr. Schwab came to the Haymarket from the east. He was hunting Spies who came to the meeting from the north. Schwab went there before Spies came, and left before he came. When Schwab left for the court house to take the car to Deering, Spies was coming to the meeting from the north west, and they did not meet that night.

Thompson's testimony is substantially as follows: He swears that before the meeting convened he was standing with his back against Crane Brothers' building, some three or four feet from the alley, and facing west. He says that while in that neighborhood

Schwab came down the street, witness not knowing him before, and that he inquired of Mr. Brazleton, a reporter, as to who that was, and Brazleton said it was Schwab. He says that very soon after that Spies, whom also he had never seen before or heard speak, rose up on a wagon and called out, "Is Parsons here?" in a loud tone of voice; that directly after making that inquiry Spies got down from the wagon, and he and Schwab entered the alley, going into it about the middle and that *there was a crowd there.* They remained in the alley about three minutes, and witness swears that standing *three feet north* of the alley, admitting that he could not see down the alley, and did not try to look into it, yet he distinctly heard a conversation between Spies and Schwab in which the words "pistols" and "police" were used, in a voice that he recognized as that of Spies, spoken in such a tone that nothing of the rest of the conversation could be caught; consequently, spoken in a low tone. Remember, he could not see the speakers and admitted a crowd to be there. He had never heard Spies speak in the world, except that loud inquiry from the wagon, "Is Parsons here?" addressed to the crowd, yet he swears to Spies' conversational tones in a low conversation, out of his range of vision. And while he had never heard Schwab speak at all, he swears he asked the question, "Is one enough or had we better go and get more?" He relates a story of then following them north on Randolph street and back to the place of meeting where the two defendants and a third party, who stood with his back toward him, yet whom he was willing to identify from a photograph as Schnaubelt, fell into conversation; that there Spies gave "something" to the third party and then they *all* went and got on the wagon.

The evidence of a score of witnesses demonstrates its falsity in every particular. Cosgrove, one of the officers of the police force and a witness for the prosecution, swore that he was present in the crowd around that wagon when Spies got up and asked: "Is Parsons here?" That there was a suggestion that Parsons was away somewhere and that some one would go and look for him. He then swears positively that Spies got down from the wagon, and that with a party of two or three men he proceeded *south-westerly* to Randolph street and then he lost him. McKeough, the very next witness, a city detective officer, following that up, swears that he also was in that crowd when Spies got on the wagon and inquired for Parsons. He also swears that Spies got down from the wagon and with a party of men moved off; and he swears that Officer Myers and himself followed Spies to the corner. Now, that is the interval when, according to Thompson, instead of going south westerly, as Cosgrove swears, to the corner, and whither

REVIEW OF THE EVIDENCE.

McKeough swears he followed him, Spies was asserted to have gone almost due east into this alley, and remained there a period of three minutes, in order to have this conversation about "pistols" and "police," and "is one of them enough?"

That is not all of the testimony. It is a matter of record that Schwab was at No. 107 Fifth avenue that evening and there received a telephone call to Deering, Spies being first called for, and that he left that place after receiving the message is evidenced by the positive testimony of Patterson, Waldo, Bach and Fielden. That the telephone message was sent from Deering is shown by the testimony of Preusser. That he was seen on the corner of Randolph and Desplaines streets, while looking for Spies to go to Deering, is evidenced by the testimony of two reporters, witnesses for the prosecution, Heinemann and Owen. No other witness except this man Thompson claims to have seen Schwab upon this alleged journey from the alley on Desplaines and Randolph streets and back again. That something after eight o'clock, *before the meeting was called to order*, Schwab went south to the corner of Randolph and took an east bound car is shown by the testimony of Hermann Becker.

That he, in fact, went to Deering and spoke there, is beyond question; that the time requisite to go there prevented him from being at the Haymarket when the speaking began is also clearly shown. Concerning his arrival at Deering the testimony of Preusser, Stittler, Radtke and Behrens confirm that of Schwab in every particular, and that he did not leave Deering, an hour's journey from the Haymarket, till after half-past ten.

Further, other evidence remains as to Schwab's non-connection with the Haymarket meeting. Carl Richter, Robert Lindinger and Frederick Liebel all swore that they saw Spies when he asked for Parsons from the wagon; that they stood at the entrance to the alley and are sure that he did not enter it. Liebel knew Schwab by sight, and although standing under the lamp-post at the corner of the alley, a few feet from the wagon when Spies asked, "Is Parsons here?" he did not see either of them go near the alley, nor saw Schwab that night.

Three different witnesses, August Spies, his brother, Henry Spies, and Henry Zohl confirm the above. Zohl swears he stood in the street southwest from the wagon; that he knew these parties; that Spies passed him going from the wagon *directly southwest*, precisely as Officer Cosgrove swore, down to that corner, to which Detective McKeough swears he followed him; and he says that the party consisted of August Spies, Henry Spies, Ernst Legner and Rudolph Schnaubelt.

The fact is worthy of attention that Brazelton, the reporter of the *Inter Ocean*, was named by Mr. Thompson as the man who pointed out Schwab to him upon the Haymarket some time before eight o'clock. Brazelton's name was indorsed on the back of the indictment as one of the witnesses for the State, yet Brazelton was not produced by the State as a witness, even when the State was notified by the defendants to produce him, thus leaving Thompson's story entirely unsupported. Another suspicious omission deserves attention. Ernst Legner, who assisted Mr. Spies from the wagon and who accompanied him when he went in search of Parsons, had his name indorsed on the indictment as a witness for the State, but he was not produced as a witness though formal notice was demanded by the defendants. This omission to produce Legner and his subsequent mysterious disappearance is extremely significant. Spies and Schwab were extremely desirous that Legner should be put on the stand, and every effort was made by their counsel to find him after it became known that the prosecution would not call him, but unavailingly. Legner had left the State and his whereabouts could not be ascertained, nor his attendance procured. The State chose to offer Thompson's testimony without attempting to corroborate it by Brazelton; and did not produce Legner although they had him as a witness before the grand jury.

Mr. Thompson's testimony being thus utterly discredited, not only from lack of support but by direct conflicting evidence, there remains not a shadow of proof connecting Mr. Schwab with the Haymarket meeting, or any alleged conspiracy, or any throwing of a bomb. The whole testimony is a fabrication from beginning to end, judged by every rule of evidence; shown such by not only the witnesses for the defense, but equally so by the witnesses for the State. The attempt, by such evidence, to implicate the defendants, or any of them, in any personal participation in that act, entirely fails. There was was no evidence against Schwab whatever, unless it be that given by Fricke that he wrote editorials for the *Arbeiter-Zeitung*, and for this he was sentenced to death!

Gilmer's testimony has been shown to be equally unreliable and he was successfully impeached. It is true that a number of witnesses were called by the State who were willing to believe Gilmer under oath, but every one of them admitted that they were not acquainted with his neighbors, did not know the opinion entertained of him by those with whom he was in daily contact, and were only casual associates. And yet on the unsupported evidence of Thompson and the testimony of the detective Gilmer, men's lives were sworn away.

Before leaving this part of the evidence let us consider the evidence regarding the locality from which the bomb was thrown. Gilmer alone, it will be remembered, swore that it came from the alley, and further that he remained standing quietly at the mouth of the alley *where the firing was the heaviest* till it was over.

Three witnesses for the State, Officer Haas, Hull and Heineman state positively that the bomb was thrown from a point south of Crane's alley, between that and Randolph street. Of the witnesses for the defense, Simonson, Zeller, Liebel, Dr. Taylor, Urban, Krumm, Albright, Bach, Holloway, Koehler, Lehnert and Bennett are equally positive; some of these stood at the opening of the alley and could not be mistaken. Bernett saw the man who threw the bomb and told the same story in the evening papers of May 5.

In conclusion, the rules of criminative evidence are: 1. All facts accepted in the conclusion of guilt must be satisfactorily proven. 2. When such conclusion rests upon a variety of facts then each fact which forms the basis of the conclusion must be proved beyond a reasonable doubt, the same as though the whole conclusion rested upon that fact.

Under these rules Thompson's evidence is worthless because it is contradicted by facts absolutely inconsistent with it. Further, the story that two men raised in Germany, speaking the German language and associates on a German paper would publicly plot revolution in English, when the subject-matter of such plotting were words to be understood between themselves, such as " pistols, police, do you think one is enough, etc.," remarks simply addressed from one to the other, is self-evidently absurd.

Yet upon the testimony of Thompson and Gilmer, the first of whom was contradicted by thirteen witnesses, and the latter contradicted by forty-six different witnesses, some of whom were called by the prosecution, and impeached by nine other witnesses, Spies and Schwab were sentenced to death!

SAMUEL FIELDEN.

That Fielden was present at the meeting is admitted by all; that he knew anything of the meeting having been called before he was asked, after eight o'clock on that evening fails to appear. He attended a meeting at 107 Fifth avenue, as treasurer, called to consider the organization of the sewing women of Chicago, with reference to the eight-hour movement, and some money was paid out by Fielden, upon the order of the meeting for that purpose. The meeting lasted till nearly nine o'clock. During the progress of the meeting, Balthazar Rau called and said speakers were wanted at the Haymarket meeting, whereupon nearly all shortly went to the Haymarket meeting. Witnesses to this effect were Patterson, Snyder, Brown, Waldo, Mrs. Holmes, Parsons and Fielden.

We have seen that the only report of Mr. Fielden's speech was that taken by Mr. English, and be it remembered English himself says his instructions from the *Tribune* office were to take *only the most incendiary parts of the speeches*. His testimony, in fact, presents only an abstract of what was said, and Fielden claims that English's report was garbled, not giving the connections, and therefore does not make sense. In Fielden's speech, however, even as reported by English, not one word can be found which has the least reference to bomb-throwing, or contains any proposition or suggestion to excite his hearers to the use of violence. In fact, in alluding to the McCormick riot of the preceding day, he spoke of the men who stoned the factory as men who acted "*in their blind rage.*" As to his figurative expression about "throttling the law," his own speech before Judge Gary is its complete explanation.

That Fielden fired a pistol-shot that night, as testified by some policemen only, we have already shown to be discredited by the wide diversity of statements made as to his position when the alleged act was committed. Captain Bonfield, Captain Ward and Lieutenant Steele, at whom, according to Detective Quinn, the shot was fired, were close to Mr. Fielden and did not see it, while Quinn admits that he "was twenty or twenty-five feet further away from the wagon than Steele or Ward." His evidence is also contradictory; he said he saw Fielden shoot and immediately returned the fire, and turning saw the bomb explode. Upon cross-examination he says that *immediately* upon hearing the order "Halt!" he turned around and repeated the command, facing his men, with his back to the wagon. He had no time to dress up his line before the bomb exploded! The whole story is absolutely inconsistent with itself as well as with the facts. Captain Ward, who was looking at him and could have touched him, knew nothing of it. Among the witnesses who were either on or close by the wagon was Freeman, a reporter, who stood three or four feet from the wagon, and when the pistol-firing commenced crouched down *behind the wagon*, where Officer Kreuger swears Fielden took cover and fired *two* shots. Freeman says there was no shooting between him and the wagon, and after a few minutes ran to the alley; that there were no shots coming from near the wagon directed toward the wagon. He failed to see Fielden shoot. Snyder, Tennes, Dr. Taylor, Messer, Holloway and Ingram were all present, and could not have been deceived had Fielden had a pistol.

The vindictive attack made upon Mr. Fielden, attempting to implicate him in shooting on that evening, besides being so grossly contradictory, utterly fails of corroborative support. On this point we call attention to the fact that when an effort was made to show by the testimony of Mr. Fielden that he was present at the examination of the various officers, upon the coroner's inquest, and that not a word was there testified as to his having fired at any time that night, the prosecution interposed objection, and the proposed testimony was excluded by the court. Further, Mr. Knox, a reporter, put upon the stand by the prosecution, testifying to an interview with Mr. Fielden on the night of the 5th of May, in the presence of one or more of the police officers, after the coroner's inquest had recommended that Fielden be held for the murder of Degan, says he does not think anything was asked of Fielden as to his having fired any shots at the Haymarket; that he did not know of such a charge at the time, and had never heard of such a claim advanced up to that time by anybody. Hume, another reporter with him, gave substantially the same evidence. The charge, therefore, is one of subsequent invention, and so clumsily presented as to make him firing from a number of irreconcilible positions at one and the same time.

As to the charge that Fielden made threats by exclaiming, "Here come the bloodhounds of the police! Men, do your duty and I'll do mine," or similar words, the evidence is equally unsatisfactory. This statement is made by detectives Quinn and Haas, the first of whom heard it when fully *fifty feet* of where the speaker was; the latter was from *ten to fifteen* feet from the wagon. Yet Haas admits on cross-examination that he was a witness at the coroner's inquest, on which occasion he said nothing of having heard Fielden utter these words. These two are the only witnesses who positively swear that it was Fielden who made the alleged remark.

Quinn further swore that he is not positive whether it was Ward or Bonfield who commanded the meeting to disperse, although he had known Ward for fourteen years and Bonfield for eight or ten years. The witness therefore confesses that he could not distinguish the voice of the officer, who admittedly gave the command to disperse in a *very loud* tone of voice, and whom he had known for fourteen years. But still he claims to have positively identified the voice of Fielden, who was a stranger to him, at the distance of fifty feet!

Five other officers heard a somewhat similar remark, though they differ in giving the words, but were unable to state who made it. This is the whole of the State's case as to this asserted threat, and it will be observed that of all the witnesses called by the State, only a few policemen, mainly professional detectives, pretend to have heard these significant words. These also claim to have heard it from all possible directions and in a conflicting variety of forms. None of the reporters heard it who were on the alert for every incident, though they were mainly called by the prosecution.

On the other hand, the following witnesses for the defendants, many of whom were in immediate proximity to the wagon, and therefore nearer than the officers, testified positively that *no such remark was made*, and they were all in a position where, if such a remark had been made in a tone of voice loud enough to be heard by Quinn at a distance of fifty feet, they could not but have heard it, and from the very nature of the remark it could not but have attracted their attention, namely: Simonson, Richter, Liebel, Taylor, Gutscher, Urban, Lindinger, Heidekmeger, Holloway, Snyder, Murphy, Bach, Ingram, Spies, and Fielden himself.

Mr. English, although he was upon the scene with instructions to report *the most incendiary utterances*, and believing that he heard all that was said, says positively that he did not hear this remark, in fact, no reporter on any paper of the city embodied that remark in his account of the meeting. The counsel for the defendants call attention to the fact that this alleged utterance, so lightly fixed upon Mr. Fielden, is one of the detectives and the police, having served on duty on previous occasions, as, for instance, in the trial of Thomas Reynolds, reported in Morgan's "Trials in Ireland," page 53, where in the attempt to procure a conviction upon a charge of riot and assault, precisely the same remark was attributed by the police swearers to the accused, and counsel claim that they are justified in saying that this charge against Mr. Fielden is also absolutely exploded, and that the respective statements of the witnesses in that behalf are shown by the whole evidence, when taken together, to be mere idle creations of professional detectives' fancy.

As to Mr. Fielden, therefore, we may affirm truly from the record:

1. That he had nothing to do with calling the Haymarket meeting.

2. That he had no knowledge that such a meeting was to be held or was in progress until hurriedly summoned as a speaker.

3. That his presence when the bomb was thrown was entirely accidental and without thought that any violence would occur.

4. That he made no threats or advised violence.

5. That he did not make use of any fire-arms, either in attack or defense.

6. That his own statement that he *never* had a revolver, and never saw a bomb in his life, remain unimpeached.

ALBERT R. PARSONS.

The testimony shows, without any contradiction, that on Sunday, May 2, 1886, Mr. Parsons was in the city of Cincinnati, Ohio, and came back from there on the morning of Tuesday May 4; that he called a meeting at 107 Fifth avenue for that evening; that in company with his wife, Mrs. Holmes and his two little children he attended that meeting; that on his way there he met two reporters, Owen and Heineman, and in answer to their inquiries said he knew nothing of the Haymarket meeting, having an engagement at another. Like Fielden he yielded to a pressing request for speakers and spoke there. His speech is admitted to have been largely statistical in its nature and containing so little of an "incendiary" character that English reported but a few paragraphs, and that he denounced a proposition to hang Gould and urged attacks to be made only on the economic system that rendered a Gould possible. This is borne out by the following witnesses: Simonson, Ferguson, Gleeson, Snyder, Bach and Freeman. His alleged call "To arms!" we have already examined and found exploded by the positive testimony of Mr. English, the reporter.

After Parsons had concluded, and be it remembered that the mayor heard nearly the entire speech, he suggested an adjournment, and upon Fielden remarking that he would be through in a few minutes, Parsons and his ladies left the meeting, and a large portion of the audience did likewise. This is established by a large number of witnesses on both sides and was not contested.

A review of the evidence touching Parsons' presence and utterances at the Haymarket meeting, accompanied by ladies, proposing an adjournment, and himself leaving the place, must satisfy any rational mind, or one not blinded by prejudice against Parsons' economic beliefs, that he had no idea of any alleged conspiracy against the police, or that violence was at all likely to happen. It is not, therefore, to be wondered at that when the trial came on, involving Mr. Parsons in a charge of participating in the murder of Mr. Degan, he should *voluntarily* come to the bar of the court, as he did, and present himself for trial. His consciousness of innocence and his strong sense of duty to his associates and the cause they represented, impelled him to this course. That, in his rectitude, he may have believed it to be to an acquittal is a reflection on the court and jury rather than on him. Honor demanded it and he has not yet given one expression of regret.

OSCAR NEEBE.

A review of the evidence against Neebe is hard to present from the lack of the requisite testimony to implicate him. He was not at the Haymarket; does not appear to have known of it, or of the Monday night "conspiracy." All in the evidence bearing upon his case is the following not very incriminating points:

1. That he was an acquaintance with certain of the defendants and had been seen a few times at the *Arbeiter-Zeitung* office by witness Gruenhut, in regard to the organization of certain branches of industry into unions.

2. The testimony of Franz Hein that on the night of May 3, Neebe came into witness' saloon, showed him a copy of the "Revenge circular" and said in reference to the McCormick riot: "It is a shame that the police act that way, but may be the time comes that it goes the other way—that they get the chance, too."

3. The evidence of two detectives, who helped themselves to what they wished without warrant in the *Arbeiter-Zeitung* building on May 5, that Neebe said, "I am in charge in the absence of Spies and Schwab."

4. Officer Stift says that he was at the house of Neebe, on the 7th of May, and there found a Colt's pistol, an old sword, a breech-loading gun and a red flag; witness admitted that the gun might have been a sporting gun.

5. A number of witnesses admitted that *they knew Neebe* and had seen him at Socialistic picnics.

6. From the testimony of Fricke, Seliger and Heinemann it appeared that Neebe had *at one time* been a member of the International Working People's Association.

7. Fricke testified that Neebe was a member of the corporation publishing the *Arbeiter-Zeitung* and that he had seen him at picnics where *some one else* had sold Most's book!

This is all; and for *this* Neebe received a sentence of fifteen years for participation in the murder of Degan! One ruling of the court has already been given showing that taking charge of the *Arbeiter-Zeitung*, in the opinion of Judge Gary, was a questionable action leaving "a debatable question which the jury ought to pass upon." There is absolutely no evidence in the record that Neebe presided over meetings where "advice to commit murder" was submitted by the speakers. Yet the court held:

"If it depended on prior knowledge or participation at the Haymarket meeting, the question would be quite different; but if there is *general advice* to commit murder, the time and occasion not being foreseen, the adviser is guilty when it is committed!"

Such rulings could not but have a direct influence upon the minds of the jurors in prejudicing Neebe's case, not even a causal relationship as accessory before the fact, as between him and the other defendants, being established.

CHAPTER XI.

THE ALLEGED CONSPIRACY.

We have reserved the review of the evidence against Fischer, Engel and Lingg to consider it in connection with the evidence of the meeting of Monday night, where the conspiracy was said to have been planned or more definitely arranged. It is claimed that all three were present on that occasion, when conspiracy was entered into and the calling of the Haymarket meeting resolved on. The witnesses were Waller, who presided, Schrade, Lehman and Greif. Waller, who distinguished himself by the alacrity with which he turned informer, was the main witness. He says he called the meeting to order at about half-past eight o'clock, and that there were some seventy or eighty persons present. The testimony of Schrade, Lehman and Greif shows that there were not over thirty or forty in attendance When the Haymarket meeting was agreed upon it was stated that the purpose of the meeting was to cheer up the workingmen so that they should be prepared in case of an attack by the police to defend themselves. Further than this no conspiracy is shown to have existed. That the Haymarket meeting was there agreed upon and Fischer authorized to issue a hand-bill, is not denied. Waller himself proposed the Tuesday meeting, and in his direct examination by the State he distinctly repudiated any conspiracy in connection with the Haymarket, as follows:

Q. What was said, if anything, as to what should be done in case the police should attempt to disperse the Haymarket meeting?

A. There was nothing said about the Haymarket. There was nothing expected that the police would get to the Haymarket.

A committee, however, was appointed of one or two from each group to observe the movement not only on the Haymarket, but in various portions of the city. If an onslaught was made by the police in the day-time, the word "Ruhe" was to be published; if at night, the different members were to be notified at their homes. The McCormick attack had convinced them that the police would on the slightest provocation attack them and they " conspired " to protect themselves in such case.

By reference to the testimony of Waller it will be seen that the witness testified that Mr. Engel said the plan proposed by him was to be followed *only* in the event of a police attack, and that the workingmen should only defend themselves if thus attacked by the police. The testimony of Waller that no allusion was made to the Haymarket, that none of the persons present at the Monday-evening meeting were proven to be present when the bomb was thrown, that he himself left to attend a meeting of the Furniture-Workers' Union, that he and Fischer were together early in the evening and on seeing the police-patrol wagons supposed that they were " getting ready to drive out to McCormick's, so that they might be out there early in the morning "— is entirely in accordance with other testimony and conclusively proves that there was no conspiracy to throw a bomb, even to resist police brutality, at the Haymarket on May 4. As to Waller's further testimony two facts are worthy of attention: 1. He, as chairman of the meeting, was in imminent peril under the reign of terror that prevailed and was willing to testify to what would save his own neck. 2. He admitted that he had received various sums of money from Captain Schaack, and that his wife also had received indefinite sums.

Bernard Schrade, testifying to the same meeting for the State, says, that arriving late at the Monday-night meeting, Waller explained what had been done, stated that six men had been shot at McCormick's by the police, and that they should be prepared in case the police went beyond their bounds to resist invasion upon their natural and civil rights. He also said that nothing was said about dynamite and that the phrase " having stuff " was not used. He said further that nothing was said at any of their meetings about dynamite or bombs, and that no discussion arose, or understanding arrived at, to use bombs on any particular occasion. This witness for the prosecution also said that he did not anticipate any trouble at the Haymarket, and that he only left on account of the approach of the storm.

Thomas Greif, the proprietor of the hall, swore that there were only twenty-five or thirty persons present, and he saw no effort made to keep the meeting secret.

If there was a conspiracy, depending upon the witnesses for the prosecution alone, we are justified in stating that it had no reference to the Haymarket meeting, and that the alleged conspiracy, even if proven, was simply one to resist what was considered unjustifiable invasion. Only two, Fischer and Engel, were shown to have been present, yet eight were put on trial for their lives on this assumption. Again, from the testimony of the prosecution it appears that the throwing of the bomb on May 4 was entirely opposed to the alleged '"conspiracy." According to the original design the "conspirators" ought to have been notified at once when the police attacked the peaceable meeting on the Haymarket square. This was not done; no part of the design alleged to have been agreed upon Monday' evening was carried out. But somebody threw a bomb into the ranks of the police. If he was a member of that conspiracy—of which there is no proof—he must have acted in direct contradiction to the plan said to have been agreed upon, he disregarded the directions of his associates, he defeated their objects and ruined the eight-hour movement for the time being. Who employed him is still a conundrum. His connection with the "conspiracy" has not been established. The evidence is conclusive that Schnaubelt did not throw the bomb. It is perhaps enough to state in regard to the testimony of Special Officer Gilmer that so completely and overwhelmingly was he impeached, contradicted and discredited, that the State did not ask a single instruction to the jury based upon the belief by them that Rudolph Schnaubelt threw the bomb as detailed by Gilmer. The testimony of Gilmer was abandoned by the representatives of the State as unworthy of credence or consideration, in the instructions asked by them. Schnaubelt had attended the Monday night meeting and we have seen that two witnesses, Lehnert and Krueger, testified to his leaving the Haymarket some time before the bomb was thrown.

Yet Fischer's presence at the Sunday and Monday-night meetings is the sole reason for his conviction. We have seen that he was at Zepf's Hall at the time the police raided the meeting at the Haymarket. No utterance of Fischer's suggesting violence upon that evening, either in speech or in print, is in record of the case. The whole testimony as to the Monday-night meeting is entirely irrelevent as to all the prisoners other than Fischer and Engel. As far as Fischer is concerned it has been conclusively shown that he was not at the Haymarket when the bomb exploded, did not contemplate either the throwing of one or that occasion would arise to exert self-defense. Further, the whole testimony presented by the State absolutely refutes the theory that the Emma-street meeting or the West Lake-street meeting had any reference whatever to the throwing of a bomb at the Haymarket meeting.

GEORGE ENGEL.

The case presented by the prosecution against Engel is nearly identical with that urged against Fischer. There are, however, some points which require brief consideration. Engel, it will be remembered, was credited with being the proposer of the "plot." There was no pretense that Engel was present at the Haymarket meeting at the time that the bomb was thrown, nor for some considerable time prior thereto. Waller testified that after the bomb was exploded he left Zepf's Hall and proceeded immediately home, stopping on the way at Engel's house. That he found Engel there with a few friends having a quiet drink of beer, and that he first informed him of what had occurred at the Haymarket. He said that upon this announcement being made, he told the party there gathered that he thought they had better go home, to which Engel fully assented, saying yes, they should all go home; and that nothing else occurred.

August Krueger says that he left the Haymarket about ten o'clock and arrived at Engel's house at about quarter past. That later Waller came in and said that three hundred men had been shot by the police at the Haymarket, and added, "we ought to go down there and do something." To this Engel responded that *whoever threw that bomb did a foolish thing*, it was nonsense and that *he did not sympathize* with such a butchery, and he told Waller that he had better go home as quick as possible; he said the policemen were just as good people as other citizens, and that the revolution must grow out of the people.

From the concurring testimony of these two witnesses, one of whom the State had secured as an informer, it appears beyond question that when the bomb was thrown Engel was quietly at home with a few friends, not anticipating any violence or conflict with the police; that he deprecated what had occurred as unwise, and advised all to go home. If the Haymarket meeting had been planned with reference to carrying out the programme of action discussed and alleged to have been agreed upon Monday night, then the natural thing for Engel and his associates, when the news was brought to them of the outbreak at the Haymarket, would have been to have gathered themselves together and inaugurated a movement against the police. The fact that no such suggestion came from Engel, and that upon Waller hinting that something ought to be done, Engel refused to entertain any such proposition, along with all the other testimony in the case, is conclusive that the Haymarket bomb was a matter of absolute surprise to Mr. Engel.

LOUIS LINGG.

The evidence introduced by the State shows that Louis Lingg did not attend the Haymarket meeting, nor was within a distance of two miles thereof during the entire evening. Captain Schaak said that Lingg admitted to him after arrest that he was present at the meeting at No. 54 West Lake street on Monday night, May 3. But the doughty captain was the only witness who made this charge. On the defense it was shown by two witnesses that Lingg passed the entire evening at a meeting of his union—the carpenters—until after eleven o'clock. These witnesses were Ernest Niendorf and Jacob Sherman.

Further, in proof that Lingg could not have been at the meeting where the alleged conspiracy was planned, it will be seen on reference to the testimony of the informer Seliger that when he (Seliger) showed to Lingg the word "Ruhe" in the paper, it was late on the night of May 4, after the bomb had been thrown, and that consequently Lingg had not thought of looking for it! He added that Lingg said it was a notice "that everything was to go topsy-turvey" and that all the armed men should appear at 54 West Lake street. According to informer Waller's testimony, however, a far different meaning was intended to be conveyed by the word. If any preference is to be given between these contradictory statements of the two informers, Waller, who was present and chairman, should know best.

The whole evidence against Lingg is that he did manufacture bombs. Yet even Seliger, who seemed willing to swear to any incriminating story, admitted that nothing was said as to when or where these bombs were to be used. He had been making them for weeks, long before any Haymarket meeting was contemplated. He was not shown to have been on terms of intimacy with the other defendants, in fact, some had never seen or heard of him. In behalf of Lingg the counsel submitted an instruction which they asked to be given to the jury, which was refused by the court. It was as follows:

"It is not enough to warrant the conviction of the defendant Lingg that he *may* have manufactured the bomb, the explosion of which killed Mathias J. Degan. He must have aided, abetted or advised the exploding of the bomb, or of the doing of some illegal act, or the doing of a legal act in an unlawful manner, in the furtherance of which, and as incident thereto, the same was exploded and said Degan killed. If, as to the defendant Lingg the jury should find beyond all reasonable doubt that he did in fact manufacture said bomb, but are not satisfied beyond all reasonable doubt that he aided, advised, counseled or abetted the throwing of said missile, or the doing of any unlawful act which resulted in the explosion of said bomb, your verdict should acquit him as far as the establishment of his guilt is attempted by the manufacture of said missile or bomb."

After examination, Judge Gary marked this "Given," and proceeded to read it to the jury. The record shows that he read it but half way through, then stopped, and marked the instruction "Refused."

This action was tantamount to an indirect instruction to the jury that a man who manufactured a weapon was accessory to the act of any man who might use it with murderous intent! How would this logic apply to Smith & Wesson, Remington, or Colt? Upon this point his counsel say:

"Whatever may be our criticism upon the matter of manufacturing dynamite bombs for any purpose, there is no law within this State which makes the mere manufacture of such missiles a crime punishable with death or otherwise. Louis Lingg could not have been convicted of murder because of all this matter detailed by Seliger and his wife and Lehmann, even if it were clear that the bomb thrown at the Haymarket had come from his hands, if it had been thrown by a third party acting upon his own responsibility and without Lingg's knowledge, consent, aid, assistance, advice or encouragement. For example, the manufacturers of revolvers, bowie knives, dirks, poisoned daggers, gatling guns, air guns, have never been held responsible for the consequences of the use of these weapons by a third party acting *sua sponte*. These weapons are harmless in themselves, and cannot be involved in the commission of crime until some free moral agent intelligently applies them to some purpose of destruction. Nor is this rule affected by the fact, if conceded, that the manufacturer must have known that the natural use to which the implement manufactured would be put would be the taking of human life. We may deprecate such industry, but we cannot say that the mere pursuit of the industry makes the man engaged in it responsible for every use of the implement produced. By way of illustration, we may suppose that some third party, an enemy of Lingg's, had obtained one of the bombs of his manufacture and use for the purpose of deliberate murder, with the design of involving Lingg himself in ruin, and with it committed a crime to which Lingg himself was a stranger, such result would not obtain.

"In order to justify a legal conviction of murder there must be satisfactory and conclusive proof of the commission by the party accused, in his own person or through another acting under his aid and advice, of the crime alleged. It will not do to allow our horror over the use of this terrible explosive to carry us away from the moorings of the law. It will not do for us to allow the realm of jurisprudence to be invaded by the mere dictates of supposed policy. We must stand by fixed principles of general application. Only thus can the law be administered as a science, and be made the protection of the innocent and the terror only of the guilty.

"We submit and insist that this record is barren of evidence justifying the conclusion by the jury that Louis Lingg was a party to a conspiracy to throw a bomb on the night of May 4, 1886, or to a common object, in the attempt to execute which that bomb was thrown. The evidence is conclusive that Lingg did not throw the bomb, did not stand by and assist the perpetration of the deed. It follows as an irresistible conclusion from Seliger's testimony that whatever Lingg did, whatever he may have attempted or proposed on the North Side, he had no knowledge that a bomb would be thrown at the Haymarket meeting. The evidence fails to show, that without being present, he had advised, encouraged, aided or abetted the perpetration of the crime charged in the indictment."

CHAPTER XII.

CONCLUSION.

But little remains to be said. We have carefully gone through the evidence, conscienciously bringing out the strongest points made against the accused, and endeavored to carefully weigh the evidence as bearing on each one of the defendants. But there still remains a matter upon which counsel for defendants lay considerable stress in their brief and argument before the Supreme Court of Illinois for a new trial. This is what they denominate the *illegitimate evidence*, which I will endeavor as briefly as possible to epitomize. The reader will remember considerable so-called evidence was introduced by the State over the protest of the defendants, but which was allowed by the court upon the assumption—before evidence—that the defendants were guilty of an illegal conspiracy.

This was shown on the very first day on which testimony was taken, when Waller was asked: "Did you ever have any bombs?"

At that time Judge Gary rendered the following ruling, which governed all subsequent proceedings:

"If the fact be that a large number of men concurred with each other in preparing to use force for the destruction of human life, *upon occasions which were not yet foreseen*, but upon some principles which they substantially agreed upon, as, for example, taking the words of this witness, if a large number of men *agreed together* to kill the police, if they were found in conflict with strikers—I believe is the phrase— *leaving it to the agents of violence to determine whether the time and occasion had come for the use of violence,* then if the time and occasion do come when the violence is used, are not *all parties* who agreed beforehand in preparing the means of death, and agreed in the use of them upon the time and occasion, equally liable?"

CONCLUSION. 171

There had been no evidence then, nor was there afterwards, that there had been an agreement between a large number of men "to kill the police," yet that assumption was taken for granted by the court. It was argued at some length, and among the various rulings of the judge the following will suffice as an exposition of Illinois law:

"If the time and occasion were left to the different conspirators, or to the different parties to the agreement, and then, when the time did come, in the judgment of *some one* of those, and he did use the force and kill, *then they are all liable.*"

Under this construction of the law anything that might tend, however remotely, to proving that the defendants were social heretics, and which might have a tendency to inflame the admitted bias of the jurors, was admitted and days consumed in matters wholly foreign to the issue in this case.

The counsel for the defendants sum up the illegitimate evidence under the following heads:

I. *Newspaper Literature.*—Whole files of the *Arbeiter-Zeitung* and the *Alarm* were paraded before the jury and days passed in reading editorials, notices, communications and reprints. Both of these papers were published by a corporation duly organized under the laws of Illinois, of which only four of the defendants were stockholders. Both were openly published and circulated, had never been interfered with and entitled to protection under the charter of the company. Every word read was general in its character, such as Victor Hugo's addresses, eight-hour editorials, scientific reprints, denunciation of capitalistic exploitation, etc. By the introduction of all this irrelevant matter it was shown, on mere newspaper authority, remember, that Oscar Neebe had presided, or was reported to have presided, at two Socialistic meetings. Therefore, fifteen years hard labor! Reprints from *Truth, Die Freiheit,* and an article by Bakounine, the Russian nihilist, which had passed into the current literature of the day, were gravely read at length to the astonishment of the middle-class jury.

II. *Johann Most's Book* on the Science of Revolutionary Warfare was introduced as evidence to convict men of murder, some of whom were unable to read the language in which it was written. The book was openly published by the International News Company of New York, and I presume is still supplied by them when ordered. Fricke had testified that it was on sale at the office of the *Arbeiter-Zeitung,* where he was a book-keeper, and had seen it sold at picnics where the defendants were present, though none of them had anything to do with its sale. Here again was the introduction of matter foreign to the issue, containing only general not specific directions and fully as permissible a production as Hardee's Tactics. The only possible use of the translation read to the jury was to still further inflame the prejudice of the jurors.

III. *Various Objects* were introduced evidently for the same reason, such as soiled and blood-stained garments said to have been worn by officers wounded on the Haymarket. It was not Degan's clothing thus paraded, showing holes made by fragments of the shell, and it was not shown in evidence that the clothing belonged to officers who died. At best it was a disgusting and vulgar appeal to passions and fears to convict men alleged to have some indefinite connection with the unknown individual who did throw the bomb, and who, it was assumed, acted upon their general advice to defend themselves.

The State also introduced a lot of cans, gas-pipes, boxes and fragments which had been fractured in experiments, to show to the now awe-struck jury the terrible destructive effect of dynamite. Said collection, upon evidence of detectives, having been found at the *Arbeiter-Zeitung* office, Lingg's room, and under sidewalks three miles from the Haymarket. These last were four tin cans, found four weeks after the Haymarket meeting and, from their very construction, altogether different from the bomb used on the night of May 4. Broken barrel staves, indented iron, torn links, tin cans containing combustible material, and even a *piece of gas-pipe* gravely termed *an empty bomb*, were used to prejudice the jury against men accused of the murder of Mathias J. Degan.

The Furnace, or "blasting machine," found at the house of Mr. Engel, where it had been for a year, and which was shown to have never been used, was introduced in order to get Bonfield's testimony that it *could be used* for the melting of metals. Irrelevant even as against Engel, it was atrocious as bearing on his comrades. Its introduction but served to insinuate into the minds of the jurors that they actually saw before them an Anarchist's blast furnace!

Various Flags and Banners found at the office of the *Arbeiter-Zeitung* were waved before the jury that all might see what a red flag or banner looked like. Waiving the point that these were admittedly seized without warrant, they had been carried in the streets of Chicago for years, for the most part belonging to trade-unions and figuring in their processions. Yet they were again flaunted as evidence against *all* the defendants!

Fischer's Armory, as it was called, was also duly paraded. We have seen from the testimony of Mr. Aschenbrenner that the articles were in a drawer in the composing room of the *Arbeiter-Zeitung* build-

CONCLUSION. 173

ing where he was employed; that Fischer was asked by witness to remove them to avoid getting others in trouble, and while doing so was arrested. There was no pretense that he had been in the habit of carrying these, or that he had them on his person May 4. Having been arrested while removing them, at the request of a fellow-workman, their introduction as evidence made him in the eyes of the jury, now already sufficiently excited a veritable walking arsenal or a modern Captain Kidd.

IV. The counsel complain that upon cross-examination the accused were compelled to answer questions not brought out on the direct examination. Thus Fielden was asked a variety of questions as to his past connection with the *Alarm*, the International, speeches delivered long before and his Socialistic views. Spies was made to identify Herr Most's letter, though he stated he had no recollection as to having received or read it, and did not think he had replied to it, and stated positively that he never carried on any correspondence with Most.

V. *Speeches and Private Utterances.*—Under this head we find in the record speeches delivered at the board of trade demonstration in April 1885; the West Twelfth street meeting and others early in 1885; remarks made at the meetings of the American Group, which were always public and open to everybody, and where the attendance was never larger than twenty-five people; private conversations of Mr. Spies in Grand Rapids, Mich., and with reporters greedy for a sensational article. Testimony of statements made in a private conversation by Spies outside of the State, a year and a quarter before the Haymarket meeting, was admitted as not only evidence against Spies, but against all the other defendants. As to Mr. Spies' "ghost story" to the reporter Wilkinson the evidence shows its weakness and Mr. Gruenhut said it was carried on in a half-joking manner; utterances at eight-hour meetings and inferences as to the tendency of these utterances had nothing to do with the charge of murder, save as foisted on the record by Judge Gary's rulings.

VI. *Injuries of Officers* as brought out by the testimony of surgeons, describing the ghastly nature of bomb wounds, etc., that the "impartial jury" might be the better enabled to discuss the question whether the defendants were connected in spirit or deed with the death of Degan.

When the jury retired each one had ringing in his ears the epithets bestowed upon the defendants by State's-Attorney Grinnell, such as "loathsome murderers;" also "these wretches here" and "assassins." Consider also the following sample extracts from his closing address in the light of the desperate effort that had been made to inflame the passions and fears of the jurors. For instance:

"Prejudice? Men, organized assassins, can preach murder in our city for years, you deliberately under your oath hear the proof, and then say you have no prejudice?"

"We stand here, gentlemen, with the verdict in our favor—I mean in favor of the prosecution as to the conduct of this case."

"Don't try, gentlemen, to shirk the issues. *Law is on trial! Anarchy is on trial!*"

"If I had the power I would like to take you all over to the Haymarket that night, and with you with tears in your eyes see the dead and mingle with the wounded and dying, see law violated, and then I could, if I had the power, paint you a picture that would *steel your hearts against the defendants.*"

From these words it will be seen, as is sufficiently shown in the testimony, that the defendants were condemned less for the murder of Degan than because they were Anarchists, because they held theoretical views at variance with those in general acceptance—in short, because they were *social heretics*.

Captain Black closed his eloquent plea before the Supreme Court in words with which we conclude. He said:

"For aught which appears in this record, your honors upon your consciences will be compelled to say that bomb may have been thrown by somebody in no way connected with these defendants, directly or indirectly. It may have been done by an enemy of theirs. It may have been done by some man acting upon his own mere malice and ill-will. It was thrown outside of the purpose of the Haymarket meeting. It was thrown in disregard of the arrangement and understanding for that meeting. It was thrown to the overthrow of the labor and the effort that these men were then giving their lives to, namely, the establishment of the eight-hour day. It brought an end to their efforts. It was not of their devising. The record shows it.

"The record fails to show who threw that bomb. And the question is, whether upon the barbaric *lex talionis*, that whenever a man was slain a man of the opposing faction must be slain, these seven men shall die because seven policemen, whom they did not like as a class, and who certainly did not love them, have died? You know the barbarians never stopped to fix individual responsibility for the crime. They simply said, 'One of ours is dead, and we cannot rest till one of theirs die for him!' It has been so here."

My rights! 'Tis easy to run o'er the score,
  For they are marked by anguish, tears and pain;
A right to add a mite to garnished store
  When I have toiled to increase others' gain;
A right to call my wife and babe my own,
  But not the muscle on which they depend;
A right to love when other joys have flown,
  But not from hunger always to defend;
A right to beg to toil from sordid greed,
  But only as a favor must I crave;
A right to starve 'mid plenteousness—from need,
  But not to claim more than a pauper's grave.
Yet aye! And may they heed who rights would spurn,
  The *right* of e'en the trodden worm to turn.

APPENDIX.

I.

CAPTAIN BLACK'S ADDRESS.

"On the morning of the 5th of May, 1886, the good people of the city of Chicago were startled and shocked at the event of the previous night, frightened, many of them, not knowing whereunto this thing might lead. Fear is the father of cruelty. It was no ordinary case. Immediately after that first emotion came a feeling which has found expression from many lips in the hearing of many, if not all of you: 'A great wrong has been done; somebody must be punished, somebody ought to suffer for the suffering which has been wrought.' Perhaps it was that feeling—I know not—which led to the unusual and extraordinary proceedings which were taken in connection with this matter immediately following the 4th of May. Perhaps it was that feeling, in a large measure, which led to the arrest and presentment of these eight defendants. Perhaps it was something of that feeling which will explain the conduct of the prosecution in this case. I am not disposed to say that there has been any willful or deliberate intent on the part of the representatives of the State to act unfairly. I am not disposed to charge that there has been upon their part any disposition to do an injustice to any man. But in their case, as in the case of all, passion perverts the heart, prejudice corrupts the judgment.

"The serious question which confronts us, in our view of the case, as we stand here to argue with you the effect of this testimony which has been presented in these past days, is, to what extent you may be influenced in your deliberations by passion or prejudice. I will not dwell at length upon that; it has been admirably presented by one of my associates. I need only to say that our hope, as against your passion, lies in our confidence that your purpose is true; that our hope, as against your prejudice, lies in the conviction that your hearts are full of human tenderness. We can only offset the one against the other. We can only hope that that human tenderness which we believe is in your hearts, and looks upon us from your faces—that that purpose of righteousness which we believe forms an element of your character, as it is inscribed upon your countenances—will stand us in stead as against the passion which has been stirred in your hearts, and the prejudice which has been sought to be instilled into your bosoms. If we can have —and that is all that we desire—a fair and impartial consideration of the testimony in this case, as the testimony in every case ought to be considered, and as the testimony in any other case would be considered, we shall be content, assured of the result.

"On the night of the 4th of May a dynamite bomb was thrown in the city of Chicago and exploded. It was the first time that in our immediate civilization, and immediately about us, this great destructive agency was used in modern contests. I beg you to remember, in the consideration of this case, that dynamite is not the invention of Socialists; it is not their discovery. Science has turned it loose upon the world—an agency of destruction, whether for defense or offense, whether for attack or to build the bulwarks round the beleagured city. It has entered into modern warfare. We know from what has already transpired in this case that dynamite is being experimented with as a weapon of warfare by the great nations of the world. What has been read in your hearing has given you the results of experiments made under the direction of the government of Austria, and while you have sat in this jury box considering the things which have been deposed before you, with reference to reaching a final and correct result, the government of the United States has voted $350,000 for the building of a dynamite cruiser. It is in the world by no procurement of Socialism, with no necessary relationship thereto. It is in the world to stay. It is manufactured freely; it is sold without let, hindrance or restriction. You may go from this jury box to the leading powder companies of the country, or their depots, and buy all the dynamite that you wish without question as to your purpose, without interrogation as to your motive. It is here. Is it necessarily a thing of evil? It has entered into the great industries, and we know its results, It has cleared the path of commerce where the great North River rolls on its way to the sea. It is here and there blasting out rocks, digging out mines, and used for helpfulness in the great industries of life. But there never came an explosive into the world, cheap, simple of construction, easy of manufacture, that it did not enter also into the world's combats. I beg you to remember also that hand bombs are not things of Socialistic devising. It may be that one or another, here and there, professing Socialistic tenets, has devised some improvements in their construction, or has made some advances with reference to their composition; they have not invented them. The hand-grenade has been known in warfare long ere you and I saw the light. The two things have come together—the hand grenade, charged no longer with the powder of old days, but charged with the dynamite of modern science. It is a union which Socialists are not responsible for. It is a union led up to by the logic of events and the necessities of situations, and it is a union that will never be divorced. We stand amazed at the dread results that are possible to this union; but as we look back over history we know this fact, contradictory as it may seem, strange as it may first strike us, that in the exact proportion in which the implements of warfare have been made effective or destructive, in that precise proportion have wars lost the utmost measure of their horror, and in that precise proportion has death by war diminished. When gunpowder came into European warfare there was an outcry against it. All the chivalry which had arrogated to itself the power and glory of battle in martial times sprang up against the introduction of gunpowder, an agency that made the iron casque and shield and cuirass of the plumed knight no better a defense than the hemp doublet of the peasant. But now, instead of wars that last through thirty years, that are determined by the personal collision of individuals, that desolate nations, the great civilized nations of the world hesitate at war because of its possibilities of evil, and diplomacy sits where once force alone was entrenched. The moral responsibility for dynamite is not upon Socialism."

Captain Black went on to urge that the sole question before the jury was who threw the bomb, for the doctrine of accessory before the fact, under which it was sought to hold the defendants, was nothing but the application to the criminal law of the civil or common law doctrine that what a man does by another he does himself. When the prosecution charged that the defendants threw it, their charge involved that the bomb was thrown by the procurement of these men, by their advice, direction, aid, counsel or encouragement, and that the man who threw it acted not alone for himself, or upon his own responsibility, but as a result of the encouragement or procurement of these men. He held that the State must show that the agent of the defendants did the deed, and that it is not sufficient to show that the defendants favored such deeds. Upon this point counsel spoke at some length. Next he took up the case of one of the talesmen examined with reference to his taking a place on the jury, who swore that, having been for three years connected with the office of the prosecuting attorney in the State of New York, he found in himself that the habit of thought and life to which he had there devoted himself had created in him a predisposition to believe every accused man guilty, which, in his own deliberate judgment before God, disqualified him from sitting as an impartial juror in a criminal case. The application of this case to the attaches of the state's attorney's office who have appeared before the jury was made the most of. The Captain then spoke as follows:

"And now, gentlemen, let us take up the real issues. I believe I can read in your faces that you are ready to give an answer to your consciences, to your fellow-men and yourselves for your conduct in the investigations you are now making. I pray you, lend me at once your judgment and your hearts.

"Has the State proven to your satisfaction, beyond a reasonable doubt, that August Spies, Michel Schwab and Adolph Fischer were personally and individually advising and providing for the throwing of the bomb on the night of May 4? Direct testimony has been introduced to prove that. It is not pretended that the other defendants are connected by direct testimony with the offense of that night. Two witnesses were placed upon the stand to prove the lighting and throwing of the bomb, Harry L. Gilmer and M. M. Thompson. I must say, gentlemen, that I think their testimony is altogether untruthful." Captain Black analyzed the testimony of these witnesses, and contended that they had laid perjury to their souls. Gilmer's story was utterly incredible and absurd. Could the jury believe beyond any reasonable doubt, beyond any substantial question, that August Spies, the brainiest man of the crowd, would commit the stupendous and supreme folly of first illuminating his face so that every man might see it and know it and then lighting the fuse of the bomb? "You saw Spies on this stand; you heard his testimony. I think I can safely leave his case in your hands. If it is a fact that Spies was on the wagon when the bomb was thrown the story of Gilmer is shattered and has not a shadow or shade of truth in it. Then this perjured witness tried to connect Fischer with this awful event, when it had been conclusively shown that this defendant was drinking beer at Zepf's Hall at the time. If there had been any effort on the part of the State to deliberately corrupt justice in one particular, and make the jurors parties to murder, they should bear that in mind in considering the whole case. Besides, there was evidence that the bomb did not come from the alley, but was thrown about twenty or forty feet south of the alley. It was not the duty of the defense to prove the falsity of Gilmer's and Thompson's testimony; their business was only to raise a reasonable doubt as to its truth, and it was the duty of the jurors, as citizens and men, acting under the law which is above all law, to give the defendants the benefit of that doubt."

Passing from the consideration of the direct testimony, Captain Black then turned to the circumstantial evidence out of which the State sought to forge the chain of conviction and bring the defendants to the extreme penalty of the law. The theory of the State was this:

That the meeting on the night of May 4 was a result and incident in the carrying out of a general conspiracy to murder; that all the defendants were parties to that conspiracy; that certain of them were active participants in the meeting, and the evidence sufficiently and incontrovertibly connected them all with and made them guilty of the murder. Now, the fact was that the Haymarket meeting was not called by any of the defendants. The "Revenge circular," which Spies wrote after the Black road tragedy, had no reference to that meeting. The attention of this defendant was called to the wording of the circular calling the meeting, and he pointed out an objectionable line. Spies had slept over the matter. Perhaps the very excess and violence of his feelings the day before had brought about a reaction; he was just and calm, and at his direction the objectionable line was stricken out. Did that look like the action of a man who was preparing for the culmination of a scheme of revolution? That day a request came through the mail to Spies to insert the word "Ruhe" in the letter-box. That was an ordinary request and Spies complied with it, not knowing the significance of the word. Upon the State's own showing the word had no reference to the Haymarket meeting. It was claimed that it was part of the general plan that the armed groups should be present at that gathering. But they were not there, and so far as known there was just one bomb with which to inaugurate the great revolution. Who is the man that had the bomb and why was he there. They knew not, nor did they know what his motive in his final action was. But they did know that August Spies had nothing whatever to do with the throwing of the bomb. In his opening remarks at that meeting Spies said they had not assembled for the purpose of rioting or making a disturbance, but for the discussion of the grievances of the laboring men. Parsons next took the stand and talked for an hour. His speech was full of statistics, and by no means inflammatory. He told them Socialism aimed at the life of no man; it aimed at the system of society and not at individuals. This remark was made in response to a cry "Hang Jay Gould," in whose place, Parsons declared, hundreds would rise were he slain.

Captain Black read the evidence of a shorthand reporter who had attended the meeting to prove the declaration that it was peaceable and orderly and no unusual remarks were made by the speakers. "There was nothing dreadful in the expression, Arm yourselves in the interests of liberty and of your rights. But still Spies, the arch-conspirator, was bent, determined, resolved irrevocably, that then and there should the inauguration of the social revolution take place! It was nonsense to advance or believe in any such proposition. Whatever might have been the ultimate desires of these men, whatever might have been the social change to which they looked forward and of which they spoke, it was more than idle to take the position and argue to intelligent men that the meeting was taken hold of by Spies and manipulated for the purpose of precipitating a conflict with the police. That idea was utterly refuted by the absence of preparations for such an event and the conduct of the speakers. It was a gratuitous assumption on the part of the State that Fischer went to the meeting of the armed groups as Spies' lieutenant for the purpose of arranging the Haymarket meeting and that Spies attended to carry out the programme which he devised for him. In a case where life and death is at stake, the imagination of the prosecuting attorneys should be brought to a halt; it is time that you as jurors should say in your conscience, and before the tribunal of your own manhood, 'We cannot guess away the life of any man.' Spies might be a Socialist, an Anarchist perhaps, but he was not devoid of the common feelings of humanity. There had been frequent contests with the police and the people, and as the editor of the workingmen's paper of Chicago, a paper devoted to the consideration of the interests of the great wage classes, he naturally took their side against the organized police. When he saw the police firing into the flying crowd on the Black road, they could imagine such a man under such circumstances going to his office and writing the 'revenge circular.' In which there was no suggestion of a meeting, in which there was nothing but the breaking out of an intense indignation, and an attempt to arouse that feeling which sometime in the future would reach such a point that such would no longer be possible or tolerated. That could be imagined without the proposition that Spies' design and intention was to precipitate a conflict.

"Who was next charged with active participation in this pretended conspiracy? Fielden. This defendant addressed the meeting. He had reached the conclusion of his speech and the whole meeting was about to separate peacefully and quietly when the police came. It was stated that Fielden fired three shots at the police. He did not believe the story told as to the first shot while he was getting out of the wagon; it was a deliberate lie. Officer Krueger testified as to the other shots, and wanted the jury to infer that he was wounded in the leg by Fielden. Officer Wessler also claimed to have had a duel with Fielden. This testimony was contradictory, and if false the State had introduced it to hang a poor teamster; it was more wicked and cowardly than the alleged conspiracy of the Socialists. 'Oh!' cried the prosecution; 'he is only a Socialist; it is only the life of one of the common herd, who has grown dangerous to the peace of those who would wrap the mantle of their selfishness about them, and he is to be put away.' The measure of the civilization of the State is the care that it has for the life and safety of its common people. If there were members of the police capable of such action it was time that the strong arm of the law laid hold of them and prevented further mischief. There was not a word of truth in the story that Fielden fired at the officers. That story is a wicked, wicked effort to bring a fellow-being to the scaffold by false swearing.

"What were the circumstances upon which the State relied to place the noose about Parsons' neck? First, that he was an American. It was a horrible thing that an American should sympathize with the common people;.that he should feel his heart respond to the desires of the oppressed workingmen! Second, he was the editor of the *Alarm;* and third, he spoke at the Haymarket meeting. It was not suggested that he knew anything about the Monday night meeting. If Parsons had ever dreamed of violence that night would his wife and her lady friend have attended the meeting? Was there anything in those circumstances to show that Parsons knew of any plan to throw the bomb?

"Against Schwab it was proven that he wrote an occasional editorial, attended meetings of Socialists, and upon that particular night he was at a safe distance from the Haymarket. If anybody was there it was a suspicious circumstance; if anybody was not there it was still a suspicious circumstance. It was the old parson's dilemma: 'You will be damned if you do, and you will be damned if you don't.' The case of Fischer and Engel could be considered together. They attended the Monday night meeting. Fischer was at the Haymarket a short time on Tuesday night, and he then went to Zepf's Hall, where he and Parsons were when the bomb was thrown.

"It is perhaps proper, that in view of the circumstance that Fischer and Engel were the only two defendants at the West Lake street meeting on Monday night, I should present briefly my opinions touching that meeting as relating to this case. Two witnesses, Waller and Schrade, testified as to what occurred at that meeting. Waller said there were seventy or eighty people present; the other placed the attendance at thirty-five to forty. Let us suppose thirty-five or forty met together in that basement. In the progress of the meeting it transpired that there had been a meeting of the north side group, of which Mr. Engel was a member, on the previous morning (Sunday). At that meeting a resolution was adopted, which was brought before the Monday night meeting for consideration, and it was adopted in the manner indicated by Waller. What was the purport of that resolution? I think I state it fairly to the State and fairly to the defendants themselves, when I say that the action then and there resolved upon was this, no more, no less: That if in the event of a struggle the police should attempt by brute force to overpower the strikers unlawfully and unjustly, those men would lend their help to their fellow-wageworkers as against the police. A plan of action was suggested by one of the group which contemplated the blowing up of police stations, cutting telegraph wires and disabling the fire department. Every particle of that resolution, gentlemen, was expressly dependent upon the unlawful invasion of the rights of the working people by the police. Nothing was to be inaugurated by the so-called conspirators, there was to be no resort to force by them in the first instance. It was solely defensive, and had reference alone to meeting force by force; it had reference alone to a possible attack in the future, dependent upon the action that the police themselves might take. I am not here to defend the action of that meeting. The question here is: Had that action anything whatever to do with the result of the Haymarket meeting? The action of the north side group had nothing to do with that, since the Haymarket meeting had never been dreamed of or suggested at that time. By whom was the Tuesday meeting suggested? What was its scope, purpose and object? As then and there declared, it was simply to be a mass meeting of workingmen with reference to police outrages that had already taken place. Were the armed men, those conspirators who met at West Lake street, present? No; they were not to be there. That is the testimony of Waller and Schrade. I am not here even to say that the proposition to call that meeting was a wise one. The event has proven how sadly unwise it was. But I am here to say that the men who in that Monday night meeting proposed the calling of the Tuesday night meeting, if we take the testimony of the State itself, had no dream or expectation of violence, difficulty or contest on that eventful night. But before the Tuesday night meeting was proposed, a suggestion was made that they ought to have some sort of signal for action, and the word 'Ruhe' was suggested by somebody. Waller could not tell who suggested it; Schrade did not know it had been agreed upon. Evidently there was no very clear idea that night what 'Ruhe' did mean, because Lingg saw it in the paper at 11 o'clock, and said: 'That is a signal that we ought to be over at 54 West Lake street.' Waller finally, under close examination by the State, said the word 'Ruhe' was to be inserted in the 'letter-box' of the *Arbeiter-Zeitung* in the event of the time arriving for a downright revolution. Had that revolution come; had it commenced when the word was put in the 'letter-box?' No. When the members saw this in the 'letter-box' what were they to do? Go to the Haymarket and attack anybody? No. They were to go to there respective places of meeting, and then, according to advices brought to them, were to determine upon a course of action. It had no reference to the throwing of the bomb at the Haymarket. Did that Monday night meeting pick out the man who was to throw the bomb? Did it provide that a collision between the police and the people was to be brought about at the Haymarket? Did it contemplate murder? Not at all. When Fischer told Spies that the word 'Ruhe' had no connection with the Haymarket meeting he spoke the truth. It was a signal that the armed men should meet at the places designated by themselves to determine what action should be taken with reference to whatever might have transpired.

"But it is to be borne in mind that the meeting of the armed section never took place. There was no meeting of the Northwest side groups; there was no meeting of any group pursuant to the word 'Ruhe.' Were any bombs to be thrown, any violence to be resorted to? No. If the police made an attack, a committee was to take word to the groups, and the groups were then, and not till then, to determine what action they should take in the line of offense. Does that make every man who was present at the Monday night meeting responsible for the throwing of the bomb? Not at all. Unless they are all responsible, it does not make Fischer and Engel responsible. Engel was not at the Tuesday night meeting. Fischer was there and went quietly away before the bomb was thrown. There was absolutely nothing in connection with the Monday night meeting which contemplated violence at the Haymarket or provided for the throwing of the bomb.

"Let me call your attention in passing to another thing. When Waller, having from some source heard of the lamentable occurence at the Haymarket, went to Engel's house he found him drinking beer with two or three friends. After listening to the details of the affair Engel said, while Waller was saying, 'Let's do something,' 'You had better go home. I have no sympathy with a movement of this kind. The police are of the common people, and when the general revolution does occur, they should be with us. I am utterly opposed to this slaughtering of them.' That is the full extent of the case against these two defendants, except the further fact that Fischer had a pistol and a dagger. It is not right to hang any man for the Haymarket murder simply because he had a dagger or a pistol in his posession.

"As to Lingg, he came from that republic sitting in the center

APPENDIX. 185

of Europe preaching the everlasting lesson of liberty. He came here in the fall of 1885, and became a member of the Seliger household. Whatever he knows of social and labor conditions in this country he learned from those about him. He joined a carpenters' union, being himself a carpenter by trade. He attended the meetings of that union. Young, active, bright, capable, he enters the band of which they speak, and manufactures bombs. There is no law against that, gentlemen; but they claim that is a circumstance from which you must draw the conclusion of his guilt, when taken with other circumstances, for the Haymarket tragedy. The State put on the stand one man, Lehmann, to whom he gave bombs. Did he tell Lehmann to go to the Haymarket and use the bombs there. No. Lehmann swears that he said: 'You take these and put them in a safe place.' And Lehmann hid them where the officer, piloted by him, found them. Does that prove that Lingg sent a bomb to the Haymarket for the purpose of having somebody killed? How did he come to make bombs; was it a matter to engage in on his own volition or responsibility? No. The Carpenters' Union at one of its meeting resolved to devote a certain amount of money for the purpose of experimenting with dynamite. You may say that was not right, but he was not responsible for it. There is no more reason in holding him responsible for the Haymarket affair on account of his experiments than there is to hold every other member of the Carpenters' Union for the same thing. That is how Lingg came to make bombs. Without dynamite a bomb shell is a toy. The man who manufactures the dynamite is the one who sets the engine of destruction in motion; but no one ever thinks when a murder has been committed through any instrumentality, of fastening the responsibility of the crime upon the man who made the instrument of death. If it were so, you could trace to the Colt Manufacturing Company, the Remington Manufacturing Company, and the manufacturers of bowie knives, all the murders resulting from the use of their weapons. But, it is said, a dynamite bomb has no use in civilization but for violence. Has a bowie knife or a revolver any known use in civilization but for violence? Lingg manufactured one of the bombs which the police officers exploded. Suppose that in exploding it some one had been killed, would it occur to anybody to put Lingg on trial for murder in that case? The State must show not that a bomb of a certain manufacture did a certain work, but that the man charged with murder exploded it. A bomb is perfectly harmless until some other instrumentality intervenes. The Lingg bombs would kill nobody unless some human independent agency took hold of them. Did Lingg know on Monday night that one of his bombs was to be used? He could not have known it, because the testimony is incontrovertible that it was understood by the men who met at 54 West Lake street there should be no violence at the Haymarket meeting. And yet the State asks you to say that Lingg shall be hanged because he manufactured bombs. The man who threw the bomb did the independent act necessary for its explosion. Who was that man? Was he connected with the defendants? The evidence does not show it.

"And a word more about that. This boy (Lingg) was dependent upon others as to his impressions of our institutions. He went to Seliger's house. Seliger is a Socialist; he has been in this country for years. He is thirty-one years of age; Lingg is twenty-one. And yet the great State of Illinois, through its legal representatives, bargains with William Seliger, the man of mature years, and with his wife, older even than himself, that if they will do what they can to put the noose around the neck of this boy they shall go scathless. Ah! gentlemen, what a mockery of justice is this."

Several cases were referred to, and he then proceeded to discuss the Haymarket meeting. There was no law that could take away the right of the people to meet and consider grievances. When it was proposed to adopt the Constitution in 1787 the States were so careful to preserve the rights of the people that several amendments were put in. Captain Black spoke of our forefathers, who had made the name of the revolutionist immortal, and referred to the meetings that had to be held as a preliminary to that great struggle. It was charged against these men that they were guilty of misdemeanors for holding meetings, and they were prosecuted for crimes. Before the Constitution could receive the approbation of the States it was necessary that the amendment providing that no laws should be passed by Congress abridging free speech should be inserted. Such a provision was incorporated in the first constitution of Illinois in 1818, and renewed in the subsequent constitutions of 1848 and 1870. The Haymarket meeting was called for the common good. Those men believed that a great wrong had been done, a great outrage committed, and the rights of the citizens in that assemblage had been invaded by an unlawful, unwarrantable and outrageous act. Continuing the speaker said:

"Bonfield, in his police office, surrounded by his minions, one hundred and eighty strong, armed to the teeth, knew that the meeting was quietly and peacefully coming to its close. Nay, he had said so to Carter Harrison. When Parsons had concluded Mayor Harrison went to the station and told Bonfield that it was a quiet meeting, and Bonfield replied, 'My detectives make me the same report.' Yet Carter Harrison did not get out of hearing before Inspector Bonfield ordered his men to fall in for that death march. Who is responsible for it? Who precipitated that conflict? Who made that battle in that street that night? The law looks at the approximate cause, not the remote. The law looks at the man immediately in fault; not at some man who may have manufactured the pistol that does the shooting, the dynamite that kills, the bomb that explodes. I ask you, upon your oath before God, in a full and honest consideration of this entire testimony, who made the Haymarket massacre? Who is responsible for that collision? If Bonfield had not marched there would there have been any death? Would not that meeting have dissolved precisely as it proposed to do? Did the bomb-thrower go down to the station where the police were and attack them? A bomb could have been thrown into that station with even more deadly effect than at the Haymarket itself. There they were, massed together in close quarters, in hiding, like a wild beast in its lair ready to spring. Did the bomb-thrower move upon them? Was there here a design to destroy? God sent that warning cloud into the heavens; these men were still there, speaking their last words; but a deadlier cloud was coming up behind this armed force. In disregard of our constitutional rights as citizens, it was proposed to order the dispersal of a peaceable meeting. Has it come to pass that under the constitution of the United States and of this State, our meetings for the discussion of grievances are subject to be scattered to the winds at the breath of a petty police officer? Can they take into their hands the law? If so, that is anarchy; nay, the chaos of constitutional right and legally guaranteed liberty. I ask you again, charging no legal responsibility here, but looking at the man who is morally at fault for the death harvest of that night, who brought it on? Would it have been but for the act of Bonfield."

Captain Black went on to say that as long as the Mayor was there Bonfield could not act, but as soon as Harrison had gone the officer could not get to the Haymarket quick enough. The police, the speaker urged, had been searching the files of the *Arbeiter-Zeitung* and the *Alarm* for years to put before the jury the most inflammatory articles. After alluding to Jesus as the great Socialist of Judea, who first preached the socialism taught by Spies and his other modern apostles, he compared John Brown and his attack on Harper's Ferry to the Socialists' attack on modern evils, concluding:—" Gentlemen, the last words for these eight lives. They are in your hands, with no power to whom you are answerable but God and history, and I say to you in closing only the words of that Divine Socialist: 'As ye would that others should do to you, do you even so to them.'"

II.

A FUND FOR THE JURY.

In discharging the jury Judge Gary addressed them as follows:
"Gentlemen of the jury, you have finished this long and very arduous trial, which has required a very considerable sacrifice of time and some hardship. I hope that everything has been done that could possibly be done to make this sacrifice and hardship as mild as might be permitted. It does not become me to say anything in regard to the case that you have tried or the verdict you have rendered, but men compulsory serving as jurors, as you have done, *deserve some recognition of the service you have performed beside the meager compensation you are to receive.* You are discharged from further attendance upon this court. I understand that some carriages are in attendance to convey you from this place. Certificates for your attendance fees as jurors you can get at any time in the future."

CHICAGO, Aug. 20.—[Editor of *The Tribune.*]—In view of the long and close confinement endured by the jury in the Anarchist trial, and the display of manly courage evidenced by their prompt and fearless verdict, I beg to suggest the propriety of starting a subscription for the purpose of raising at least $1,000 for the benefit of each juryman. I am far from being rich, but would gladly give $25 for this purpose, and will deliver same at your office the day you may start the subscription.

W. C. E.

CHICAGO, Aug. 20.—[Editor of *The Tribune.*]—The long agony is over. Law has triumphed. Anarchy is defeated. The conspirators have been promptly convicted. Let them be as promptly punished. The "twelve good men and true" whose honesty and fearlessness made a conviction possible should not be forgotten. They have performed their unpleasant duty without flinching. Let them be generously remembered. Raise a fund — say $100,000 — to be presented with the thanks of a grateful people.

E. A. MULFORD.

Mr. N. B. Ream, in speaking to a *Tribune* reporter, thought it would be eminently proper to start a fund for the purpose of indemnifying the jurors who so patiently sat for eight weeks at the trial, thereby losing in business and time and endangering their health, for which they were so meagerly paid by the county, and then in vouchers which will be cashed, nobody knows when. Mr. Ream thought it was not proper to mention this while the trial was in progress, but now that it is over he is willing to head the list with the sum of $500. Thus will the schoolmaster, who so nobly sacrificed his vacation, be in a measure repaid, and so will the others who, being mostly, if not all, business men, were greatly inconvenienced by their selection as jurors.

III.

A. R. Parsons on the Eight-Hour Movement in March, 1886.

(From an Interview in the *Daily News*, March 13, 1886.)

A. R. Parsons, the Anarchist, said:

"The labor question is up for settlement. It demands and commands a hearing. The existing disorders threaten not only the peace, but the destruction of society itself. The movement to reduce the work hours is intended by its projectors to give a peaceful solution to the difficulties between capitalists and laborers. I have always held that there were two ways to settle this trouble—either by peaceable or violent methods. Reduced hours—or eight hours—is a peace-offering. It is for capitalists to give or laborers to take. I hold that capitalists will not give eight hours. Why? Because the rate of wages in every wage-paying country is regulated by what it takes to live on; in other words, it is subsistence wages. This subsistence wage is what political economists call the 'iron law of wages,' because it is unvarying and inviolable. How does this law operate? In this way: A laborer is hired to do a day's work. In the first two hours labor of the ten he reproduces the equivalent of his wage; the other eight hours is what the employer gets and gets for nothing. Hence the laborer, as the statistics of the census of 1880 show, does ten hours work for two hours pay.—Now, reduced hours, or eight hours, means that the profit monger is to get only six hours instead of, as now, eight hours for nothing. For this reason employers of labor will not voluntarily concede the reduction.

On the other hand, fewer hours means more pay. Capitalists and laborers know this. Reduced hours is the only measure of economic reform which consults the interests of laborers as consumers. Now, this means a higher standard of living for the producers, which can only be acquired by their possessing and consuming a larger share of their own product. This would diminish the surplus or profits of the labor exploiters. Labor can therefore, for this reason, get only what it can take. Can labor force capital to reduce the work-hours? How can it?

The legalized possession and control of capital puts the wage-worker or propertyless class at their mercy. Capitalists can deprive labor of its bread by lock-outs and discharges. The laborer is forced to yield or perish. If he becomes disorderly he is suppressed by the militia and police. The last resort is force. The servitude of labor to capital is now and always has been maintained by force. If the labor organizations arm and force the concession of eight hours from employers, then the employing class will have to pay as much for eight hours work as they now do for ten. Employers will put labor-saving machinery to work instead of these high-priced laborers. The laborers will then, for the same reason that they reduced the hours to eight, have to reduce them to six hours per day. A voluntary reduction of the work hours is a peaceful solution of the labor problem, by which no disarrangement or confusion would occur. Wages in this way will increase until they represent the earnings, instead of, as now, the necessities, of the wage laborer. This would result in making every laborer a capitalist and every capitalist a laborer; a system of universal co-operative production and distribution. Reduced hours would melt the wages or profit system out of existence and usher in the co-operative or free-labor system.

I do not believe that capital will quietly or peaceably permit the economic emancipation of their wage-slaves. It is against all the teachings of history and human nature for men to voluntarily yield up usurped or arbibtrary power. The capitalists of the world will for this reason force the workers into armed revolution. Socialists point out this fact and warn the workingmen to prepare for the inevitable."

IV.

WHY THIS BOOK WAS WRITTEN.

COOK COUNTY JAIL, Chicago, Illinois.

Comrade Lum:—It has been resolved by our friends outside, that the proceedings, etc., of our late trial should be published in book form. We request you herewith to assume the editorship of this publication,—in fact, we know of no other man who could undertake this work with the same degree of competency and discriminative capacity as yourself, and trust that you will comply with our request.

The work should be begun at once. Will you to this end confer with our friends? Fraternally,

A. SPIES, A. R. PARSONS,
MICHAEL SCHWAB, SAMUEL FIELDEN,
ADOLPH FISCHER, O. NEEBE,
G. ENGEL, LOUIS LINGG.

AUGUST SPIES'
Auto-Biography;

HIS SPEECH IN COURT,

AND GENERAL NOTES.

By *NINA VAN ZANDT.*

Bound in Paper, 25 Cents.   **Bound in Cloth, 65 Cents.**

→ THE ✢ ACCUSED ✢ THE ✢ ACCUSERS. ←

THE FAMOUS SPEECHES
— OF THE —
Eight Chicago Anarchists
IN COURT,

When asked if they had anything to say, why sentence should not be passed upon them,

On October 7th, 8th and 9th, 1886, at Chicago, Ill.

PRICE 15 CENTS.

Published and For Sale by the

SOCIALISTIC PUBLISHING SOCIETY,

274 W. 12th St., Chicago, Ill.

Made in the USA
Lexington, KY
02 January 2015